MW01123871

From Here to Heaven

Our Family's Story of Tragedy, Triumph, and the Best Yet to Come

Sarah J. Hartrum - Decareaux

WestBow Press books may be ordered through booksellers or by contacting:

WestBow Press
A Division of Thomas Nelson & Zondervan
1663 Liberty Drive
Bloomington, IN 47403
www.westbowpress.com
1 (866) 928-1240

ISBN: 978-1-5127-2013-6 (sc)
ISBN: 978-1-5127-2015-0 (hc)
ISBN: 978-1-5127-2014-3 (e)

Library of Congress Control Number: 2015918909

Print information available on the last page.

WestBow Press rev. date: 12/4/2015

For Dave, Dominic, and Grant: may this story of your journey, endurance, strength, determination, and bond be a lasting testimony to the power of family, love between a father and his sons, and strength in the face of seemingly unbeatable odds. May the world see that this is not the end of your story. Victory was yours. The best is yet to come; you are more alive than we are here, and your journey was not an ending but a glorious beginning. "May the Lord watch between you and me when we are absent one from the other" (Genesis 31:49 NASB). Until then, my loves.

This book is also dedicated to all the hurting. It is a message of hope. When you find the smallest ounce of hope, grab it tightly and do not let go. No matter your circumstance, there is hope. Allow God to be your hope, and while the road may not be easy, it will be bearable. There is calm in the midst of the storm. Step out in faith—one foot in front of the other, one breath at a time.

It is a slap in the face of the Enemy when I share my testimony.

"They triumphed over him by the blood of the Lamb and by the word of their testimony" (Revelations 12:11).

Contents

"I pray that Your Son, Jesus Christ, lives in our hearts forever in everything and that every day we live to honor and worship You. I pray that the blood He shed may become the love we share as we continue to live by His example. Use us, guide us, and teach us Your ways so that we may do Your bidding, gather souls for Your kingdom, and be witnesses of Your glorious Word to each person we meet. We know that Your will shall be done, that You know what is good for us, and that the strength we have comes from You, Lord. We are the vessels; we are the soldiers; we are Your lovely creation. We pray that You bless us and send us forth replenished and fueled to spread Your mighty Word. In this we pray. Amen."

I found this prayer, written by my husband, as I was cleaning off a shelf in my bedroom in late 2013 after the accident. I came across the Bible that Dave had used most often in men's Bible study while we were stationed in England and Italy from 2005 to 2008. The prayer was on an index card tucked inside. It was the first time I had laid eyes on it.

Introduction

Standing at the trailhead, I looked as far as I could through the early morning mist on that cold January morning in 2013. Perhaps if I willed it enough, I would see Dave, Dominic, and Grant returning to me from another Decareaux family adventure. They had left the day before, hiking the Ozark Trail in Mark Twain National Forest in Missouri.

I strained my eyes, hoping to see any hint of them coming over the horizon through the trees. I felt them so strongly. I felt as though they were standing right next to me. I thought I felt this way because they were close to home and I would soon see them walking toward me. Looking back, however, I believe that I did feel their presence. Their spirits and the Holy Spirit - preparing me for what was about to happen.

Part I

Unexpected Journey

Chapter 1

A Beginning

I was trying desperately to lose him in the crowd. I weaved through and dodged people, all the while looking behind me—ducking, hiding, walking ever faster in the opposite direction from the guy following me.

He is not taking no for an answer, I thought.

That cold December night in 2000, I found myself trying frantically to lose a guy who had made it his mission all night to chat me up at the club on Laclede's Landing in downtown St. Louis. I tried for several minutes to politely make my disinterest clear. When that didn't work, I walked away—and he followed. My casual pace quickly became brisk weaving through the crowd as I tried to avoid another awkward encounter with him.

And then I saw him, a different man at the rear of the club, standing with his back against the wall. He had a gentle look on his face as he took in his surroundings. This man was not obnoxiously hitting on ladies or acting crazy like half the people in the club that night. In fact, he looked a little bored.

Perfect, I thought. *I'll stand by him and make it look like we're together.*

I walked toward him and stood close enough to make it look as if we were a couple but not close enough to make him think I was strange.

My pursuer had caught up with me, but to my relief, I saw the expression on his face change as he looked at me and then at the man next to me. He walked away in defeat, assuming we were indeed together.

Relieved, I leaned against the wall to catch my breath. Suddenly I heard a voice say, "What kind of people come here, anyway?"

I looked up to see the handsome face of the man beside me, my safe haven. He was smiling.

"What?" I responded, offering a coy smile in return.

"I said, what kind of people come here, anyway? Everybody seems so young."

"I'm probably older than you are. How old are you, anyway?" I asked.

"Twenty-three."

"What? Me, too!"

Those were the first words Dave and I spoke to one another. We wound up talking the entire evening.

Over the loud beat of the music, we introduced ourselves.

"I'm Dave," he said.

"I'm Sarah. Nice to meet you," I responded.

We spoke casually, exchanging general information. I told him I was a student teacher in Illinois, and he said he was an airman stationed in New Jersey but on assignment at Scott Air Force Base in Illinois for a few months. We laughed and joked as we watched the crowd around us. Then we stepped outside the club so we could talk where it was quiet. Deep in conversation, we began to explore the historic sidewalks of Laclede's Landing.

As we were walking, a homeless man stopped us, hawking a big, thick book about the Beatles. Dave, an avid Beatles fan as I would learn, stopped to haggle with the man about the price. Later I would discover that we had met on the anniversary of John Lennon's passing, and the significance of finding the book for sale that night had not escaped Dave.

After a few minutes, Dave and the homeless man agreed on a price. As Dave handed him the money and retrieved the book, the man thanked him and started to walk away. However, he turned to tell Dave one last thing.

"Take care of that beautiful wife you have there," he said.

Having met only hours before, Dave and I stood on the sidewalk outside the club a bit dumbstruck as we looked at each other. We knew we were in the midst of something magical. We were at the beginning of something beautiful.

The next day, Dave called and asked if I'd like to go out for a steak dinner. Living on my own in an itty-bitty apartment on a student teacher's budget, I suggested he come to my place to eat, and he agreed. We talked over pizza and pink lemonade until four in the morning, discussing our families, our dreams, and our goals and sharing many funny stories.

I laughed to tears as Dave shared stories about his crazy high school days. He and his buddies once duck-taped a friend from head to toe like a mummy, left him on the front porch of his parents' home, rang the doorbell, and hid in the bushes. They succumbed to uncontrollable laughter when the boy's mother opened the door and screamed at the sight of her son taped over every inch of his body except for his nose and his mouth.

Dave could make me laugh from the start. I knew there was something different about him, something special, but I also realized as we continued dating that he was soon due to fly out to his next duty station with the military, Portugal's Azore Islands. I didn't want to get too close, knowing he was leaving the country in a matter of weeks.

But each time we got together, I put that thought further from my mind and enjoyed his company. In fact, we talked and/or saw each other every day after the night we met, and I had the three-hundred-dollar phone bill to prove it.

As we continued dating during December of 2000, we discovered that we shared similar goals, passions, and dreams. We both loved to travel and wanted large families; we shared similar values and had the same political views. I told Dave of my deep commitment to my faith in Jesus Christ. Dave, raised a Catholic, listened with interest as I explained what my faith meant to my life and how I tried to live out that faith. He, in turn, told me how his Catholic upbringing influenced his life decisions. We recognized similarities and differences in our faith traditions.

We hit no snags in our budding relationship until one night when we were supposed to meet to see a movie. My car broke down on the way to the theater. And since this was before the days of cell phones, I had no way to tell Dave what had happened, and he assumed I had changed my mind and stood him up. Safely home after hitching a ride from my brother-in-law, I called Dave, who had left the theater and returned to his room at the base to relax. I assured him I was not brushing him off and explained that my car had broken down. Laughing about it, we picked up where we had left off and continued to grow our newfound relationship.

As Dave's departure date neared, we knew we wanted to be together, but we fought our feelings.

How could this be possible? How could I be in love with a stranger? I thought.

I didn't admit the truth until late December when Dave went home to Louisiana for his birthday and for Christmas. While he was gone, I missed him. One evening while out to dinner with a friend, I asked, "Becky, what if I love him?"

Dave started to acknowledge his feelings around the same time, but he revealed later that he had thought, *How can I possibly love someone I just met?*

Before going home for Christmas that year, Dave tried to convince me to go with him. I said no. Amazingly, I turned down the invitation because in my deepest spirit, I knew that we were going to get married, that I would move around the world with him, and that I needed to be home at Christmas because this was the last holiday season I would spend with my family for a while. God had already laid that on my heart.

I didn't tell Dave that just yet. He settled for the next-best thing and brought my cat, Maggie, home with him for Christmas. While we were apart those few days, Dave routinely called me from his parents' house to talk, instructing Maggie to "say hi to Mommy."

In early January, Dave proposed in the living room of my apartment and asked me to go to Portugal with him. I immediately said yes. We had met only four weeks prior.

We thought it was time we told our families about our relationship and the fact that we were getting married. I did not introduce Dave to my parents until we were engaged. The day they met him, January 5, 2001, he and I stayed at their house until midnight, visiting and laughing. My mom and dad loved him immediately; Dave and my parents hit it off from the start.

Dave wore his Beatles tie and a sport jacket, and I wore a simple blue dress with a white jacket for our wedding on January 11, 2001. Because our marriage was a surprise to everyone and because the ceremony took place on a weekday afternoon, my parents and my brother-in-law, Doug, were the only guests at the small courthouse ceremony. My dad was our photographer; my mom gave Dave a boutonniere and presented me with a single red rose. My parents served as witnesses. It was a simple, beautiful ceremony.

After our wedding, my parents treated Dave and me and Doug to lunch at an Italian restaurant. While eating, I looked around the table at the intimate group toasting our marriage. I was grateful to my parents for their support and to my brother-in-law for taking time out of his one day off from work to show his love and support. Most of all, I was grateful to be married to the man sitting next to me. I couldn't wait to start out on our adventure together.

The brand-new Mr. and Mrs. Decareaux. We were married in a small courthouse wedding in Waterloo, Illinois; this photo was taken at our reception in New Orleans, Louisiana, in February 2001.

In late January my parents hosted a special dinner in Missouri. It was the first opportunity our families had to meet. Several members of Dave's family had driven up from Louisiana for the occasion. My parents, Dave's parents, and members of our families enjoyed a festive evening together, getting to know one another at the Cheshire Inn in Clayton, Missouri. Dave and I were spoiled with gifts, cards, and toasts by loved ones, and we all enjoyed a wonderful steak dinner by candlelight. Surrounded by so many people who loved me and my brand-new husband, I was overcome with excitement and gratitude.

Dave and I at a family dinner in Missouri in January 2001.

In February, we traveled to New Orleans to visit Dave's family at his parents' home. We were treated to a traditional reception with all the trimmings: a DJ, a catered meal, decorations, a cake, and a toast to the couple. Some of my family members made the trip to celebrate with us. Our reception was exactly what I had pictured as a little girl. It was fun, it was festive, and it was beautiful.

Finally, after all the wedding festivities had ended, we left for New Jersey—on my first flight—to finalize the paperwork assuring that I could go with Dave to the Azores.

Left: Dave and I at our wedding reception in New Orleans in February 2001.

Right: Dave and I the day after our reception, opening gifts and sharing a private joke. We laughed and lived much during our marriage.

Dave was stationed in New Jersey. He was on assignment in the St. Louis area, at Scott Air Force Base, for only a few months before he was due in the Azores. He had left New Jersey without even a girlfriend and had come back with a wife.

How did this happen? Why did a girl with a good head on her shoulders, a bookworm who never had a serious boyfriend and didn't date much, marry a guy she had just met—in a club, not in church as planned—after five weeks together? We married because we knew we were meant to be partners. We knew from the night we met. Our connection was instant.

On a March morning, several weeks after our wedding, Dave and I climbed aboard an air force cargo plane and flew to our new home—the Azores. The crew members, knowing we were newlyweds and that I was new to military life, were friendly, talkative, and helpful. Dave and I could hardly hear each other speak over the roar of the plane as we sat near the netted military cargo, strapped in as if we were wearing jumpsuits and preparing to parachute out of the plane. But it was all an adventure to me, and I was as happy as I could possibly have been. In fact, I was so ecstatic that after we landed, I was eager to get a picture of the plane that had just taken me across the ocean for the first time.

As I snapped a picture, a woman walked briskly toward me, saying, "Ma'am, Madame, no! No photo!"

I quickly learned that it was forbidden to take photos of military aircraft on the flight line, and my introduction to overseas military life was a Portuguese woman trying to confiscate my camera. Dave and the friendly crew convinced her to let me keep it. My first photo of the Azores was of a woman reaching for my camera.

In ten weeks Dave and I had met, married, met each other's families, and moved overseas. A student teacher who had received a degree in education from Greenville College in late December and was living in an apartment in my hometown, I was now a wife living in a foreign country. Dave, an airman on temporary duty at Scott Air Force Base, was now a husband at his new duty station in Portugal.

We were newlyweds in a foreign land, and the adventure had just begun.

While Dave and I were waiting for our base apartment to become available, we stayed in the base hotel for a few weeks. Eager to prove myself a good wife and a good cook, I decided to make dinner one night in our hotel suite kitchenette. I thought BLT sandwiches would be a good choice. While I had the best intentions, the bacon didn't turn out as I had hoped. I burned it so badly that the smoke alarm went off in our room. In fact, all the smoke alarms in the hallway on our floor went off as well. I quickly called the front desk and said that I had merely burned bacon and that there was no fire. But I learned quickly that when a smoke alarm went off on base, the fire department was automatically notified. The hotel evacuated every room in the multilevel hotel until the source of the alarm could be found and the problem could be officially determined. With Dave laughing at me, we obeyed the order to evacuate. I left my failed bacon in the pan in a sink full of water, and he and I evacuated along with everyone else in the hotel. The fire department soon gave the all-clear for everyone to return. As we walked up the stairs to the hotel entrance, Dave and I heard a conversation between two people in the crowd trying to figure out the reason for the evacuation.

"I don't know," one of them said. "I heard some lady burned bacon really bad."

I shot Dave a look that said something like, "Be quiet," hung my head low, blended into the crowd walking toward the hotel, and acted as annoyed as everyone else was with whoever had burned that bacon.

Left: I survey our new home on Terceira Island, Azores, Portugal, in the spring of 2001.

Right: Dave explores Angra City Park, Azores, Portugal, in 2001.

Life could not have been more beautiful. Dave and I had the stereotypical magical first newlywed year. We always joked that we didn't get a honeymoon but had opted for two years in the Azore Islands instead—good trade, we reasoned! We got to know each other after having been little more than strangers. We learned the lay of the land in our new home—traveling all over the small island, exploring, swimming, and taking pictures—and decided to add to our brood. We bought two puppies, huskies we named Bo and Cleo. Still waiting for Dave's Jeep to be shipped to the island, we called a taxi and had the driver drop us off at a pet store in the nearby town of Angra, a short distance from the base. Having bought our new husky babies, we carried them up and down the streets of Angra, looking for another taxi to take us home. Finding one, we piled ourselves and our two new additions into the back seat. We smiled at the Portuguese driver as he stared at us in the rearview mirror. Unlike him, we did not find it strange at all to be hauling two good-size dogs around town in a taxi.

It was that day, after picking out Bo and Cleo and walking up and down the sidewalks of Angra, that I started to feel sick. Mere days after that, we found out we were expecting our first baby.

Dave with our first "babies," Bo (lying) and Cleo (sitting), Portugal, 2001.

On December 2, 2001, we welcomed our first child, Kathryn Elizabeth—Kate, as we would call her. My first labor was interesting, to say the least. I had gone into labor the day before Kate was due to be born, and by the next morning I had had enough. The Portuguese hospital offered only mild pain-control medicine, and my breathing was not up to par as demonstrated in the labor and delivery videos I had watched. My face and extremities were going numb because my poor breathing and my inability to handle the pain of many hours of nonprogressive contractions were causing me to hyperventilate. I am sure the Portuguese hospital staff had much to talk about after my discharge, as I routinely screamed, "Jesus, help me!" as I progressed through labor. As Dave held me from the side, and I buried my face in his shoulder, I bit him in the collarbone while bearing down on a particularly painful contraction—so hard that he yelped and jumped up out of his chair. During another especially painful contraction, a nurse pulled her hand away from mine. I was squeezing it so hard as I screamed in pain that she said, "Ouch!" Despite my condition, I managed to look at her incredulously, as if to say, "Really? I'll trade places with you."

Though I bit Dave twice on the collarbone during my labor ordeal and I screamed for the doctors to "just knock me out and cut me open," we were overjoyed to have our baby girl safe and sound in our arms. Dave got to meet Kate before I did. Because the doctors eventually decided to put the crazy American woman out of her misery and knock her out to perform a C-section, I awoke hours after Kate had been born. As I was wheeled from recovery to my hospital room, I saw our Kate bundled in a yellow sleeper. I heard Dave enter the room right after I had been wheeled in.

"Dave! Look! Look at her!" I said, excited as a kid on Christmas morning, in awe of what we had made together.

"I know," he calmly answered, walking toward Kate and placing his hand on her tiny body. "We've met."

I found out soon after that while hospital rules prevented Dave from being in the operating room when Kate was born, the nurses carried her to him moments after her birth as he waited in the hall. He and Kate got to bond for three hours before I met her.

After many days at the hospital, we were finally ready to take our new baby home. All the beautiful visions of our first baby's homecoming quickly went out the window, however, as Kate screamed to the point of losing her breath while Dave tried to dress her in a special coming-home outfit. Kate continued to protest being prodded and bothered as Dave attempted to strap her into a car seat to be carried out of the hospital to the little foreign car waiting in the parking lot. The idea that the three of us would serenely leave the hospital, Dave and I hand in hand, soon vanished. With Kate screaming, Dave walked as quickly as he could to get our baby down the hallway and out of the hospital as I hobbled after him.

After we finally got Kate secured in her car seat, Dave helped me get into the car, we buckled up, and he turned the key in the ignition. The engine did not start. Dave sat for a moment as if plotting his next move. As I remained in the car and Kate wailed in protest at being disturbed (and probably feeling hungry at that point), Dave searched the parking lot for anyone able and willing to help start our car with jumper cables. I watched him approach many people, none of whom had the cables.

Finally, through a good number of hand signs and charades, Dave was able to convey to a dear Portuguese man that we needed help with our car battery. Having a set of jumper cables, the man eagerly drove over and helped us get our car started. I had taken Kate out of her seat to nurse her in the passenger seat while Dave hunted down help. I handed Kate over to Dave, who quickly buckled our baby back in her seat. With our forty-five-minute ordeal ended, we were finally on our way home. We drove twenty minutes across the island to our base apartment with our brand-new baby girl.

That coming-home story became classic Decareaux family lore as the years passed. Kate always enjoyed hearing the story of our first adventure (or misadventure) as a family. That experience taught me that God will allow my dreams to come to fruition—though maybe not in the way I had planned. Dave and I got our baby girl home safe and sound but certainly not in the way we had pictured. I was grateful as I cradled Kate the first night we had her home. Though I had dreams of getting her home in some storybook way, God had one-upped me. While our trip home may have looked messy, it was full of unforgettable moments. I was thankful for a God who brought laughter and family memories out of messy places.

Back home at our tiny base apartment, Dave and I felt like the world consisted of only the three of us. With some leave time saved up, Dave was able to stay home with Kate and me for three weeks after her birth. We had precious time in our apartment during the Christmas season as a new family of three with a cat and two dogs to boot. Life was beautiful.

The Decareaux family, Christmas Eve 2001, Azores, Portugal.

Dave was holding his baby girl one afternoon in our apartment when he looked at me and said, "Sarah, I just want to be her best friend."

His love for his girl was instant and full. Dave was inseparable from Kate. He hated having to go to work since this meant he couldn't see her for hours. When Kate was a few months old, I substitute taught at the base elementary school a few times, and Dave brought Kate to work with him for a few hours each day when our babysitter was unavailable. He loved it. At Dave's office Christmas party, just days after she was born, we made Kate's debut to our friends and Dave's coworkers, including many Portuguese civilians. While we were enjoying ourselves at the party, talking to those at our table, Dave held Kate and attended to her every need. An older Portuguese couple got my attention from a table away, pointed to Dave, and with huge smiles on their faces said in their thick accent, "Good daddy. He good daddy!"

Dave and brand-new baby Kate on his twenty-fifth birthday, December 22, 2001, Azores, Portugal.

Kate was only five months old when we found out we were a month along with our second child—Kate and Dom are only thirteen months apart.

In the first trimester of all my pregnancies I got very ill and was basically bedridden from about week five until about week thirteen. In early 2002, I had a new baby to care for while suffering intense morning sickness. Dave came home with a beautiful card most days, helping in any way he could. Because I was almost incapacitated by first-trimester sickness, he would often work all day and then have to clean the entire house, do laundry, make himself dinner, and take care of Kate. During those early months of my pregnancy with Dom, it was all I could do to meet Kate's basic needs while Dave was at work.

Dave and I were partners from the get-go, true companions.

While I was in the second trimester of my pregnancy with Dom, I returned to the States with Kate and got a little apartment in my hometown while Dave finished the last six months of our Azores tour.

We hated the separation, but I had to make the move so I could have Dom at an American hospital near family. While having Kate at the Portuguese hospital was a great experience, we wanted something different since our second baby would be born so soon after his sister. My family helped me with baby Kate as they could, while still having to adhere to their own busy work schedules; and kept me blissfully occupied as we awaited Dominic's birth. My parents and my siblings gathered in my apartment for Thanksgiving dessert, along with Dave's parents and sister, who had driven to Illinois for the Thanksgiving holiday and for Kate's upcoming first birthday party.

Dave came to Illinois for extended visits in August, October, and December, and in January for Dom's birth. I learned early on as a military spouse that to be content I would have to be flexible, self-sufficient, and self-motivated. Separation is part of military life, and I quickly gained an admiration for wives who rose to the occasion and were partners to their husbands, managing on their own when necessary. They carried on when their husbands were called to duty and the family was stationed far from relatives, many times overseas. With no parents, siblings, or old friends around, women were asked to take care of the family, to pay bills, and to do what had to be done to keep a family and a house running. They had little to no outside support.

That is why military friends become as close as family while stationed abroad. They become each other's family, each other's support. In the first year of my marriage, God showed me many air force wives, and military wives in general, who modeled just how that was done through every deployment, training exercise, temporary assignment, and separation.

In my years as a military wife, I was privileged to become friends with a woman giving birth to her seventh child while her husband was in a war zone and with a woman, a veteran military pilot herself, who elected to stay home and to teach her children there. I met many women who had to move their entire households both cross country and overseas while their husbands were deployed. I quickly decided that I would pattern myself after these women. Their example served me well early in my marriage when Dave and I were an ocean apart, I was due to have Dominic, and I was raising our infant, Kate. And I was lucky—I had family all around me.

God is a good God, and He knew I needed to see strong women in action—motivated, capable, proactive, competent women taking care of their families—to guide me as a new military wife. He also knew I would need to recall those examples and that training many years down the road when Dave would be called home.

Dominic Christian was born January 4, 2003, in Belleville, Illinois.

Our nine-pounder came into the world as a quiet crier and a gentle spirit; *that* he would make up for as a high-strung, energetic toddler and preschooler. As with Kate, I went into labor despite the C-section already planned. Dom was ready for his debut before his due date. I had learned from my failed attempts with Kate how to breathe properly while in labor with Dom. And I did it with gusto (or perhaps overcompensating for my failed attempt with Kate). As I battled contractions the night before, Dave slept next to me. I eagerly awoke him at 5:30 a.m. and told him to get me to the hospital. I admit I may have been too eager, since I was a bit bitter that he was sleeping peacefully while I was in the pangs of early childbirth.

I managed not to bite Dave this time, instead breathing, staring, and concentrating on my "focal point" as I had been taught to do. I fought every contraction as it came. This became a mission for me, almost an attempt to settle the score with the contractions, which had so clearly won while I was in labor with Kate the year before. My staring became tunnel vision, and I honed in on my focal point, speaking to no one and answering no questions. My concentration, my silence, and my determination to "beat" the contractions were so intense that a nurse checking me in at registration asked Dave if I was "all right". Dave, almost rolling his eyes at my gung-ho attempt to fight the contractions, answered, "Yep. She's 'concentrating,'" and I'm pretty sure I saw him do air quotes as he said this.

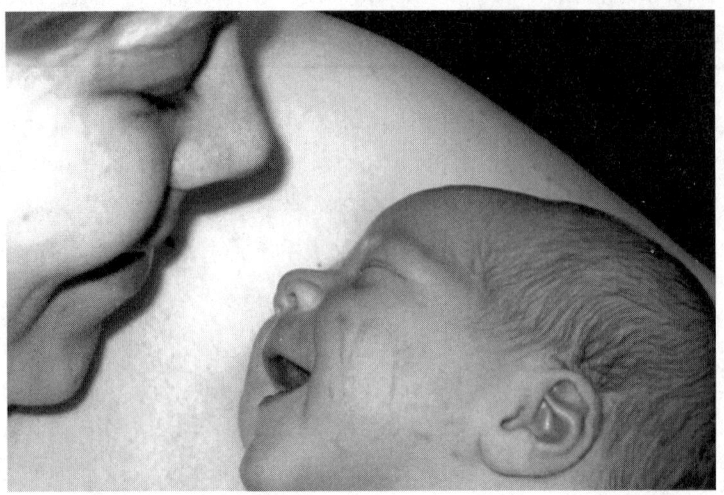

Dominic Christian and I in Illinois, January 2003.

In the labor room, I fought the contractions as long as I could, but when a nurse presented with the choice of remaining in labor or having the C-section, my focus broke, my silence ended, and I yelled, "Let's just stick with the plan! Give me a shot right now!"

I couldn't get the spinal block fast enough and was calm and content as I felt all pain vanish and I awaited the birth of Dominic Christian. His was the first birth Dave saw and the first I was awake for and able to experience. At first, Dave stood beside me, rubbing my forehead, talking softly to me, and reporting everything the doctors were doing. Then he shifted to where the action was, watching the doctors work and awaiting Dom's appearance.

I noticed Dave's concerned expression as the birth progressed. Later I found out he was concerned that the doctors had to pull on and twist our baby to free his shoulders and to remove him from my belly. Days later, as Dave recounted Dom's birth, he finished the story by saying, "I mean, they were being pretty rough. I was about to say somethin'."

I reassured Dave that the doctors knew exactly what they were doing. I said that birth is not pretty and that sometimes babies need extra help being removed, especially when they're big babies. Dave seemed satisfied with my explanation, but I smiled as I thought how protective my husband was of his boy even as he was entering the world.

I remember the first cry I heard my baby boy make, and I remember my first sight of him. I looked to my left after he had been removed from my belly and saw the nurses carry him away for his initial tests. I watched, tears streaming down my face, as one of his tiny arms and one of his tiny legs flailed about in protest as he was prodded and examined.

While Kate was in the capable hands of my sister, who stayed with her throughout my hospital stay, Dave and I spent time together in the hospital, knowing he would soon have to fly back to the Azores to finish his tour there. Those days at the hospital were a blessed time and have become sacred memories. We welcomed many visitors and my parents came to meet baby Dom. Dave tenderly cared for me, attended to Dominic, and kept me company. We talked, laughed, and admired our baby boy. We felt blessed beyond words to have such a beautiful family. We couldn't have asked for more.

Dave had to return to finish out his last two months in the Azores when our son was only a few days old. After Dave's short sojourn overseas, we would prepare for our move to a new post at Mountain Home Air Force Base in Idaho.

The morning I was to say good-bye to my husband before his return to the Azores, I peeked into the bedroom in our little apartment to see him holding Kate and sitting next to Dom's cradle—talking to the children and introducing the two. I grabbed my camera and quietly filmed the moment.

I knew that this was a sacred moment, but I didn't know how or why I would treasure it in my heart for the rest of my life. In the video, you can hear me softly whimpering tears of joy as I witnessed that moment of love between a father and his babies.

Nineteen-month-old Kate with six-month-old Dom,
Mountain Home Air Force Base, Idaho, summer 2003.

In early 2003, Dave returned to the States, and "rescued us" – the babies and me; as we moved to Mountain Home Air Force Base, Idaho. Another chapter had begun in our whirlwind lives. We had just celebrated our second anniversary, and we already had two children, had lived in the Azores, and were now in Idaho. Life was crazy, but life was good.

We certainly had our ups and downs adjusting to life with two small babies and getting reacquainted after having been apart on and off for several months, but we always worked through our kinks.

Dave's love for the outdoors was kindled in Idaho. I have since journaled, "Dave was complete out in God's nature. Life made sense to him out on a hiking trail."

Dave and Dominic, Grand Tetons, Wyoming, 2003.

My husband's love for the outdoors—for creation, mountains, rivers, trails, streams, and wildlife—took hold in the Gem State. As a family, we made day trips to locations throughout Idaho. We camped with two little babies, we swam in Payette Lake, we admired the beauty of the Sawtooth Mountains, and Dave went winter hiking with friends. We traveled to nearby Yellowstone and Grand Teton National Parks twice in two years. The summer I was pregnant with Grant, Dave took whitewater rafting guide courses.

Dave and Dominic, Idaho, 2003.

In March of 2004, we found out we were expecting our bonus child.

We had itty-bitty toddler Kate, an infant Dominic, and were already looking forward to baby number three. We were ecstatic. Dave badly wanted another boy. We had a beautiful summer while I was pregnant with Grant. We visited Yellowstone National Park in nearby Wyoming, we moved into a bigger house on base to better accommodate our expanding family, my parents came for a great visit, my birthday was in July, and we knew we had a baby boy on the way that fall.

Grant David arrived on November 3, 2004. When he was born, his daddy carried him to me and said, "You have to look at this," pulling off Grant's tiny cap to reveal our only baby thus far with a crop of dark hair.

Grant's birth, unlike Kate and Dom's, was absolutely effortless. I had planned a C-section, and he did not try to come early. The entire procedure went smoothly. Grant's peaceful entrance into the world gave every indication as to the calm, pleasant baby and child he would become. However, we did capture one moment on video, at what we could only guess was Grant's first time being offended. As Dave filmed, I held Grant David hours after he was born. Dave and I doted over our new son, giggling at his precious coos, touching his tiny fingers, and unfolding his baby blanket to count his little toes. I exclaimed, "Welcome, Dom! We are so glad to have you join our family."

Grant immediately burst into tears as I realized too late that I had just called him by his brother's name. All efforts to console him were fruitless, so we ended the video. Struggling to be heard over his protests and cries, we said we would try to film more later after he had calmed down. Grant David was his own little man, and he wanted to make sure we knew that and wouldn't make the mistake of calling him by his brother's name again.

My mom had flown to Idaho to take care of Kate and Dom while Dave and I were in the hospital with Grant. The day we drove the few blocks from the hospital to our house on the base to bring Grant home, Dave and I were tired but giddy at the thought of having our whole family under one roof. And just as Grant's smooth birth gave every indication of the child he would become, what we heard walking up our driveway and sidewalk to the front door foretold what kind of toddler and preschooler Dominic would become. My mom had made several signs welcoming "Mommy and Grant" home and had taped them on the door, along with balloons, to welcome the newest addition. As Dave and I approached the front door, we heard my mom coaching the kids on how to welcome us when we entered the house, not knowing we had already pulled up and were nearing the front porch. In absolute exasperation, she added, "Dominic, get *off* that table right now! No, you may *not* stand on the table."

Dave and I looked at each other and grinned, knowing we were in for an adventure with three very small kids so close together.

Dave and his babies the day Grant David was born, November 3, 2004. Kate was not quite three, and Dom was not quite two.

While Grant's birth and hospital stay went smoothly, a misunderstanding following his birth reduced me to overly hormonal tears, leaving Dave to pick up the pieces and to calm his wound-up wife. Shortly after Grant's arrival, I had to return to the doctor for a postbaby checkup. We left baby Grant, along with toddlers Kate and Dom, at home with my mom, since the appointment was right up the street from our house and was not expected to take long. As Dave and I rode the hospital elevator up to my doctor's office, we discussed how my mom was due to fly back home to Illinois in a matter of days. I started crying, absolutely overwhelmed that she had to leave. Trying to console me but aware that my crocodile tears were in large part due to my postbaby hormones, Dave simply put his hand on my shoulder (and I'm sure inwardly rolled his eyes several times). When the doors opened, a woman entering the elevator as we were leaving noticed my tears and asked Dave, "Aw, is she in labor? Well, you're on the wrong floor for labor and delivery."

As I breathed in, preparing to unleash the fresh wave of tears that question brought, Dave, appearing desperate, tried to speak to the woman through wide eyes, conveying to her the message, "No, no, no. Don't say that. Be quiet." As she finished speaking, he shook his head slowly in defeat, looking at her as if to say, "Really, lady? Now? You had to say that now?" Then he guided me briskly away from her down the hallway.

After Grant's birth, we settled into life in our new house in Idaho. Dave was working, I was taking care of three babies ages three and under, and life was blissfully crazy and wonderful. We were blessed, and we knew it. We were grateful that we had three healthy children and that we loved each other.

In March 2005, Dave got orders for RAF Alconbury, England. We were excited to be returning overseas. Born with the travel bug, we were anxious to explore Europe.

In early 2005, Dave and I prepared for our move to the American military base at Alconbury, but first we took a road trip in true Decareaux fashion.

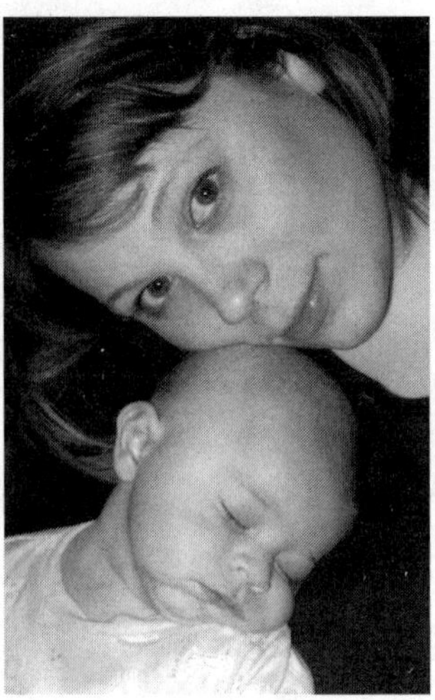

Grant David and I in Idaho, 2004.

As we said good-bye to Idaho and the United States, we did it in grand style. We headed out in our minivan from Idaho to Wyoming, stopping at the Grand Teton Mountains for the third year running. From there, we traveled to South Dakota, where we spent a few days exploring the Black Hills and Mount Rushmore. We drove down to Arkansas and eventually to Louisiana, where we visited Dave's family for several days.

We dropped Cleo, our husky, off with Dave's parents, who graciously agreed to let her live with them for two years while we were in England. Then we headed north to see my family in the St. Louis area. We visited for several days, and then we were off, ready for our flight to England to begin our European adventure as a family of five.

Left: Kate and Dom examining their brand-new baby brother, Grant, Idaho, 2004.

Right: The kids at Mount Rushmore, South Dakota, April 2005: Kate, three; Dom, two; Grant, five months.

England brought something we did not expect, however. We moved in May 2005, and by July of that year, Dave and I were having severe marital problems.

Looking back years later, we attributed our difficulties to the stress of our whirlwind life. We had three small children, and moving overseas was tough. Dave had to adjust to the stresses of a new job, and I felt isolated at home with three small babies. The stress took its toll on us.

We were trying to live as faithful Christians. As an outward sign of an inward transition, Dave had even gotten baptized on our third wedding anniversary the year before. However, we were still overtaken by the strains that the move to England caused.

Our troubles grew to the point where we were convinced divorce was our only option. We started to plan how life would go when I returned home. I would teach at a school and raise our kids, and Dave would work on getting stationed near us.

It was a challenging time. But thankfully, God had mercy on us and put us back on track. He took off our blinders and revealed to us again the beauty of our lives, the love we had for each other, the bond between us, the laughs we shared, and how we had let earthly stress get us off course.

Once we had received good counseling and had brought the sources of our stress under control, Dave and I got back together, and we never went to that place in our marriage again.

No, it was not always perfect. There were days when I wanted to give up, and there were days when he wanted to give up. Dave and I still had arguments; we were authentic people, and we did not hide what upset us about each other. But we loved deeply and expressed frustrations with each other deeply.

That was Dave and I.

Sometimes I felt that he was the male version of me and that I was the female version of him. We were so alike that we shared each other's faults. Both of us were stubborn and would cling to our ground.

It took God's grace, good counseling, and our love and commitment to each other and to the family we had created to overcome that and to learn how to be a family. We had been married for only four years by that point.

That hard time at the beginning of our stay in England in 2005 was the best thing that could have happened to our marriage. We learned from that experience what rock bottom was, and we never wanted to return there.

And we never did. We took full advantage of living overseas.

Dave and I.

We had no children in England; we took a four-year break from childbearing, but it wasn't our decision. God did not allow us to get pregnant, and that turned out to be a blessing. He gave us time to raise the children we had.

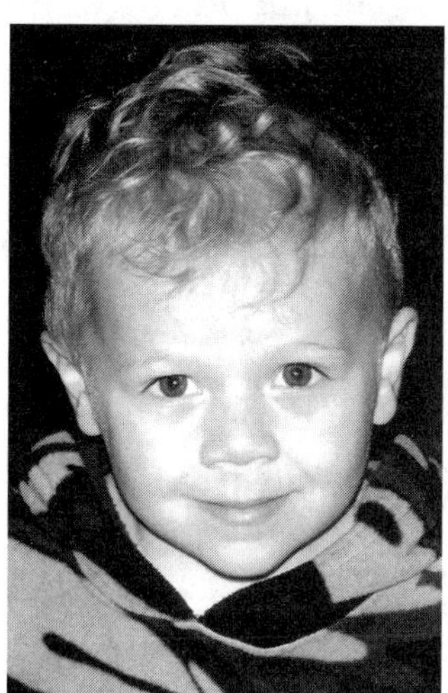

Left: Dominic Christian, two years old, England, 2005.

Right: Grant David, one year old, England, 2005.

We were an adventurous family, traipsing all over Europe in our American minivan. We took a ferry across the English Channel to mainland Europe and did a nine-country tour in ten days, visiting the German Alps, northern Italy, the cafés of Paris, and the French countryside. We drove through Belgium, Switzerland, the Netherlands, Austria, and Luxembourg.

Many times, we traveled by the seat of our pants. While on a trip to Scotland, we stopped in Sherwood Forest in England to explore the fabled stomping grounds of Robin Hood before entering Scotland days later. We arrived at Loch Ness in the middle of the night. We intended on spending one night and the following full day there before moving on to explore the rest of the country. Not having booked a hotel ahead of time, we pulled into the parking lot of a century's old palace turned hotel, and decided to let the kids who were sound asleep, stay asleep. We spent that night sleeping in the van.

We awoke the next morning to Loch Ness to the front of us, a huge statue of the famed Loch monster to our left, and tourists and locals alike walking behind our van in the parking lot. From a distance, they were peering into our windows at the strange family sleeping in their van. Despite not having been official guests in the hotel the previous evening, therefore not entitled to any of the amenities of the hotel, Dave and I coached the kids on walking into the hotel like we "belonged there" or "owned the place". We headed straight for the restroom in the lobby to freshen up for the day. Dave and I laughed with each other as we brushed our kids' teeth, changed their diapers and washed their little faces in the hotel lobby restroom we had commandeered into our own private washroom. We snickered at our flexibility in traveling with small kids, and at our adventurous spirits. Even if those adventures had to be accompanied by some quick thinking.

While staying in Paris the fall of 2006, Dave and I found ourselves hungry for a snack, so we took our three itty-bitty kids to a restaurant at midnight. They slept on the bench at our table while Dave and I had a late-night Parisian date. Some memories will be forever etched in my spirit, and that night is one of them.

Whether it was four-year-old Kate getting her head stuck between rungs of a fence at the Tower of London, Dave and I counting our kids and realizing we had left two-year-old Grant at the front of a cathedral in Cambridge, or Dominic walking out of a store with a nice family that realized a three-year-old stranger was following them to their car, our travels across Europe were filled with adventure.

Left: Dave and the kids in front of Neuschwanstein Castle, Germany, fall 2006.

Right: Dave at Farchant Waterfall, Bavaria, Germany, fall 2006.

Left: Dave and I and our kids at Warwick Castle, England, fall 2005.

Right: Dave and I on a ferry, crossing the English Channel, headed for Belgium on a twenty-four-hour date in 2006.

Our family's faith deepened in England. Dave was part of the praise team/worship band at our chapel. He was a gifted musician. After playing the trumpet all through high school, he had taught himself to play guitar, bass guitar, and some piano. Dave enjoyed many hours of practicing, writing music, and singing. On many evenings, Dave would sing into his voice recorder so he could listen and identify how he could improve as he practiced his music. I have a recording of Dave singing a praise song he wrote for Jesus; the lyrics are a prayer from his heart to the Father. I still listen to that song. It brings me much comfort as I picture Dave singing those words directly to Jesus as he stands before His throne.

I was active in the chapel ladies' groups, including the Protestant Women of the Chapel, teaching and leading Bible studies and writing and teaching a workshop on spiritual heritage. I attended ladies' Bible conferences all over England. Dave attended men's groups through the chapel, and rallies and workshops across the country.

We grew in our faith as a family and as individuals. We attended couples' Bible study and went to chapel on Sundays; the kids joined Awana Bible Club when they were old enough.

Dominic was a high-strung and energetic toddler and preschooler, and soon after he joined, his co-leader (me) forbid him from returning to his Awana cubbies class until he was a little older and able to sit through a lesson. Dominic had a lot of energy as a small boy and kept Dave and me on our toes. Whether he was trying to escape out of the back window of the car when I stopped to pump gas or to empty our fifty-gallon fish tank of all its pebbles and to relocate them onto our dining room floor, Dom kept things lively in the Decareaux house.

We realized Dominic had a fairly tight grasp on the concept of standing in the corner as a consequence for poor behavior when one day we found his teddy bear standing with its face against our dining room doorway. When I asked what his teddy bear was doing, Dom responded that his friend had been "naughty."

But whatever Dom lacked in self-control he made up for in wit and charm, even from an early age. He was so intense in his make-believe that we couldn't help but laugh. One evening, he climbed atop a stuffed horse, donning his plastic knight's helmet and holding a shield, sword drawn high in the air. Through roaring laughter, Dave and I tried to explain to him that it was hard to take him seriously as a fierce knight while he was sporting only his Bob the Builder undies.

Dom's personality as a three-year-old can be summed up this way: he was the only one of our five children who ended up getting a spanking from each of his four grandparents. As he grew into a mellow and quite mature young man, he grinned when I reminded him of that fact. Dom was quite proud of his accomplishment.

Grant, by contrast, was a calm child from the moment he was born. He had a silly streak but was by far the most agreeable of our kids. One afternoon in England, I had run with two-year-old Grant to the BX (base exchange/department store) for a quick errand. In a hurry, I was anxious to make my purchases and be on my way. I was getting a little frustrated at the amount of time it was taking the checkout lady to ring up my items. As I looked more closely, however, I could see the woman looked sad; she wore an expression of concern and heaviness on her young face.

Calming down a bit, I decided my rush did not outweigh my need to show compassion for a woman obviously not having a good day. As I put my remaining items on the counter with one hand while holding Grant in my other arm, he tried to get the woman's attention. She was oblivious to baby Grant's attempts to get her to giggle by making silly faces and blowing bubbles with his lips. Finally, as the woman looked up to tell me the amount I owed, Grant caught her eye and rewarded her with the biggest, brightest, chubby-cheeked toddler smile I had ever seen. The woman immediately burst into a radiant grin. Her smile shown through her eyes, and for a brief moment, she and Grant held each other in a wondrous stare. As Grant and I walked through the lane, she exclaimed, "That baby has just made my day," and her beautiful smile remained.

Smiling at her and then at Grant as I walked out to the car, I realized that God had used my boy to bring that woman joy, and I was overwhelmed with the thought, *I am holding a real live angel. My boy is a real live angel.* I kissed the top of his curly-haired head, taking in the smell of my precious little boy.

The years in England were a time of discovery and the reapplication of our faith. We enjoyed adventures as a family with lots of cooking, traveling, and love. Life was also certainly full of laughs. Kate tried to cut her own hair one winter, resulting in a lopsided 'do her entire year as a four-year-old, with one side clipped clear to her scalp and the other in a cropped bob to her chin. Another time, Grant crashed the Christmas pageant at Kate and Dom's British Montessori preschool one year, storming up the front rows at midsong and calling out, "Hi, Kate! Hi!" On another occasion, Kate was caught by her preschool teachers after taking a candy bar from the school kitchen and barricading herself in the restroom until she had stuffed the entire thing in her mouth. Then there was the time Dom was so rambunctious that Dave and I had mercy on a babysitter and left only Kate and Grant with her, bringing Dominic along on our date. I try to forget the time I again mobilized the base fire department by burning minipizzas in our oven. Life was crazy, and life was beautiful.

We were stationed in England from 2005 to 2007, and after eleven years in the air force, Dave thought it was time to leave military service. Having finished his bachelor's degree and earned his master's in the years since our marriage, we figured he might make more money in the civilian world.

So, in the summer of 2007, Dave separated from the military and we moved back stateside. It was a huge leap of faith, since we had no job, only a little money in the bank, three kids, and a dog. But we totally trusted God.

After finding our footing—staying with Dave's family in New Orleans, staying with my family in the St. Louis area, and taking the kids to Disney World in August—we decided we would take a road trip to Idaho in search of work. Though we had enjoyed our European travels, Dave had always pined to return to Idaho; the wilderness called him.

Left: Dave and the kids, England, Christmas Eve 2006.

Right: My baby boys and I on my birthday, England, July 2007.

So, with a few thousand dollars stuffed in our pockets, we packed our minivan with all our earthly belongings, besides what was in storage, and headed northwest with our three kids and the dog.

We made an adventure of it, traveling through Louisiana, Texas, Oklahoma, and New Mexico. In Colorado, we stopped at Durango,

Silverton, Mesa Verde, and Rocky Mountain National Park before moving on to Utah and Wyoming and heading into Idaho.

We hoped Dave would find work there with contacts from his military days but quickly learned this was not in God's plan. We stayed in a cheap hotel for a few weeks while Dave explored job leads that turned out to be utterly fruitless.

Our life had never fallen lower. We had been to Loch Ness in Scotland on vacation in May and to Disney World in August, but by October we were homeless, jobless, and directionless. Our plan to leave the military had certainly not turned out the way we had hoped.

With our heads hung low, we decided to use the last of our money to drive to St. Louis. We would stay with my family until we could find work and would see what God did.

Looking back, we felt that we had diverged from God's plan for us. Dave and I had selfishly thought we would make more money if we left the military and took life into our own hands, and we were left with no work and no home.

We lived in the St. Louis area from October 2007 to early 2008. We were able to afford to rent a little farmhouse on the grounds of a church in southern Illinois. Dave got a job at Scott Air Force Base as a civilian contractor for the Department of Defense, making a fraction of what he earned while in the military. I started substitute teaching.

We had intended to homeschool our children but put Kate in kindergarten at my childhood elementary school so I could work. I also waited tables at the place where I had worked in college.

That was a humbling time for us. We had gone from making a good income in the military, having all of our needs met and traveling throughout Europe, to Dave making a fraction of his air force pay as I returned to my college job.

Once we had traipsed across Europe, eaten in Paris at midnight, and driven to three countries and said hello in three languages in one day. We had been to Scotland just months before, had flown from England to Ireland and back again just for the day, and had taken a ferry from England to Belgium on a twenty-four-hour date. Now we slept in sleeping bags on the floor of our rented farmhouse because we could not afford to get our furniture and belongings shipped from storage in England and delivered to us.

To make matters worse, the trusty minivan that had taken us all over Europe broke down for good in Illinois, and we could afford only a used car that we borrowed a thousand dollars from my dad to buy.

We were devastated at the turn our lives had taken, but our kids were healthy, we were near my family, and we were getting by, so we made the most of it. Dave continued to apply for Department of Defense contractor jobs overseas, anxious to get us out of our difficult situation. We wanted our life back.

After months of humble living, on my dad's birthday, January 18, 2008, Dave got *the* call from Italy.

He had been hired as a civilian contractor at a US naval base there. He would be making triple what he was making in Illinois, more than we had ever made. God had provided for us, and we were overjoyed to be returning to our old life.

On top of that, we found out we were expecting baby number four!

Kate had just turned six, Dom five, and Grant three. Again, life was looking beautiful.

Dave had to leave for Italy in February 2008. I had to stay in Illinois with the children to get our belongings from England delivered to our new Italian address. Since Dave was now a civilian, we had to arrange the move ourselves and could no longer rely on the government to arrange the move for us.

I had to get any belongings we weren't taking put into local storage (with my dad and my brothers doing all the heavy lifting) and to drive to Chicago to obtain visas for the children and me to live in Italy. My mom came along to keep the kids under control during the eight-hour round trip. Finally, I had to get the paperwork to have our dog Cleo shipped with us to Italy.

I made all these preparations while in the first trimester with our fourth baby and suffering extreme morning sickness. But God provided a strength I had never had during any of my previous pregnancies. As long as I had apples, pecans, and a daily foot-long BLT sub sandwich, I was good to go, feeling well enough to do everything needed to prepare for the move. In April 2008, I flew to Rome with three little kids, my dog securely in the cargo hold.

Dave was waiting at the Rome airport to retrieve us, and our family was reunited. We lived near the US naval station in Naples. I quickly recovered from my first-trimester sickness, Dave was making decent money, and we were paying off debt, anticipating our new baby, and traveling all over Italy.

Even though we were civilians in the military community, because Dave worked for the Department of Defense, we felt as if we had returned to our old lives.

Life was again beautiful. We took day trips to the beach, to Rome, to Pompeii, to the Amalfi Coast. We were grateful God had restored our prosperity, and we were joyful.

Grant and Dominic at an Italian beach twenty minutes from our home, 2008.

Left: Kate, Dom, and Grant exploring at the Mediterranean Sea, Italy, 2008.

Right: Grant, three, and Dominic, four, at our home in Italy, 2008.

Left: The Decareaux family at the Coliseum in Rome, 2008. I was twenty-eight weeks pregnant with Finn.

Right: Dom, Grant, and Kate acting silly after an afternoon of homeschooling; Italy, 2008.

Dave and the kids in Italy, Father's Day 2008.

On October 17, 2008, Finn Nathaniel arrived.

We had another healthy baby boy. Finn's birth, like Grant's, was smooth and effortless. This was another planned C-section, and Finn came as scheduled. I laughed as I was wheeled into surgery, as Dave and I donned our surgical caps—what the naval medical team assisting the doctors called our party hats. Dave stayed at my side during the C-section, rubbing my forehead and videotaping the entire birth process. When we heard Finn's first cries as he was removed from my belly, Dave stroked my forehead, bent down to kiss me, and said, "Good job," before walking over to meet our brand-new son. Dave bonded with Finn and filmed their first encounter. I have the most precious video of baby Finn, just moments old, crying softly into the camera as nurses assess his condition. Over the commotion, Dave's voice is soft and gentle as he introduces himself to our son, "Hi, Finn. I'm your daddy. I'm your daddy, Finn."

We had one girl and then three boys. I bought books on mothering boys, thinking God had some kind of message for me in sending so many sons.

Finn and his daddy, Italy, 2008.

In secret, I had dearly hoped for another girl. But in retrospect I see my God knew I would need another boy years later. Not only did He give me Finn and therefore allow me to continue parenting a son after our tragedy, but He granted me my long-desired baby girl, in Elise, two years after Finn was born. What a good God.

Big brothers and big sister meeting baby Finn for the first time, Italy, October 2008. Dom was five, Grant was two weeks away from his fourth birthday, and Kate was six.

In true Decareaux family fashion, the adventure continued.

The day after Dave and I welcomed Finn into the world, Dave came to my hospital room and said, "Oh, by the way, our company lost the contract here in Naples, and in two weeks we are moving to Stuttgart, Germany."

I was holding our brand-new son, and while I was usually excited at the prospect of a new move, I burst into tears.

My mom had flown to Naples and was watching our three small kids while Dave and I were at the hospital with Finn. We soon returned home, but a few days later, a bloating in my abdomen had me concerned. I was terrified that a complication had taken place with my internal incisions and asked Dave to drive me to the emergency room immediately. After the birth of four children, Dave knew the effects of my postbaby hormones, and though he assured me I was okay, he realized it was best to get me to the hospital. Arriving at the emergency room, I was crying and quite worried. Dave sat next to me, holding Finn. He was convinced I was fine, but understood my need to have a doctor examine me and tell me I was all right.

As the minutes passed, my concern became annoyance that I had to wait so long in the emergency room. Unwilling to rock the boat any further, Dave refused to ask the hospital staff what was taking so long. One inquiry had been enough. I decided to take matters into my own hands, and despite Dave's protests, I wobbled over to the nurses' station and told the two people behind the counter, apparently on break, to "put their sandwiches down and get to my room to see what was going on". I returned to the examination room, awaiting a doctor. Dave and I sat in silence. He sat in stunned and embarrassed silence, and I remained in concerned silence, occasionally shooting him a defiant look that said, "What?...What?" Dave simply shook his head, a grin ever so slightly visible upon his face.

A doctor arrived shortly after to assess my condition and assured me that I was okay, that I was simply taking on extra fluid, and that I could go home and continue to heal. Days later, after those postbaby hormones had subsided, I thought over the emergency room incident. I was grateful for a hospital staff that knew how to roll with the punches from a hormonal new mother and for a husband, who, in his wisdom, let me have my say and do what I needed to do to feel some control over my seemingly out-of-control situation.

Dave always knew how to calm me down, allowing me to work through things my own way and to come to conclusions using my own method. I was grateful for a husband who loved me through my good, bad, ugly, and in-between. And many times it seemed, knew me better than I knew myself.

In the days following Dave's news of our pending move to Germany, we had to see my mom off at the airport and to get ready for a move to another country in two weeks' time.

I usually loved the moving process, but I could hardly walk after having had our son, so Dave did everything to prepare. The movers came and packed us out, but Dave cleaned the house, prepared all of our moving paperwork, and made all hotel arrangements.

Two weeks after Finn's birth, we drove eleven hours up to Germany. On the way, we stopped overnight in Verona, Italy, and also took a detour to see the Leaning Tower of Pisa. The night before Grant's fourth birthday, we arrived in Stuttgart.

Dave and I two weeks after bringing Finn into the world, ready to set out on our newest adventure in the fall of 2008. We were heading for Stuttgart, Germany, the next day.

A beautiful hotel suite in downtown Stuttgart was home for three months. We filled that suite with a four-year-old Grant, five-year-old Dom, six-year-old Kate, two-week-old Finn, our dog Cleo, and our newly acquired cat from Italy, Ulysses.

We lived in the hotel for three months while awaiting our German home. Grant turned four, Kate seven, Dom six, and Dave thirty-two in our hotel home, and we celebrated Thanksgiving and Christmas there. We sometimes got a little stir crazy living in a hotel suite for months, and I had to break up fights between the children that I never thought possible. In their boredom, they got into some interesting ones. One evening, while Dave was at work, I was sitting on the bed nursing Finn. I never did find out fully what the fight was fully about, but Kate, Dom, and Grant were arguing in their little bedroom, and the dispute ended with one of them saying, "I don't know where it is. Check his pants."

Still nursing Finn, I decided to let that one go and allow them to work it out.

Dave and Grant on Grant's fourth birthday, November 3, 2008.
We had arrived in Stuttgart, Germany, the night before.

Dave settled in nicely to his job as a civilian contractor at the US army garrison in Stuttgart, and we moved into a charming home in Renningen, Germany, in February 2009.

We started traveling all over Europe again with gusto, all the while homeschooling the children. We finished Kate's first-grade year, Dom's kindergarten year, and Grant's preschool year.

The kids were finally old enough to start activities outside of home: T-ball, the Awana church club, homeschool co-op classes, Girl Scouts, and Cub Scouts. Dave could not wait for his boys to reach the age for Scouting. He had developed a love for the outdoors while we lived in Idaho, and Scouting was a perfect marriage between time spent with his boys and with nature.

Dave helping Dom get ready for his first Cub Scout meeting, Germany, 2009.

Our days in Germany were filled with travel, adventure, homeschooling, and activities.

Dave and I got involved in parent leader roles. Dave was a Cub Scout master, and I was the Cub Scout pack secretary; I taught a homeschool co-op class and was team mom for our kids' T-ball and softball teams.

Dave and I took turns strapping baby Finn to our backs in our backpack hiker. We were true partners. As Finn entered his toddler years, he and Dave became very close. Finn was a rambunctious toddler and reminded me so much of Dom at that age. We let Finn's hair grow out, and he sported an Einsteinesque bleach blond 'do for a couple of years. His crazy hair matched his crazy personality, and Dave was often the only one who could calm our boy down. I referred to Dave as the "Finn whisperer". Finn was certainly a daddy's boy, and Dave loved every minute with him.

Dave loved being a daddy and spending time with his kids. His love of all things *Star Wars* rubbed off on the children. On many weekends Dave and the kids would sit through a marathon of all the *Star Wars* movies that culminated in a battle after each screening. Dave would duel the kids with the many light sabers we had in the house. Whether it was drawing with Kate, assembling Lego creations with Dom, or playing music while Grant hummed to the tune, Dave shared his interests with our kids. He was born to be a father.

Left: Dave and Finn, Germany, 2009.

Right: Brothers and buddies—Grant, four, and Finn, one, Germany, 2009.

Life stayed blissfully crazy during those years in Germany. Finn often times, left us all in stitches or shaking our heads in bafflement. One day, Dave returned from work as I was in the living room folding laundry. It had been a long day, and I barely looked up as he entered the room.

"Hey. How was your day?" I asked him.

"It was pretty good. How was yours?" he said.

"It was … interesting," I said.

Just as I spoke, Dominic entered the living room sporting a jagged green stripe from his eyelid to his eyebrow. Dave looked at him confused and asked, "What on earth is on your eye?"

Without hesitating, Dom responded, "Oh, Finn tried to stab me in the eye with a marker," and walked out of the room like it was no big deal.

Dave, horrified, looked to me as if asking for further explanation. Without skipping a beat, I said, "Dave, that's just how we do while you're at work," and continued folding laundry.

We traveled extensively throughout Europe while living in Germany, hiking the Alps and the area around Lake Eibsee in Bavaria. We visited

Hitler's Eagle's Nest, Poland, and the Czech Republic. We journeyed across the border into France too many times to count, sometimes just to grab a nice dinner. Whether we were on a train across England, the underground "tube" in London, the Paris Metro, the Autobahn in Germany, or the Metro of Rome, we were always on the go.

Dave and I took solo trips with friends to give each other time to relax and refuel. For instance, I went to the Alps with my dear friend Kim, and when I got back, Dave visited the Spanish islands of Ibiza and Majorca with a buddy. We had a great system going.

Our kids were growing, healthy, and adventurous. If the sun was shining and Dave wasn't working, we were in the van headed somewhere—a castle, a museum, a hiking trail.

Dave, Finn, and I ringing in Finn's first birthday, Paris, 2009.

One afternoon, Dave called from work and said, "I'm coming home early. Have everybody packed. We're driving to France."

I did not argue and waited for details later.

When I am told we are headed to France, I just do as I am told, I thought.

As it turned out, we saw the Tour de France and ended up making a tradition of traveling to the bike races in 2009 and 2010.

Our lives were full of adventure and love in Germany—blessed memories indeed.

Left: Finn trying to take big brother Dom's Cub Scout hat, Germany, 2009.

Right: Kate and Grant, buddies always, Germany, 2009.

Dave and the kids, Germany, Father's Day 2009.

In late 2009, we found out we were expecting baby number five.

I remember the day we told the kids they were going to have a baby sister. Dave and I had asked a friend to babysit while we went for my 3-D ultrasound appointment.

We found out that the baby would be a girl and drove to the playground to retrieve the kids from my girlfriend. We pulled up and asked the children to gather around.

"Guys, *Elise* will be joining our family in August!" Dave said.

Everyone was so excited. Of course, at age seven, Dominic had to say, "Aw, man! I wanted a brother!" He fooled no one though, as he said this with a sly smile on his face.

I looked at Grant, my gentle soul. His grin at hearing he would have a new sister was so big that it looked as if he would crack his cheeks. My sweet boy.

On August 20, 2010, Elise Marianna arrived. As the nurses were helping me onto the operating table in preparation for the C-section that would bring Elise into the world, one of them expressed amazement that I was giving birth to my fifth child, since large families were uncommon in Germany.

"So when is the sixth?" she asked.

I looked at her stunned and managed to say, "Um, let me get through this one first and I'll let you know."

Dave entered the room and held my hand as the procedure started. Completely numb from the waist down, I asked him for a progress report. "Have they started cutting yet?" I asked.

Looking fascinated yet grossed out, he answered, "Oh, they've started," and immediately after I heard Elise's first cries.

I could not believe how quickly she was born. Having had babies in a Portuguese hospital, a civilian hospital in Illinois, a military hospital in Idaho, and a US naval hospital in Italy, all wonderful experiences with highly competent care, I was amazed at the proficiency of the German doctors. Elise's birth was effortless. The nurse placed her directly on my chest moments after birth. It was the first time I was able to experience that, since with C-sections, my babies were generally cleaned up and measured before I got to touch them. Dave and I bonded with our new daughter and cried tears of joy as we listened to her make those first few baby sounds.

Back in my room many hours after Elise's birth, I realized one way in which the American birthing process was unsurpassed: Americans knew how to ward off pain. In the German hospital, many doctors preferred a holistic approach and minimal meds. Thus I found myself repeatedly having to ask for pain medication. As each time I was presented with the minimum, I tried to break through the language barrier to ask the nurses for something stronger.

"Much pain. I am in much pain," I said very slowly and very loudly, as if that would make it translate any better.

The nurses seemed a bit annoyed and reminded me to take the pills before the pain started to ward off discomfort. Dave held my hand through it all and got a chuckle out of my attempts at translating. However, he couldn't stay with me in the hospital as long as he had in previous times, since we now had four children back home. And while Dave's mom had flown in and was at our house caring for our brood, he didn't want to leave her with our crazies for too long without being there to help keep everyone in line.

Dave's mom cooked, cleaned, and kept our kids occupied, and we were grateful to have her there.

Elise was an easy, pleasant baby and reminded me so much of Grant at that age. She was content as long as she was held, and there were always many eager hands willing to hold the youngest of five children. On many nights, Dave fell asleep with baby Elise in his arms. After having three boys following Kate, I was overjoyed to see Dave handle a baby girl for the first time in so many years. As he snuggled Elise, smiled at her, and blew kisses on her belly, I was reminded of the long ago days when he showed his love for baby Kate in just the same way. In the late evenings Dave and I would put our kids to bed and settle down to relax on the couch next to each other, each with our laptops. Dave spent many an evening playing a video game with one hand as he held Elise with the other.

Dave holding our brand-new Elise Marianna, Germany, 2010.

Dominic became a hands-on, protective big brother to Elise. He was terrific with her and learned early on how to change a diaper. Kate, the oldest of our brood, was an excellent big sister, and she is still a minimomma. Grant loved to make his baby sister laugh, and I have many videos of him making silly faces at her. She rewarded her brother's efforts with full-on belly laughs, much to Grant's delight. Finn was not so sure about his little sister at first, since she was taking over his turf as the baby of the family. But one afternoon we realized that Finn had warmed up to Elise when he asked in his twenty-two-month-old way if he could hold her on his lap. As Kate tried to take Elise, thinking Finn was finished holding the baby, Finn growled at her. He actually uttered a low guttural growl that left Kate with no doubt that Finn had claimed Elise as his new buddy.

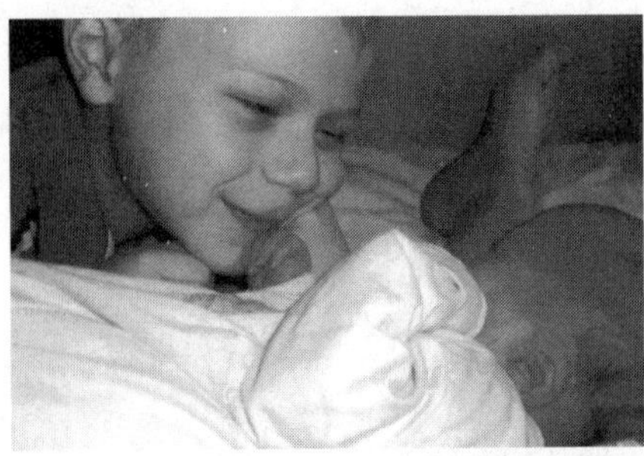

Left: Dominic meeting his baby sister, Elise, Germany, 2010.

Right: The Decareaux kids, Germany, 2010.

We stayed active after Elise's birth, continuing the adventure even as a family of seven. We took day trips, overnighters, weekenders, and vacations. In 2011, we went to Salzburg, Austria, in May; to Pisa, Italy, for a beach vacation in August, and to Venice, Italy, for vacation in October. One day Finn insisted on chasing peacocks at the Stuttgart Zoo in Germany until one of them had had enough and went after him, eventually catching him and pinching his belly with its claw. We recalled that Finn had chased birds in many countries—pigeons in the Venice city square, birds at a fountain in the center of Salzburg, seagulls at the beaches near Pisa. It dawned on us how well traveled our kids were, and we were exceedingly grateful for the life that we led.

Left: Dave and I with baby Elise in the Snuggie, returning to our day trips when she was only a few weeks old, Germany, 2010.

Right: The Decareaux kids, Triberg Waterfalls, Black Forest, Germany, 2010.

Left: Dave and our kids in Pisa, Italy, 2011.

Right: The Decareauxes in Pisa, Italy, 2011. We toured the city in this bike cart, as we called it. I had never laughed so hard.

Kate and her brothers. Celebrating Daddy's thirty-fourth birthday, Germany, 2010.

We traveled to Normandy, France, for a vacation in May of 2012. Our family was nonstop. The many vacations we took were punctuated by small trips in between: a weekender here, a day trip to a castle there, and weeklong Cub Scout camp each summer. We lived a full existence as a family of seven.

Our trip to Normandy was life-changing.

Dom was an avid war and history buff. He educated himself and all of us about the world wars, the Civil War, and other major events. He collected war action figures and built a boot- camp obstacle course in our backyard. We got him minicamo pants, and he whittled a stick into a smooth weapon he called his gun. He even made Dave and me military IDs out of index cards.

The trip to Normandy was a living history lesson about much of what Dominic already knew, even at nine years old.

We visited Normandy's American cemetery on Memorial Day, and we had the boys wear their Cub Scout uniforms to show respect. I have the most precious photos of Dom standing in front of a grave and contemplating the scene. I would love to know what was going through his beautiful mind.

My three big kids—Kate, Dom, and Grant—scoured the cemetery with the mission of finding all grave markers that read, "Known But to God," so they could pay special respects to the unknown soldiers.

I had no idea that less than a year later, my nephew, their cousin, would be at another military cemetery, across the ocean in Missouri, paying respects to my boys in his Cub Scout uniform on Memorial Day. Only God could have known.

Left: The kids at Utah Beach in Normandy, France, May 2012. This was a life-changing trip for all of us.

Right: Dominic and Grant, in Cub Scout uniform, at Pointe du Hoc, Normandy, France, May 2012. We were all astonished at the tenacity shown by the men who scaled those cliffs so many years before.

Left: Dave, Omaha Beach, Normandy, France, May 2012. He was moved beyond words by this place where so many lives were lost.

Right: The Decareaux kids outside our cabin in Normandy, France, May 2012.

Grant was not a war or a history buff; he was my animal lover. By the time he was eighteen months old, he could identify several animals. I have video of him accurately naming animals for his daddy: "rhino, hippo, horsy, butterfly, dinosaur."

In Germany, we would take walks to a creek across the street from our home or to the woods behind our house. Grant would put on his zookeeper vest, a fishing vest Dave had bought him for Christmas in 2009. Grant would grab a memo pad and a pencil and record all the animals he encountered on the way to our destination. They might be real or imaginary: spider, ladybug, lion, black panther.

Kate, Dom, Grant, and I would spend hours after school on a lazy afternoon gathered around my computer, watching episodes of History Channel's *Monster Quest*, Syfy's *Destination Truth*, and R.L. Stine's *Goosebumps.*

My kids have always been my friends.

We were a tight-knit family living overseas; we had only each other. Of course we had friends, but holidays were spent as a family. As we were overseas, we couldn't attend parties with extended family.

Dave and I homeschooled and were with the kids at all times. The children couldn't wait for Daddy to get home from work so the family could go out to eat or cook together, they could tell him about their day, or attend a Cub Scout meeting. Our life was indeed blessed.

Dave and Kate headed to a father-daughter dance, Germany, 2011.

Left: Dave and Elise on our Italian beach trip, August 2011.
Right: Dave and our kids on his thirty-fourth birthday, Germany, December 2010.

Left: Dave with Dom and Grant, Germany, Christmas Eve 2011.
Right: Dave, Grant's daddy and den leader, awarding him a Scout badge, Germany, May 2012.

St. Patrick's Day 2012, Germany.

Left: The kids on a day trip to a dinosaur museum, Germany, 2011.

Right: Dom and baby sister, Elise, Germany, 2011.

By July 2012, we were moving from Germany back to the States.

While working in Germany as a civilian contractor for the Department of Defense, Dave had gotten a General Schedule government job with the military. He had even received a promotion within the GS system. He was on the fast track to success.

Because some of my family members back home were experiencing health problems, we preferred that Dave be stationed back stateside. God did us one better and arranged for Dave to get a job at Scott Air Force Base, Illinois, forty-five minutes from my hometown.

On July 28, 2012, we arrived in St. Louis.

We were prepared to forgo overseas life for a time, to purchase a home, and to put down roots until we were ready for another foreign adventure. We anticipated staying stateside for about five years. Our goal was to reach Hawaii or Asia next, but for the time being, we were overjoyed to have an assignment so close to my family.

After we had decided to leave Germany, Dave had applied for Department of Defense jobs all over the United States, and the only two interviews he got were for positions at Scott Air Force Base.

Our God knew why we would need to be near family.

We embraced living close to relatives. The kids had play dates with their cousins, and we enjoyed dinners out with my friends, cousins, and sisters. We welcomed Dave's parents up to Illinois for Elise's second birthday celebration at a local park. Elise was celebrated that day by her brothers and sister, my parents, Dave's parents, many family and friends, aunt, uncles and cousins. Dave and my brothers became hiking buddies. Dave's goals were to section-hike the entire Ozark Trail and then move on, work schedule permitting, to the Appalachian Trail or even trails in the Rockies.

We lived on Scott Air Force Base for two months while we sought a home. On September 28, 2012, we moved into the first home we had owned, in Millstadt, Illinois.

Dave settled in nicely to his GS-13 job on Scott Air Force Base, while I concentrated on making our house a home and teaching our kids.

We got Kate into art classes and the boys back into Cub Scouts. They were in the same pack as their cousins. With his extensive Cub Scout experience, Dave volunteered to lead the wolf den for our boys' pack. Dave had founded a pack in Germany for boys at the Robinson barracks and was knowledgeable about all things Scouting.

Dave was excited that his boys were finally at the age he had always eagerly anticipated. They were Cub Scouts, and he had built-in hiking buddies.

My boys were always up for adventure. Dominic and Grant were not video game kids, athletes, or art students; they were hikers and loved spending quality time with their dad. Hiking was in their spirits. They took great pride in shopping with Dave for hiking gear, backpacks, special hiking shoes, and trekking poles.

Dave, Dom, Grant, and Bear headed out on a two-day hike in the Ozark Mountains of Missouri, November 2012. Finn is upset he can't go along.

Left: Dom on a two-day hike with Dave and Grant, Missouri, November 2012.

Right: Dave, the Missouri Ozarks, 2012.

The weekend we moved into our home, Dave and Dom picked up another hiking partner—our new Lab puppy, Bear. Dom was Bear's master. Dave and I decided that Dominic was old enough to take full responsibility for our new canine companion, and Dom was excited by the challenge.

Dom was a diligent master, following directions and mixing Bear's puppy food just right, making sure it soaked for a full ten minutes before allowing Bear to eat it. One day, Bear was whining for his food, trying to get at the bowl on the countertop. I reached for the bowl to place it on the floor. Entering the kitchen, Dom saw what I was doing and reprimanded his momma. "Mom! His food has to soak for exactly ten minutes! He can't have it yet." Apologizing, I realized that Dom had Bear's care completely under control and that I should let him look out for his dog in his own way. This was part of growing up, part of becoming a young man, and I was proud of my boy and how seriously he took his role as Bear's master. He worked tirelessly to train Bear and had the many T-shirts with holes from the puppy's teeth to prove it.

Dominic bringing home Bear at ten weeks old, Illinois, September 2012.

My guys displayed their love for the outdoors soon after arriving in the St. Louis area. We had been in town for two weeks and were still in our temporary lodging on Scott Air Force Base when Dave and our boys went with my brother, my nephew, and other family members on a canoeing trip.

Only two weeks after that outing in August of 2012, our family of seven went on a camping trip to a lake in Illinois. In September, Dave took an overnight backpacking trip with my brothers along a section of the Ozark Trail in Missouri. In November, he led our sons on that same stretch of trail. They ran into bad weather, but carrying overnight gear, they were more than prepared. They hunkered down under an overhanging rock and stayed safe. In fact, they made such good time, having hiked twelve miles in one day, that they called me to pick them up a night early.

We dove in to adventure with both feet living back stateside.

Dave, Grant, and Elise apple picking, Millstadt, Illinois, fall 2012.

Grant doing schoolwork, Illinois, fall 2012.

Left: My boys headed to a fall festival, Illinois, 2012.

Right: Grant and Finn on the way into our woods for an afternoon adventure, 2012.

Left: Dominic and Grant delivering Christmas cookies to our neighbors, Illinois, 2012.

Right: Dominic running through our pine clearing with Bear and Cleo, 2012.

Left: My crazy kids on Grant's eighth birthday, Illinois, fall 2012.

Right: Brothers Dominic, Grant, and Finn out on a lake adventure with their daddy, Illinois, fall 2012.

The Decareaux family, Illinois, Christmas 2012.

Our trip in January of 2013 was nothing out of the ordinary for the Decareaux family. We planned to stay in a cabin, and Dave and the big kids (Kate, Dom and Grant) would hike. We were always on the go.

Since arriving stateside in July, we had gone on the outdoor adventures mentioned above and had traveled to New Orleans to see Dave's family in November. I had taken a Caribbean cruise with my cousins in November, and we had returned to New Orleans in early January for a late Christmas with Dave's family and to celebrate Dom's birthday.

Our anniversary hiking trip came only days after we had arrived back home from New Orleans. We never sat still. Dave worked hard, played hard, loved much, laughed much, and lived much.

In January of 2013, Dave had gotten an unexpected three-day weekend. He excitedly told me he had been researching a lodge in the Ozarks and wanted to take the family there to celebrate our wedding anniversary. He was also excited that the place sat by some great trails. Dave had arranged for the lodge to prepare us a special anniversary meal on the evening of our arrival.

We packed up hiking gear, camp food, and wine and headed out with our kids and the dogs for another Decareaux family adventure on January 11, 2013, our twelfth anniversary.

Our plan was to arrive on the late afternoon of the eleventh and to have an anniversary meal. The next day Dave and the big kids would take a short hike. Once they returned, we were to enjoy a family campfire in the evening.

On Sunday the thirteenth, we were to stop by Johnson's Shut-Ins State Park for photos before driving back home after what we expected would be a fun weekend.

Only God could have known how drastically our plans would change.

Chapter 2

That Weekend—from Here to Heaven

I awoke the morning of Friday, January 11, with a mental list of all we would need to pack and to do before leaving on our anniversary trip to the lodge. But Dave quickly reminded me that he had everything in order. The trip was, in part, an anniversary gift to me, and he had taken care of all arrangements. I was responsible only for packing a bag and rounding up a few more clothes for the kids. Dave would even do the grocery shopping so that we would have enough food for our stay in the cabin.

But first, before the day began, before duties beckoned, before kids awoke, we snuggled. I laid my head on Dave's chest, and we talked. In a house with five kids, eleven years old and under, running around, we rarely got a peaceful moment together. We were reflective that morning of our twelfth wedding anniversary. We talked about the past, about how we met, and about our hopes and dreams for the future. This was one of those precious moments spouses share before the kids awake, before the dog whines to be let out, before the day begins, and I treasured it.

Our snuggling time was short-lived. We had to jump into action as the kids got up and routine family life began. The baby needed her diaper changed, breakfast had to be made, and the dog needed to be let out. I spent the late morning and the early afternoon packing a few last- minute items for the kids and myself, while Dave and Kate headed to the grocery store to get the groceries we would need for meals at our cabin. Finally, around 2:00 p.m., we got on the road.

Dave and I were in the front seats of our minivan, with the kids sitting in the two rows behind us; our dogs, Cleo (our longtime husky companion, twelve years old) and Bear (our newly acquired Lab puppy, five months old) rested securely on the floorboards. We were on our way to the Ozarks to celebrate twelve years of marriage.

As we pulled out of our lane and onto the road, we repeated a family ritual. When we would leave on a trip, we would look back at the house and say, "Bye, house! See you in a couple days." As was also routine, I said a silent prayer for traveling mercies on our two-hour drive to the Brushy Creek Lodge in the Missouri Ozarks.

As our family of seven said good-bye to our house that afternoon, I did not know that only four of us would be returning two days later.

About thirty minutes into the drive, Dave remembered he had not picked up hot cocoa. Wanting the trip to be perfect, he pulled over at a gas station to buy cocoa packets for our family campfire later that weekend.

Our drive was peaceful. There were no big sibling spats in the seats behind us, the dogs rested, and Finn and Elise slept most of the way. About an hour into the journey, Dave and I held hands as he drove. Because this was our anniversary, we were nostalgic, contemplative, and hopeful. We told stories about our families. We reflected on what we wanted to do the same as our families and what we wanted to do differently. Deeply grateful for our children, Dave said, "I just don't understand how some men walk out on their families. I just cannot understand walking out on your children."

I squeezed his hand more tightly, grateful for the man of character and integrity beside me, the man I got to call partner and friend, and said, "Dave, don't worry. That is not our story. This is when we do for our family what others were not able to do for theirs in our past, and we are going to be sitting in rocking chairs on our front porch one day, both with white hair, holding hands, watching our twenty grandchildren play all around us."

Dave squeezed my hand and looked straight ahead. I watched his face in the moment after I spoke. He smiled a content, far-off smile, as if he were picturing what I had said.

We were only about twenty minutes from our destination when we suffered the only hiccup on our drive: poor Dominic, succumbing to car sickness, threw up all over the back seat of the van. And in typical Dave-and-Sarah fashion, despite the beautiful drive and the moments of bonding on our anniversary, we had a spat. As Dom threw up, the kids and I frantically searched for a container of some kind, and Dave worried about vomit getting all over the back seat. It was a typical moment of frustration and confusion on a family road trip, and I finally yelled, "Dave, shut up! Your son is sick!"

While Dave had every reason to want us to act quickly so we could avoid a mess, I was also feeling the stress of the situation, and we had a classic family fight. We got Dom cleaned up and the mess contained as best we could, and the last twenty minutes of the drive were silent. Needless to say, Dave and I were no longer holding hands.

We loved much and aired our frustrations much, and our anniversary was no exception. But as we saw the sign for the lodge grounds, Dave stopped the van. He turned to me with a smile on his face, grabbed my hand, and said, "Are you ready?" Then he gave my hand a squeeze. After twelve years of marriage, I knew what that meant. This was his way of saying, "I'm sorry. You're sorry. Let's be friends again."

I broke into a grin, squeezed his hand, and said, "Yeah, I'm ready. Just let me get a picture of the sign first."

And all was well again in the Decareaux van.

We pulled into the parking lot, anxious to get checked in, to find our cabin, to get Dom and the van cleaned up, and to start our weekend vacation. Dave and I asked Kate to hold down the fort in the van, and he and I headed for the lodge to check in. As we entered, our excitement grew. The lodge was beautifully decorated and laid out; it was exactly what our family needed to bond that anniversary weekend. We were greeted at the front desk by Annette, the manager. After Dave got us checked in, I said, "We had a mess on the way down here. Can you tell me where the washers and dryers are? Are they in the shower house?"

I assumed that Dave had booked us a rustic cabin and that we would have to use a shower house on the grounds.

"I'm sorry, ma'am. I don't understand. Shower house? You have a shower in your cabin, and I can show you here in the lodge where the laundry facilities are," Annette answered.

"We have a shower in the cabin?" I said.

"Yes," Annette replied.

I looked at Dave. A silent satisfaction showed all over his face.

"Well done," I said slowly, slapping him in the belly with the back of my hand.

Dave's grin widened. He knew he had done well. He had planned the trip, and he had done an amazing job, making sure we had a deluxe cabin with shower facilities.

We found our cabin, unpacked the van, got Dominic and the van cleaned up, let the dogs stretch their legs, and changed the baby's diaper. When everyone was settled, Dave reminded us that we were having dinner at six in the lodge. Along with planning the trip, grocery shopping, and making sure we had showers in our cabin, Dave had arranged to have a special anniversary meal prepared for our family that evening.

After cleaning up, we found ourselves with about thirty minutes before dinner. We walked the grounds and took pictures, and the kids played on a wooden teeter totter next to the lodge. Five rambunctious kids were bound to break something, and that weekend, it was the teeter totter. Somehow my lovelies managed to knock it off center, and the whole thing came tumbling down, with each blaming the other. Dave tried his best to right the teeter totter, but to no avail. We decided to inform Annette upon arriving for dinner and to offer to make up for it.

We sat down to a meal of breaded and baked chicken, green beans, mashed potatoes, and bread. Dave had additionally arranged for kid-friendly fare, and sure enough, the children were served homemade mac and cheese. We had chocolate cake for dessert. Annette had outdone herself with the cooking, and Dave had outdone himself with the planning.

Our meal that night was magical. We were content, well fed, jovial, celebratory, grateful, and humbled at the family's good fortune. We had a good conversation with Annette about homeschooling, the kids did not fight us about finishing their meals, and at one point, Annette's four-year-old daughter joined us at our table. Annette told her girl to move to her table so we could eat in privacy on our special day. Dave quickly piped up, "We have five kids; what's one more?" he said with a smile; and Annette's adorable daughter joined us for dinner that evening.

As I ate contently, surrounded by my children, across from my gracious, generous man, I had no idea that this would be our last meal as a family of seven.

After dinner, we were anxious to return to the cabin and get the kids tucked in for the night. Dave had developed a migraine during our meal. He suffered migraines constantly, and the only thing he could do was to take Motrin and sleep it off. So, although we had wine waiting for us back at the cabin to celebrate our anniversary, we put the kids to bed early and were all off to sleep by about 8:30 p.m.

Around four in the morning, Dave woke up, his migraine having worn off. I awoke when I heard him stirring. We lay there in the dark, going over the day's events. Dave apologized for cutting our anniversary celebration short due to his migraine. I assured him there was no problem, and we continued to snuggle and talk. "Wasn't that meal magical?" Dave said. "It was just a magical night." That was the last thing I remember him saying before we fell back to sleep.

Our family awoke at about nine on the morning of Saturday, January 12, 2013, having slept in a bit. This was a vacation, after all. "We are getting a late start to the day," Dave told me. "I think we should just go to Johnson's Shut-Ins today as a family and skip the hike."

Dave was referring to a spot in the Black River just miles from the lodge where boulders made a natural swimming playground. Of course, in January, we couldn't swim, but we were anxious to take photos of that beautiful place at some point on our weekend getaway. "That's fine, Dave," I said. "You just let me know what we're doing today. I'm fine with whatever."

I am so grateful God allowed me that gracious response. When the game plan changed unexpectedly, I was usually thrown off kilter and had to readjust my thinking for the day.

But for some reason, when Dave proposed changing the plan that day, I was not phased. In fact, I welcomed the idea of staying together as a family and not having to entertain the babies (Finn and Elise) for hours alone while Dave and the big kids hiked. The plan had been for Dave and the big kids to hike for a few hours while the babies and I stayed on the grounds of the lodge. Annette had agreed to show the babies and me the horses that afternoon. If we had any time left before the guys returned from hiking, I thought we would spend it in the rec room at the lodge or napping back at the cabin.

But when the boys heard Dave say he was contemplating canceling the hike, they cried out in protest.

"I want to hike! You promised us we were going to go hiking!"

Not wanting to disappoint his boys, Dave quickly reverted to his original plan and decided to hike after all. But it would be a short hike, he assured me, since we had gotten a late start to the day.

While everyone was getting ready, Kate cried out, "Mom, I brought the wrong shoes. I am not going hiking."

"Kate, you don't want to hurt Daddy's feelings," I said. "He's looking forward to hiking with you big kids. You should go. It doesn't matter what shoes you brought."

"Mom, I am not going to get my new shoes dirty. I'm not going," Kate told me.

"Okay," I said. "You are going to be bored with me. The babies and I are just hanging out here today, but it's your choice."

Kate assured me she was not hiking and was staying with the babies and me.

We got dressed and ate our Cheerios, and Dave made coffee. Sometime during this morning routine, he decided that since this would be a short hike and Kate wasn't going, he would take Finn along. Again, I told him I was fine with whatever he decided to do.

Always the outdoorsman, Dave made his single-serve coffee on a camp stove even though he had a coffee maker in the cabin. Cup in hand, Dave stood in the open doorway as the kids ran outside and played. The bright morning sun created a brilliant picture of Dave silhouetted in the beautiful scene. I grabbed my camera to capture the moment. Seeing this, Dave said, "This is the perfect vacation pose, isn't it?"

I took the photo, and Dave, adjusting a bit, coffee cup still in hand, said, "Okay, take another one."

I have the most brilliant photos of Dave, the sun creating a glow all around him as he stands at the door of the cabin. He appears almost angelic, almost heavenly. Looking back, I feel heaven was preparing to greet three more faithful souls that night, and we were seeing a glimpse of the glory that morning.

As the boys readied their daypacks and supplies, I asked Dave to wait a moment while I tied Finn's shoes and got his coat on.

"Oh, no. I've changed my mind," Dave said. "I'm not going to take him."

"Dave," I protested, "he is going to throw a fit. You have to take him now."

"He doesn't even know I was considering taking him, so be quiet and he'll never know," Dave assured me.

Again, I relented, which was out of character for me. I reasoned that Dave and the boys could surely do this hike more quickly without Finn in tow.

I had Dave, Dom, and Grant, along with Bear, gather under a tree in front of our cabin for a few photos, and then they were off. There were no long, drawn-out, or special good-byes. Kate, Finn, Elise, Cleo, and I would await their return later in the afternoon for family campfire time. We knew a storm was coming that night but thought we had plenty of time for a short campfire before it hit.

As Dominic and Grant ran ahead of Dave with Bear on his leash toward the trailhead within view of our cabin, I called out to them, "I love you! Have fun!"

As Dave set out to catch up, Finn jumped out of my arms and ran toward his father, crying, "Daddy, Daddy. I want Daddy."

He wanted to desperately to go along. I was outside in my slippers and ran inside the cabin to throw on my shoes to go retrieve Finn. In the time it took me to do that, Finn had reached his daddy, and Dave was carrying him back up the hill to me. Finn was screaming and sobbing; he wanted his daddy so badly. Dave spoke calmly and reassuringly to Finn, saying that Daddy loved him and would see him soon. Then he handed me our son. That was our last exchange as husband and wife, as mother and father. I took Finn from my husband and walked back up the hill to our cabin, reassuring Finn that Daddy would soon return.

The whole while I carried him up the hill, Finn was reaching out behind me for his daddy, calling out to him. I took Finn to the back porch of the cabin, and through the bare trees, we could see Dom, Grant, and Bear, with Dave having just caught up to them, heading out on the trailhead below. Finn and I watched and took pictures of them from a distance, calling out our good-byes.

"Say bye to Daddy, Finn. Say 'Bye bye and we'll see you soon.'"

And then they were out of sight. That was the last time I saw my boys alive on earth. No one could have known where their journey would take them that day.

After seeing off Dave, Dom, and Grant, the rest of us prepared to start our day. We planned to meet up with Annette, who had offered to show us some of the horses belonging to the lodge. As we dressed and walked the short distance to the lodge to connect with Annette, I was grateful for the adventurous life our family led. We never sat still. We were always exploring and learning, and I liked it that way.

We followed Annette to a nearby barn and found many horses in their stalls. The children and I walked from stall to stall, petting the faces of the outgoing horses and staying clear of the ones Annette said didn't welcome unfamiliar company.

The kids had a great time on that peaceful early afternoon. I took several pictures to remember the moment. When we opened the doors of the large barn to head back to the lodge, we saw that an unexpected drizzle had started. As the kids ran in the pasture near the barn, I noticed they were getting a bit too wet for the cold temperatures and told them it was time to return to the lodge so they could stay dry.

On the way to the lodge rec room to play games that afternoon, I thought, *Well, Dave and the boys will be back any minute. That rain started way earlier than we thought it would, and there is no way they're hiking in the rain.*

At about 2:30 p.m., I told the kids it was time to head back to our cabin. I wanted to take a short nap before Dave and the boys returned and we commenced with our family plans for the evening—a campfire and s'mores. However, as I looked out of the rec room windows, I guessed we probably wouldn't be having a campfire that night, not with the rain coming down harder and sooner than we expected.

Back at the cabin, the babies lay down for a nap, Kate occupied herself with a game she had brought, and I sat on the bed to journal. I liked to keep a record of all the trips we took as a family, a travel log of sorts. After spending time on my journal, I decided to play solitaire with a deck of cards we had taken along for family games that night. After several rounds of solitaire, I realized that a good amount of time had passed and that Dave and the boys should be back soon. It was about 4:00 p.m. They were due back by 4:30 p.m., but I was surprised that they hadn't returned early with the rain arriving sooner than anticipated.

Finn and Elise, having woken from their naps, were playing with Cleo and otherwise keeping themselves occupied. Finn decided it would be fun to roast marshmallows with one of the two space heaters in our cabin.

"We already broke the teeter totter, Finn. I don't need you gooing up the space heater as well," I told him. *Although,* I thought, *you might as well roast marshmallows by the heater, because it does not look as if we are getting a family campfire tonight.*

The drizzle of early afternoon became a steady rain and then a downpour. I thought how miserable Dave and the boys must be and how they would come back dejected and soaking wet. I periodically looked out of the cabin windows toward the trailhead, watching for any sign of them. I had done that for several minutes when there was a knock on the door.

Annette was at the door and asked if Dave and the boys had returned.

"No," I said, adding that I was a bit concerned, since the weather had gotten colder.

Annette offered to drive her van to the forestry roads that intersected the trail Dave and the boys would have taken. She hoped to intercept our guys and bring them the rest of the way back to the cabin. Annette thought she could fit my guys and Bear more comfortably in the van than in her truck.

I agreed that would be a great idea, thanked her, and closed the door.

Nightfall began at about 5:00 p.m. Noticing the slight air of concern in the room, Kate threw on her jacket and started for the door.

"Where on earth are you going?" I asked.

"I'm going to the trailhead to see if I see them coming."

"No you're not, hon. It's pouring out there. Annette is going to pick them up. They'll be fine."

But even as I said that, I picked up my phone. Though I knew there was no cell phone service where we were, I attempted to text Dave.

"Where are you?" I typed, to no response.

As we waited for Annette to return with our guys, I continued to watch from the windows. It was now completely dark, and I could see headlights coming to and fro from the lodge parking lot. Knowing we were the only guests that weekend, I wondered what all the activity was about. I had no idea that Annette, in her concern, had called the lodge owners to help her look for Dave, Dom, and Grant.

Finally, I heard a vehicle outside of the cabin. I opened the door and saw through what had become a deluge that Annette had returned in her van. Squinting through the rain and the darkness, I thought I saw figures beside her in the vehicle. Certain that she had brought the boys back, I felt relieved. I couldn't wait to get them inside and into warm clothes and to ask them about their journey.

But when Annette opened her car door and the light came on inside the van, I could see she was alone.

I could have sworn I saw several figures in the van with her, I thought.

Worried, I met her on the porch.

"You didn't find them?" I asked.

"No," she responded, adding, "and I've called George and Joann, the owners of the lodge, in to help. They've got a couple of the lodge workers in their trucks looking too."

Worried and aggravated, I asked what I could do, and she recommended I stay put in case the boys returned to the cabin. I agreed, and Annette left to continue driving the roads near the trail to see if she could spot my guys.

I watched through the windows as several trucks drove to and from the lodge. Each time, I hoped and prayed that one of those trucks contained Dave, Dom, and Grant.

Around 6:30 p.m., hours after Dave, Dom, and Grant were due back, Annette returned to the cabin and told me to come to the lodge. A search party had been organized. My heart dropped to my feet. I hurriedly left, asking Kate to sit with the babies for a few minutes at the cabin. But my spirit was soon calmed. Inside the warm, bright, almost cheery lodge, I found several cowboys, wearing hats, coats, and spurs, sitting at the tables, and talking over bowls of chili. Annette had made chili and fixings to feed the many cowboys and lodge personnel who had come to help look for Dave and the boys. Seeing that the mood was calm, almost jovial, I was embarrassed that those men and women were willing to go out in that weather and to get cold and soaking wet because my husband had seemingly lost his way.

One of the cowboys noticed me off to the side.

"Is this the wife?" he asked with a smile.

"I'm the wife," I answered, returning his smile. "I am so sorry, you guys. First we break your teeter totter, and now this; we have got to be the worst guests you have ever had stay here!"

Everyone chuckled and assured me it was no big deal. This was not the first search they had made, they told me.

My mood lifted, my spirits calmed, and I talked with the searchers for some time before Annette approached me and said, "Sarah, go to your cabin and get a warm change of clothes for your guys. When they are found, they are going to need to get warmed up right away, so we are going to have them shower here at the lodge. I have towels, so go get those warm clothes."

I agreed, and as I walked back to the cabin to get the clothes, my spirit was burdened with the thought of my guys out in those woods in the downpour, soaking wet and cold.

Returning to the lodge with a change in clothes for each of my guys, I stood by the front desk with Annette and other workers as we watched the weather forecast on the computer and listened to radio calls coming in from those searching the woods.

As I saw on the computer screen that the temperature was dipping into the thirties, a man in uniform entered the lodge. He introduced himself as a deputy from the sheriff's department and asked to speak with me. He explained that the lodge owners had requested an official search since their search was becoming increasingly difficult. My heart fell out of my chest. He asked for copies of the trail maps indicating where Dave and the boys would be hiking, and he was off.

As I continued to listen to radio calls and to watch the forecast, my mind swirled with thoughts, with theories, with questions. I turned to

Annette and asked, "Are there any wild animals out there we should be concerned about?"

"Not in this rain," she answered.

"Well, what about hypothermia?" I asked. "Should we be worried about them being wet and cold?"

Annette hesitated for a moment and then, looking me right in the eyes, said, "I have considered that."

The way she answered left me feeling as if there was something she was not telling me. Perhaps unwilling to hear anything more, I did not press for a further explanation.

The night had started with Annette out in her van looking for my guys and with lodge personnel driving their trucks up and down forestry roads and riding trails on horseback, seeking any sign of Dave and the boys. Now the search had become a full-scale effort. Fifty-plus people from multiple agencies had been called in and were searching the pitch-black woods in a downpour on horseback, on foot, on ATVs, and in trucks. They had ambulances ready at spots where the trail connected with forestry roads.

I stayed behind at the lodge, wanting to be near the cabin in case my remaining kids needed me or Dave and the boys arrived there. But I also wanted to be near what had become command central at the lodge's front desk to hear any information that the searchers relayed by radio.

As each hour passed, my hopes dwindled. I told myself that Dave and the boys were in good hands with the capable searchers and that there was no reason to alarm anyone. I decided not to call my family or Dave's yet.

A few of the searchers and I reasoned that Dave, a skilled outdoorsman, must have hunkered down out of the storm somewhere with the boys. It was starting to seem that he and the boys had left the trail, having found shelter at some unknown point.

With a sure confidence in the searchers' ability and in Dave's skill, I was worried but not hopeless. I assumed the best—that Dave and my boys were holed up in a barn, a hunting shack, or somewhere else away from the storm.

A call came in on the radio saying that a horse trailer on one of the trucks had almost been washed away by a creek that had become a raging river in the deluge.

That was about midnight, and at that point we got word that the search would be called for the night. Everything inside me cried out, *Do not call off this search!*

But I looked at the faces around me—tired, worn, wet, and miserable but still confident— I was sure that the searchers believed as I did or there was no way they would call a halt. I was certain we all agreed that Dave had to have hunkered down off of the trail. There was no other way to explain why he hadn't been found, and finding him off of the trail in the pitch black would be impossible. Meanwhile, the storm was becoming increasingly dangerous for the searchers. It was inconceivable that they would leave a man and two little boys to the elements if they did not have confidence, as I did, that they were somewhere safe and would come home when the storm had subsided.

My spirit calmed, I walked back to the cabin a little after midnight.

I went to bed thinking Dave would return to the cabin in the middle of the night, having waited out the brunt of the storm in a barn somewhere along the trail, and would bring our sons to the door cold and miserable but safe and sound and with a story to tell. I had always had full faith and confidence in Dave. In fact, I turned on both space heaters in the cabin, thinking, *When they come back, they are going to be cold and wet. I want to have it warm and cozy in here.*

Then I slept heavily. The emotion of the evening's search had taken its toll, and I was more exhausted than I realized. As I drifted off to sleep, I thought, *It's okay. He's a skilled outdoorsman. They're in a barn or structure of some kind, hunkering down. I'm just going to rest until they make it back to the cabin.*

I didn't know that while I was sleeping in the cabin with two space heaters going, Dave, Dominic, and Grant were succumbing to hypothermia.

I woke to a hard, urgent knock on the cabin door.

Finally, I thought, *they're home.*

I jumped out of the bed, fully clothed since I had fallen asleep that way, and ran to throw open the door. I was expecting to get my boys inside and out of their wet clothes, I was not prepared to see the person at the door. It was not Dave and our sons but Annette, telling me to come down to the lodge because the search had resumed.

"What? What time is?" I asked.

I was completely disoriented. It was 7:30 a.m. I had slept through the night. Dave had not returned to the cabin in the middle of the night. I had to stop and think for a moment to get my bearings.

Wait a minute. Dave didn't come back here. It's 7:30 a.m. and they're still searching.

I knew then deep in my spirit that the outlook was not good.

I left sleeping Kate, Finn, and baby Elise in the cabin and walked through the early morning mist to the lodge just yards away. Each step seemed heavy. I felt adrenaline, hesitancy, dread, and urgency all at the same time. I couldn't get to the lodge fast enough, yet I didn't want to go there, knowing deep inside that the situation wasn't good.

I believe that God had spoken to my spirit in my sleep, warning me that all would not be well. My spirit seemed to know my boys were already in heaven, even if my head and heart didn't yet.

What I didn't know then was that based on best estimates, my husband and my sons had passed to heaven between four and six that morning as I was sleeping. I was waiting for them to come home to me that night. Around the time I was expecting them to knock on the cabin door, they were going home. Home. Their eternal home. And it's as if my spirit already knew they were there.

I walked into the lodge to see men at a table sitting around a map of the forest, talking, planning, and making notes. The scene was very official looking, and it made me even more worried. But something rose up in me, one last surge of hope, and I dove in, wanting to know how I could help.

I never offered to go along on the searches. I felt I would be best served staying at command central as a couple of dear ladies worked the radios and took calls coming in from the search vehicles to the lodge. I wanted to hear all the information as it arrived. I felt an urgent need to help, to look at a map. I asked questions. I wanted to know where the men had already searched. They asked for detailed descriptions of Dave, Dom, Grant, and even Bear, our Lab. I asked about their game plan. As the men left to search around 8:00 a.m., I went to the front desk where Annette and Nikki were manning the radios. As each call came in, I listened.

"There's small footprints here."

"We found a fanny pack."

My heart fell to my feet. Grant had been wearing a fanny pack and a small backpack. *If Dave shed Grant's fanny pack, it must be because he needed to carry him. What's wrong with my baby Grant that Daddy needs to carry him?* I thought.

My breath caught in my throat as each clue came in.

"What direction are the prints going in?" I wanted to know. "Do the prints look fresh?"

The clues started to arrive steadily over the next several minutes.

At this point, I thought it was time to call family members to let them know what was happening. I had refrained from doing this, assuming that Dave had the situation under control, assuming that the searchers would find him and the boys. I didn't want to worry anyone, thinking that Dave, Dom, and Grant would eventually appear with quite a story to tell.

I called my parents.

"Dad, we have a situation going on here. Dave and the boys went on a hike yesterday and haven't come back yet."

As I explained the situation and the search efforts, he bombarded me with questions.

"When did they start hiking? Who's searching?"

I was overwhelmed. I was scared; the worry and urgency in his voice made me realize just how dire the situation was despite my best efforts to deny it to myself. When my dad said he and my mom were leaving right away to drive the two hours to the lodge, I knew it was time to call Dave's parents.

His mom picked up the phone, and I briefed her of the situation, much the same as I did my dad. Very concerned, she assured me that she and Dave's dad were on their way up to Missouri right away. They had to drive ten hours from Louisiana.

Hanging up with Dave's mom, I started to whimper. And then my whimper became tears as I realized the reason for my whimper. The urgency in responses from both my dad and Dave's mom, forced me to face the reality of the situation I was trying desperately to downplay in my head. I knew deep in my spirit, that my boys were probably not going to come home to me.

Walking back to the front desk, I looked out of the window to see a light snow had started to fall. My hopes faded even more. The searchers were considering sending up a search helicopter, but the snow canceled that plan. As each clue came in and the search continued, my hope diminished more.

There's just no reason Dave wouldn't be back by now even if he had hunkered down through the night, I thought.

It was after 9:00 a.m. Annette, Nikki, and I started talking.

"Someone must be injured; there's just no reason they wouldn't be back yet," I said.

I pictured Dave having broken his leg and struggling to walk back; that would explain why he and the boys were not back yet and why it was taking so long for the searchers to find them. Theories abounded: Dave had broken a bone; one of the boys was injured, and Dave had to carry him; Dave had had a heart attack. At one point I was even briefly questioned by sheriff's officers, who wanted to know if Dave and I were having marital problems and if perhaps he had taken off with my boys.

"Of course not," I assured them.

I needed some air. I walked out of the front doors of the lodge to the edge of the gravel parking lot in the direction of the trailhead. As I stood near the trailhead that foggy morning, the chilly morning air heightened all my senses. I said aloud, "Where are you, Dave; where are you guys?"

I turned from the trailhead and walked back toward the lodge. As I passed an empty truck in the parking lot, a call came over the radio inside of it. I heard someone say, "We found …"

Then there was fuzz and inaudible talk. I couldn't make out clearly what was being said, but something told me it was important. I ran into the lodge.

"A call is coming over the radio in the truck outside!"

The ladies assured me they had heard the same calls coming in to the lodge. Then a call came over the radio.

"We found them." I heard the words come over the waves. *We found them.*

"Oh thank God!" I said as Nikki, manning the radio, repeated the message.

They found them! my spirit shouted.

I cried tears of relief like I had never felt before. A weight lifted off of me that I hadn't even known was there. They found them.

But then I heard Nikki say, "Okay, okay, okay."

I saw that she had put down the radio and was talking on the phone to someone I could not hear.

"Okay, okay," she kept saying.

Immediately that feeling of relief I had just a millisecond before left me. The look on Nikki's face told me all I needed to know.

"What's wrong?" I demanded. "Who's not okay? Which one's not okay?"

I feared in my spirit that Grant David was seriously injured or had not made it. Nothing could have prepared me for what I was about to hear. I walked toward Nikki. I was going to take the phone out of her hands and demand answers. She handed the phone to Annette and walked around the counter to me.

"Baby," she said. "Baby, they're not okay."

"Which ones?" I demanded. "Who's not okay?"

"Baby, they're not okay. They need to be warmed up."

"Which ones?" I asked.

Nikki paused just a moment. "All of them."

My mind started racing. I backed away from her, as if I could distance myself from what I was about to hear. Adrenaline, emotion, and sheer terror coursed through me, and I thought, *If I ask a question about the worst-case scenario, any answer I hear will at least be better than that.* So I screamed, "Are they dead? Is my family dead?"

Nikki's face gave me my answer; she did not try to scale back my worst-case scenario as I had desperately hoped she would.

"They're not okay," she said, clasping my hands in hers.

"No," I said. "No." I pulled my hands away from hers. "Take me to them right now. I will warm them up. Take me to them *now*."

I turned and dashed for the lodge doors. I wanted to run. I needed to run. I needed to be with Dave and my boys right then. I had no idea how to get to them, but I needed them. The feeling was primal.

The ladies hopped into action, preventing me from leaving. I demanded over and over to be taken to them. Finally, Annette told me to get into her truck; she would take me to them. Instead she took me to a barn and told me to go inside so we could make phone calls and I could calm down. I didn't need to be calmed down, I told her. I needed to get to my boys to warm them up. Annette became firm with me and demanded I get out of the truck and into the barn.

I obeyed and waited for her to make calls to find out where to take me to see my boys. Pacing, waiting, crying out to God, screaming, and pleading, I finally broke. I grabbed a windowsill in the barn and sank down to the ground.

I kept praying aloud, "I'm sorry, Father, for any of my sins," as if anything I had done could have, would have caused any of this.

"Please, God," I said, "warm them up. I have seen You do miracles, Father. I know You can. Do one *right now*."

I sank into the fetal position. My screamed prayers became whispered pleading as I lay on the cold barn floor.

"Please, God. Please," I cried over and over.

And then He answered me. Not audibly but strong and sure, He said to my spirit, *They are already home with Me, daughter. They will not be coming home with you, so get up off the floor.*

As soon as I heard this in my spirit, I obeyed, and slowly I started to stand. I did not know what was next, but I knew what had just been spoken to my spirit, and I knew I had to get off of the floor. I stood and looked out of the barn window.

Okay, I answered inwardly, *but if I accept this, You'd better be with me.*

Finally, I was calm enough to tell Annette I was ready to see my boys or at least to get information about them. Recognizing that I had calmed down, she agreed. We walked out of the barn to find a man had just pulled up in a truck.

"Can you take me to my boys?" I begged him as Annette guided me to her truck. She and the man shot each other knowing looks.

Any resolve I had mustered in the barn crumbled when I saw someone I thought might be able to help me. The man looked at me in a way I had never seen, have never seen since, and never want to see again. It was look of sheer sorrow and pity. It was the face of a man who had no words to tell me—or none I wanted to hear.

I had no idea who the man was, but I found out later he was the one who had found my boys. He had found them on the trail, already having passed to heaven. He had made the phone call saying they had been found. I later learned that he had told the ladies at the lodge to put down the radio and pick up a phone out of my earshot, because my boys were gone. He looked at me with the face of a man who knew he had no words for the wife and the mother of the three he had just found.

Annette and I got in her truck. As she drove, she got on her radio and said, "Sarah is here and she wants any information you can give. She wants the truth."

"Tell her," a female voice said, "that her husband is gone and they are trying to save her boys."

Those few words crushed every dream I had for the rest of my life. All at once, life was over. I knew in my spirit that my boys were also gone and that the confirmation was just coming out in pieces. With those few words, the life drained out of my spirit. I almost felt it go. A hardness settled in. And as emotionless as you can imagine, with a stone face, I stared straight ahead and said in a hushed tone, "I knew it was too good to last too long."

We drove back to the lodge to get my purse. Annette found out that first responders had worked on the boys on the trail and were taking them to the hospital in ambulances. But I knew what I had to do first: I had to call my family and Dave's parents before I went to the hospital. Everyone deserved to know Dave was gone.

I called my parents, who were on route to the lodge. My dad answered. I whispered, "Dad … Dave is dead."

"Oh my God, Sarah. Oh my God," he repeated in utter disbelief. "Mary, Dave's dead!" he quickly reported to my mom.

I heard her scream in the background.

Saying the words out loud and hearing my parents' reactions, my hard façade cracked and I screamed into the phone, "My husband is *dead*. My husband is *dead*, Dad!"

I was sobbing uncontrollably but managed to say, "I have to go, Dad. They are trying to save my boys. I have to go."

But I knew what I had to do next. I had to call Dave's parents.

I dialed and waited only a moment before Dave's dad picked up.

"David, I have to tell you something," I whispered. "Dave didn't make it…"

Even after our brief conversation and I hung up the phone, Dave's parents' reactions played over and over in my ears. I don't like to think about that moment much. I got just a taste of what the man who found my family felt when I faced him outside the barn and asked him to take me to my boys. Sometimes there are no words when you face a parent who has just lost a child.

I was told we had to wait a few minutes before going to the hospital, because the ambulances had just left the trail scene. Any sense of urgency to get there, however, was muted in me. The moment I learned that Dave was gone, the life drained out of me. And I knew in my spirit that my boys were gone too. Getting to the hospital simply meant having to face the confirmation of that fact.

I decided to lie down on the couch in the common area of the lodge, awaiting that trip to face good-byes to my baby boys. My knees were weak. I felt drained. I felt dead. I felt sick. I felt I would faint or vomit if I didn't lie down. My movements were on auto pilot. I was empty. I had no energy to fight or to insist on going to the hospital immediately. My will was broken. My husband was gone, and I knew my boys were gone even if the news was not official yet.

The adrenaline I had felt after hearing the boys were found was wearing off. Everything had taken a toll—the emotional roller coaster of my breakdown and my brief resolve in the barn, my emptiness after hearing confirmation that Dave was gone, my emotional release as I screamed to my dad that my husband was dead, and having to tell Dave's parents that he didn't make it. And it had been only about an hour since my husband and the boys had been found.

At some point while I was resting on the couch, a kind pastor and his wife tried to talk to me. But as they were speaking, I looked up and saw Finn. Some workers at the lodge, checking on the kids in the cabin when the tragedy started to unfold, had brought him down to play at the lodge while the girls rested at the cabin.

I ran to my boy, fell to my knees, and scooped him up. I held him as close as I could and sobbed into his tiny shoulder. As I clutched him, I cried for all the things he would never do with his daddy, for all the moments his daddy would miss as Finn grew. I sobbed—and Finn had no idea why.

Eventually, some lodge workers led him away from me and I continued to rest. They assured me they would check on and watch Kate and Elise as well. Finally, after what was only about twenty minutes but seemed like hours, it was time to head to the hospital. I went to the cabin to get my purse and there were Kate and Elise. Kate, a minimomma at eleven years old, was playing with her little sister.

"Is everything okay, Mom? Is there any news yet? Have they found them yet?"

I paused and stared at her. I knew I had to get to my boys at the hospital and didn't have the time to properly tell Kate the news about her dad.

"No, Kate. Nothing yet. I have to go."

And I walked out of the cabin.

The drive to the hospital seemed to take hours although it probably lasted about thirty minutes. Annette and Nikki—who had manned the radios during the search, who had received the call that my loved ones were found, and who had to tell me, "Baby, they're not okay"—drove me to the hospital. These two dear ladies were like guardian angels to me the entire morning.

The day was sunny and beautiful, but as I looked out of the truck window, there was only emptiness. I knew what lay before me, and there was absolutely no way to prepare, so I didn't even try. I had given up. I didn't feel God. I didn't feel resolve. I didn't feel sorrow. I felt nothing.

I was so deep in hopelessness that I could no longer see or feel anything around me, good or bad. But while I did not know it then, at my absolute weakest, at the point where I had given up any strength of my own, God moved in and gave me His strength to deal with what I was about to face.

I walked into the hospital and found out the boys' ambulances had not yet arrived. I was led to the ER where they would be taken and found a hustle and bustle of activity. There seemed to be fifty people in every kind of uniform possible—police, EMTs, firefighters, nurses, doctors, even people running around in civilian clothes. Hospital staffers were warming towels, talking, and prepping equipment. They seemed to be preparing for battle. And they were. They fought valiantly.

I was approached by a nurse named Karen, who asked me all the necessary insurance questions. She explained what would be going on as soon as the boys arrived. Karen was amazing. She seemed to be an angel assigned to guide me through the time at the hospital, much like Annette and Nikki were assigned to see me through the morning at the lodge.

Finally, the boys arrived and there was a flurry of activity. Then I saw them. Finally, I saw them. My boys.

We found you. Boys, we found you! my spirit screamed.

Each boy was wheeled in on a stretcher and rushed into a room. They were surrounded by such a cloud of people that I could hardly see the two of them. But I got glimpses. I cried out to them above the noise, "Mommy's here, boys! Mommy is here. I love you."

I saw them just briefly as they were rushed in front of where I stood into the ER room to my right, but that was enough. I needed to see them, to know, regardless of their condition, that they had been found. Though I knew in my spirit that they had joined their daddy in heaven, seeing them, and seeing the hospital staff work so heroically to try to save their lives, gave me a glimmer of hope that God might let them come home with me.

Police officers, EMTs, nurses, and doctors worked relentlessly on my boys. I was humbled and grateful as I watched these strangers work with such resolve and determination to try to bring my boys back to me. For better or for worse, emotion started to come back to me. I was opening myself up to the pain of the situation, but I could also embrace the magnificent acts of courage, love, and sacrifice happening all around me.

The medical teams were doing nonstop chest compressions on the boys; the crew members' arms would give out and other team members would step in and continue CPR. They were warming blankets in a dryer and immediately running them to the boys. They were pumping warm fluid through their little bodies. The efforts were continuous.

I watched from the doorway and called out to the boys as the crews worked. I don't remember everything I said, but I had simple goals: to let my boys know that Mommy was there—"we found you"—and that I loved them deeply and to be sure they heard my voice.

I had to sit periodically to avoid having my knees buckle underneath me. As I sat, I spotted a woman in uniform to my right in the distance. She stood in the double-door entrance of the emergency room and looked at me. From the corner of my eye, I saw her walk toward me. I was surrounded by people: lodge personnel, nurses, a local pastor and his wife. As the woman in uniform approached, I could tell she was an EMT. She knelt in front of me, took my hands in hers, and with concern, compassion, and a Christ-like love showing in her young eyes, asked, "Can I pray with you?"

"Yes," I managed to say gratefully.

As she prayed, I was overcome with thankfulness. In boldly taking me by the hands and praying with me, she had delivered a message from God that He was indeed with me.

Weeks later, talking with one of the first responders, I found out that this woman was among those who had worked on my boys at the place where they were found. She had done her best to bring Grant back to me before releasing him to hospital personnel, and that afternoon, exhausted and drained, she had come to a grieving mother to offer her encouragement and prayers.

On several occasions during the two hours the team members worked on my boys, they let me go to their bedsides. I looked first at Dominic—my boy, my kindred spirit, my friend, my handsome son, my wise old soul in a little boy's body.

I looked in his eyes. They were open, but my boy was no longer there. I had an urgent desire to tell him and Grant, "We found you, boys." *Jesus in heaven, no mother should ever have to see the baby she brought into this world lying lifeless before her,* I thought.

Then I looked toward Grant—my baby, my joy, my sweet, smiling, gentle soul. His eyes were closed. He looked like he was sleeping. He had tubes taped to his nose so warm fluid could be run through him. (I learned later that the crews worked extra hard on Grant because he was the warmest when found, and they thought they had the best chance of saving him.) Each time I kissed him, I tasted and smelled that tape. I pried his eyelid open momentarily as I spoke to him so I could see his eye color one last time on earth. That's the kind of crazy, desperate thing you do when you're preparing to say good-bye to your babies.

I knew in my spirit that my boys were already in heaven with Daddy and Jesus, and that reality was cemented for me when I saw them in those hospital beds. There was no life in Dominic's eyes, and Grant was already sleeping peacefully. I knew those forms lying before me were only their shells. Talking to them, kissing them, touching them, and lying on the beds with them—all that was for me. This was my good-bye. And looking back, I feel that the boys were standing right there with me as I was saying good-bye to their shells.

I felt a desperate need to breathe air into them. If I could just put my mouth to theirs, I could breathe life back into them. I kept begging the doctors, "Let me lie on them like preemie babies. I can warm them up if they feel Mommy's touch." *Dear Lord, no mother should have to go through this*, my spirit cried.

It's unnatural. It's sick. It's wrong. Oh God, please have mercy. I ache. I ache for my boys, I prayed.

Gently, tenderly, God whispered to me, *Release them to Me, daughter. They have already been home with Me for a while now. They are alive with Me here. Let their shells go.*

As I was lying with Grant, dozens of strangers surrounded me, crying as they watched this sacred moment. My brother David, the first of my family to arrive, was at my side. Then I heard my dad's voice. I lifted my head, and in my anguish, all I could call out was, "Daddy, come see my boys."

My mom entered the room and got emotional. I stopped her; I needed to keep that space sacred.

"Mom, no. Don't do that here. They are okay. They are okay."

God provided me with something I had never felt before and have never felt since; there were no words, only emotions. I felt on a mission: *We will give these boys a proper transition to the other world.*

I feel almost privileged to have gotten to say good-bye to my boys. Though their spirits had left them hours earlier, I was able to hold them and to have my closure with them. My good-bye.

After I was led away from my sons' shells by the tender arms of my mom and dad and my angel of a nurse, Karen, I needed to see my husband.

As I was taken into a hall, the world consisted of only the three feet in front of me. I had one objective. People were talking all around me, leading me here and there, and all I could get out was, "I want to see my husband."

My parents drove me to the coroner's office, and I walked in to see my Dave—my strong, vibrant husband. I had the same reaction I had upon seeing the boys wheeled into the emergency room: I just wanted him to know we had found him. It meant nothing then, but I just wanted Dave to know "we found you."

I asked for privacy, and I closed the door. Dave and I were alone in the starch-white room. Dave, ever handsome, looked like he had just come out of the shower. He had been cleaned up by the coroner and seemed to have a slight grin of contentment on his face. I spoke to him. I held his hand. I put my head to his chest as I so often would when we lay down to sleep at night. Nothing. No familiar beat. I wanted him to know how much I loved him. I spoke words to him, but my heart's feeling is all I remember.

Arriving back at the lodge, I had to tell our Kate that her dad and her brothers were not coming home with us. I led her outside of the lodge. I found a place where we could have privacy and told her as I looked into her pleading blue eyes, "Kate, Daddy and your brothers are going to live with Jesus now."

She collapsed into me, crying, "Mom? Mom, no!"

I held her. I quickly led her back to the lodge, where almost my entire family and lodge workers were assembled, and covered her in blankets. She was going into shock.

I felt a primal need to gather my chicks under my arm and to return to our home. My brother Richard drove us there. As were pulling away from the lodge, Finn asked why we were going home without Daddy, Dom, and Grant.

As my brother drove Kate, Finn, Elise, our dogs, and me home in our minivan—the one Dave had driven with all five of our kids and our two dogs to the lodge just two days before—my cell phone went off, indicating I had a text. In an absolutely robotic, emotionless state of mind, I glanced at my phone, assuming it was Dave's parents updating me on their location as they traveled to my parents' home in Illinois.

Instead, I saw a text from Dave sent the night before while the search was going on but just coming in to my phone as we were leaving the lodge and my phone starting receiving a signal. The message had been sent about seven Saturday night, and it had only one word: "Help."

While I am on this side of the veil, I will never know fully what happened as my boys trekked through those woods or why they couldn't be found. I will know only when I am in heaven.

The hours of mystery run from 2:00 p.m., when the boys were last seen at Sutton Bluff, to 10:00 a.m. the next day when they were found along the trail. Most people believe that Dave and the boys left the trail sometime during this period, trying to find shelter from the storm.

We do have solid information about their time line. Dave, Dominic, Grant, and Bear headed out from our cabin for a short hike at about 10:30 a.m. Saturday, January 12, 2013. They were expected back by about 4:00 p.m., and Annette and I knew that.

Dave had prepared for a day hike with Dom and Grant and left all the overnight gear in the cabin. Dave brought trekking poles, water, a water filter, waterproof matches, a flashlight, a pocketknife, a phone, and snacks. Grant brought snacks (sunflower seeds and oranges) in his backpack and fanny pack, and Dom took Bear's leash and dog treats in his backpack. Each boy had a water bottle. During the Saturday night deluge when the temperature dropped twenty degrees in an hour, the searchers asked me to check in the cabin to determine what gear Dave had taken. They specifically asked me to check for cold-weather gear. A sense of dread came over me as I examined the gear left behind: a tent, a tarp, bivy sacks for warmth were all left in overnight packs. Everything they would have needed to save their lives remained in the cabin.

We know from the photos found on Dave's phone that the first portion of the hike was enjoyable. Grant and Dom were smiling and happy. There are no pictures of Dave. I wish there were.

We know that the weather was pleasant, in the low sixties and high fifties when they set out. Judging by the photos found on Dave's phone, both boys were apparently warm. Each had shed their top layers of clothing—Dom a sweater and Grant a fleece—and were wearing them tied around their waists.

We know they made extraordinary time, covering the eight miles or so to Sutton Bluff in a little more than four hours. We know this based on an eyewitness account. The last man to see my boys alive put them there at around 2:00 p.m.

Saturday evening as the search was in full force, Annette received a call at the lodge front desk from a man asking if searchers had "found that man and his boys yet." Annette regretfully told him they had not. The man identified himself and told Annette that while out on a drive that afternoon, he and his wife had happened upon Dave and the boys at Sutton Bluff around 2:00 p.m. He and Dave had had a pleasant conversation. He said Dave was talkative, friendly, and eager to learn anything the man could offer about the surrounding area. He told Annette that Dom and Grant were in good spirits, running around with the dog, and were a little damp from the sprinkle that had just started but no worse for the wear. Their cheerfulness indicated they were under no stress.

The man said that he bid Dave and the boys farewell and that he and his wife drove on. He recalled that moments later he realized the storm was arriving sooner than had been forecast, and he decided to turn around and offer Dave, Dom, and Grant a ride back to the lodge to save them a hike in potentially dangerous weather. He and his wife returned to Sutton Bluff, but there was no sign of Dave and the boys. They had already started their hike back toward the lodge.

We know more about the events surrounding the time Dave and the boys spent on the trail. My brothers, experienced and fit, have since hiked this section of the Ozark trail together and separately and have said that even with no children or dog to hinder them, they struggled to cover the same amount of ground in the same amount of time as Dave and the boys did.

There is much speculation, backed by solid theories, about all that happened next on their journey. Searchers looked from about 7:00 p.m. until about 12:30 a.m. but found no trace of the boys. A prevailing theory is that with the rain picking up and the temperature dropping dramatically as they left Sutton Bluff, Dave thought the best plan would be to leave the trail and to look for shelter in the woods.

Any structure would have helped ward off the downpour—an upturned tree with big exposed roots, a rock overhang, an old hunting shack, a barn. During the search that night, I asked one of the men to show me on a giant poster-size map of the forest where the search was taking place and where the trail and Sutton Bluff were located. I was encouraged because he pointed out that all the shaded areas on the map were privately owned land. So the chances were good that Dave had stumbled upon a structure where he and the boys could take refuge. That became my peace the entire evening as the fruitless search progressed. *It's okay*, I thought. *They can't find them because Dave found somewhere off trail to hunker down.*

The speculation is that by about 7:00 p.m., Dave and the boys had found some kind of refuge and may have hunkered down for several hours, trying to wait out the storm. They may even have intended to spend the night in their shelter and to hike back at daybreak. However, Dave may well have seen our boys faltering, perhaps already starting to succumb to hypothermia, and felt he had no choice but to begin the trek back to the cabin in the middle of the night at the tail end of the storm with creeks swollen and trails flooded. His cell phone had run out of charge, and his flashlight, which he may have lost, has never been found.

We do know that Dave carried our boys across a raging creek in the pitch-black night. The only way to reach the spot where he and the boys were found is to cross a creek along the trail. Dave had to have carried our sons across that river one at a time, subjecting himself to the brutal cold and raging currents at least three times. He carried one boy across, returned to retrieve the other, and crossed again. And Dave may have carried Bear across as well; he was only a small puppy and likely could not have crossed the creek without assistance. It is believed, given that Dave and our sons were found a short way from that point on the creek, it is likely that this crossing was the last big chill their bodies could take and that they all succumbed to hypothermia soon after passing through the water.

I can't fathom the bitter choice Dave had to make when he was confronted with the raging creek obstructing his path home. He had to have known the boys needed warmth as soon as possible, but the only way back was across a cold, swollen creek. Dave was infused with the strength of a mighty man that night. Our heavenly Father gave him the will to carry our sons across those frigid waters, and I will forever be grateful for my man, who did everything in his power to try to save our sons' lives.

The belief that Dave and the boys left some sort of shelter and started their trek back to the cabin in the middle of the night is based on evidence found along the trail.

The searchers had someone posted in a truck at the intersection of the trail and a gravel forestry road until about 12:30 a.m. They did not see Dave and the boys and saw no indication that they had come through there. Yet, when the searchers returned to the same intersection the next morning, they found two rock cairns had been built on each side of the road near the trail. A cairn is a rock mound, typically built in a pyramid to indicate location and direction. That's the way Dave built it. He was trying to signal anyone looking for them that they had been there. That is a perfect example of what a skilled outdoorsman he was.

Further, orange peels were found all along the trail in the same area, bright orange side up, likely another attempt by Dave to signal their location to searchers. The searcher on post at that intersection until 12:30 a.m. did not see any of these clues, leading us all to conclude that Dave and the boys headed through that intersection sometime after that.

Therefore, it is quite likely that Dave and the boys left their shelter and continued their trek on the trail, where everyone was searching for them only hours before, and that they did this just after the search had been called off for the night.

If I dwelled on things like this, they would drive me over the edge and I would start pointing fingers: "If they hadn't called off the search, someone would have been at that intersection when Dave and the boys passed by."

But if I started down that road, where would I stop? Would I blame myself for not calling family sooner to help search? (Dave's mom and my brothers have said they would have searched the entire night until Dave and the boys were found.) Would I blame Dave for not taking his cold-weather gear on the hike? Would I blame him and the boys for taking a long hike instead of the short one they had planned? Would I blame somebody for the lack of cell service? Would I blame one of the searchers, who later lamented, "If I had just left my truck there at that intersection with the keys in it when the search was called off"?

Or would I blame my boys? Dave had decided Saturday morning that a hike wasn't a good idea and that we should drive to Johnson's Shut-Ins instead. The boys protested that they were promised a hike, and Dave, unwilling to disappoint them, returned to his original plan.

Or how about blaming God for the storm coming in harder and sooner than expected? When would I stop? I could blame myself, Dave, the world, or God for the rest of my life, and it wouldn't change the outcome.

One point that took me some time to process and to accept is that at another intersection on the trail, a right turn brings you about a mile away from the cabin and the lodge, but Dave, in his hypothermic state, went straight at that intersection.

When Dave and the boys were found on the trail, they were about one mile in, having gone straight instead of right. Had they gone right for about the same distance, they would have reached our cabin and come inside to the warmth and safety of the heaters, of shelter, of my arms. Instead, they went the same distance in the wrong direction, until their bodies could do no more.

My boys had gone the distance. They had trekked those miles and had walked those slippery, muddy trails, soaking wet and freezing. They had endured. But the last mile that would have brought them home to me brought them to their eternal home instead.

My boys—my ten-year-old and my eight-year-old—had the bodies and the wills of men that night. They had the resolve, the endurance, and the determination of grown men as they trekked with their dad those last few hours of their earthly lives, and I am proud. Dom always wanted to be a soldier or a marine when he grew up. Well, my boys were as valiant and as strong as warriors that night. My spirit overflows with pride for my sons.

Dave and the boys were meant to go home that night, home to heaven. Twelve or more things would have saved their lives, and not one of them did. God has asked me to trust His sovereignty, to trust His knowledge, and to trust His design for Dave, Dominic, and Grant going home to Him that night.

Chapter 3

What Now? The Hands and Feet of Christ

We arrived at my parents' house at about seven Sunday night. Dave's parents had arrived from New Orleans. My siblings, my aunts and uncles, my dear friend Becky, and many from our church family gathered at my parents' home for about an hour that night to mourn, to get information, and to be together. We gathered in the living room, sometimes in virtual silence, trying to grasp what had happened. So many of us were in shock.

But all I wanted to do was to go home with my children. I don't remember who drove my children and me home that night, but I knew I wanted to get to my house, where Dave and I lived, where my boys' things were, where I would be in familiar surroundings, and to crawl under the covers of my bed.

That night as I lay down, I had no thoughts, just emptiness. Becky spent the night down on the couch, Finn and Elise slept with me, and Kate slept in her bed. I didn't know what was next. I was going through the motions, almost by rote memorization or reflex. I awoke with a start in what I thought was the middle of the night and jumped out of bed, wanting to know where my dog was. My heart was pounding and my mind was racing.

Where's Cleo? Is she safe? It's cold outside.

I went downstairs and saw her sleeping peacefully, curled up on the living room floor. All the commotion woke Becky, and I ended up sitting on the couch in the early morning dark next to my dear childhood friend. There were barely any words between us. Sometimes there are no words.

I don't know why I had that irrational concern for Cleo's well-being. Perhaps my mind was trying too hard to process everything that had happened and started to short out a bit.

Each time I awoke for the next several weeks, I had a huge hole in my chest. I can hardly describe the feeling. It is sickening, a feeling of absolute emptiness, hopelessness, and darkness. Everything had lost its color. There was no past, present, or future, only present pain. That hole was terrifying. It was almost paralyzing.

I found that deep sorrow had a taste. It started in a deep chasm in my chest, inched up into my throat, and then into my mouth. It was the sick taste of sorrow.

One afternoon that first week home without Dave, Dom, and Grant, I was in my bedroom writing down things I wanted to say about my husband and our sons at their funeral services. I was also gathering mementos, items that represented them, to display at the funeral home. I picked out Dave's guitar and his Bible, Dominic's Lego creations, Grant's dinosaur collection, and the boys' Cub Scout uniforms. I knew immediately that I wanted their services to be a celebration of their lives. I resolved that despite how I was feeling, I was going to honor my man and my sons.

As I was busily gathering items, I heard my dad say from behind me, "I can't believe you are able to go through these things already."

Immersed in the job in front of me, I hadn't heard him and my mom come up the stairs to my bedroom, so I was startled at first. I answered, "I want their services to show who they really are. They are not the shells that will be lying motionless in those caskets. They are more than that."

I had an intense need to make their services a beautiful reflection of them, their loves, and who they truly were. Despite my resolve, my spirit was crushed.

Dear Jesus, I thought, *no mother should have to go through her sons' dresser drawers to pull out the outfits they will wear in their caskets.*

I went through the preparations for their funeral on autopilot, as if in slow motion. Looking back, I am amazed at how God provides that supernatural shield enabling you to do the unthinkable.

It dawned on me one morning that first week home that I had not eaten in a few days—not a bite, not a taste. I had had water. That was all. In fact, I hadn't eaten since before the search on Saturday night. I was hungry but refused to eat. I willed my hunger away. I had told myself I was not allowed to enjoy a bite of food, much less a meal. My boys could no longer eat, so why should I? My boys had suffered, so I deserved to suffer. I decided to make myself suffer with hunger. Someone must have noticed, because it became one dear woman's mission to make me eat.

Dave's parents had come up with forty or more friends and family members from the New Orleans area. They converged on Millstadt/ Columbia, Illinois, to offer help.

David Sr.'s fireman friends, longtime Decareaux family friends, Dave's grandmother (Maw Maw), aunts, uncles, and cousins all came show their support, most having driven or flown in from the New Orleans area.

Ms. Toni, or Aunt Toni, as she came to be called that week, started bringing me toast and hot tea each day. "Have you eaten?" she would ask. "Why don't you take a bite?"

I was hungry and grateful but conflicted about whether I should eat. Finally, God knocked some sense into me and made me realize that to properly honor my husband and my boys at their funeral services, I had to be on my feet, alert, well, and nourished. I would be no good to anyone if I got ill, so I took a grateful, ravenous bite of toast. I told myself that I needed nutrients to survive and to stay strong but that there was no reason for me to eat anything beyond what was absolutely necessary. I was sustained by toast and hot tea for a week.

That became increasingly hard to maintain. As I discovered, one way people help in times of sorrow is to bring food. Dave's fellow workers at the Defense Information Systems Agency, located on Scott Air Force Base, brought food by the trunkload: sandwich fixings, desserts, pastries, salads, and hot meals. My aunts Lee and Nancy brought hot dishes cooked by several ladies in our family and by family friends. Dave's great-uncle Kenny and his aunt Chris cooked dishes in my kitchen. Further, they prepared cookies, pastries, and more and spread them out on my dining room table. Anything and everything that smelled great was coming out of my kitchen that week.

I found that with tragedy when so many people were in and out of the house, one way God had people minister was to make sure everyone on hand was fed. It was such a blessing.

Horrific circumstances had brought family members and friends from across the country to my house. Thirty or more of them were visiting in my living room at any given moment. This huge family gathering was a reunion of sorts.

I knew why they were there, but deep down in my spirit was a ray of something. I will call it gratitude rather than hope. Whatever it was, I started to feel loved and covered.

That week in my home the hands and feet of Christ (1 Corinthians 12:27) were manifested in family and friends from near and far who did everything imaginable to keep my home, my family, and my will going.

Dave's mom and his godmother, Aunt Edith, took down and put away all the Christmas decorations and ornaments that Dave and I had not put away before our trip. I didn't change a diaper on Elise for two weeks. The children were cared for by many loving hands. In fact, Dave's mom had to take Finn and Elise to the doctor for me that first week, since they had developed severe colds.

Friends from past and present came to console, to hug, to talk, and to cry. I found the leader of the church youth group from my high school years standing in my foyer one day when I came downstairs. Sue, my Sunday school teacher when I was a child, visited. Dustin, Dave's dear friend since their military days, came bearing gifts for the children. Officials from Scott Air Force Base came by to offer their support. Dave's supervisor, Tony, offered to act as a liaison between Scott Air Force Base and my family and to handle all logistics related to Dave's job and benefits.

I found Tony, a brother in Christ, to be a great spiritual comfort as he offered prayers and words of wisdom from Scripture during his visits.

Dave's sister, Brittany, and her husband, Joel, took on the job of taking care of Bear. Only five months old, full of energy, and without his master, Dominic, he was a handful.

Every time I turned around, someone was doing something to help. Dave's cousin Angela and his uncle Bob cleaned out my van. The church down the road brought boxes and boxes of paper products. Dave's dad and mom, my sister, Deanna, and my dear friend Becky's husband, Greg, moved and stacked boxes in my basement to make it possible to walk down there. Dave and I had just moved into the house in September. We had many boxes of household goods shipped from our home in Germany and had barely begun to sort through them.

Colleen and Hilary, dear friends as well as cousins, held me and comforted me. They knew my family well because of our many travels together and loved Dave and my boys dearly, so they were in their own deep mourning.

Dave's aunt Kathy, his cousins Jamie, Angela, Jennifer, and Michael, his uncle Larry and his uncle Ted offered support and help. One early afternoon, Aunt Kathy was holding down the fort at my home. Everyone had left for the day, and I had gone upstairs to take a nap. I rested securely, knowing she had everything under control. Everyone played a part in keeping my head above water that first week home.

Dave's Maw Maw, whom he loved very much and was very close to, sat in my living room most days, taking it all in. I often found myself wanting to sit by her. Having lost my own grandmother, to whom I was very close, years before, I found Maw Maw's presence comforting for many reasons, including the fact that Dave and his grandmother shared the same eye color. Grant shared that eye color, too. Therefore, being around her made me feel like I was near Dave and my boys. I also found comfort in her grandmotherly presence and liked when she held my hand.

Dave's uncle Bob took on the monumental task of acting as the liaison between the benefits people in Dave's human resources department and my family, making all necessary arrangements for me to simply sign the documents. My sister Elizabeth came to console, to offer her company, and to help occupy Finn. My brother David, among so much more, gathered dozens of trash bags, which in the commotion of that first week had collected in my shed, and took them to the dump. My sister Deanna was in and out that first week and well beyond, organizing photos for the funeral services and diving in wherever she could help. My brother Richard and his wife, Roxanne, came to visit and took their turn spending the night at my home.

Deanna, Dave's parents, my friend Becky, and my aunts Lee and Nancy also took turns spending the night at my house the first few weeks we were home. Calls and messages flooded in from all over the world; friends from every base in every state and country where we had been stationed showed their support in droves.

My parents came each day to console and to comfort. They helped me with the arduous task of unpacking from the lodge trip. All the bags from that weekend had been piled up in my loft. They contained the food that was supposed to provide our campfire snacks, the jammies that my boys were supposed to wear to bed, and the unopened wine that was supposed to help Dave and me celebrate our anniversary. I was grateful that I had those two people beside me as I took apart the bags that were packed just a week before in preparation for a fun family weekend that had gone terribly wrong.

One day in that first week home after the tragedy, I looked around my living room to see the most eclectic mix of people sitting in one place: my parents, Dave's parents, Dave's many aunts, uncles, and cousins; Great-Uncle Kenny, Great-Aunt Mae, David Sr.'s fireman friends, my aunt Lee, my sisters, my brothers, Dave's dear friend Dustin, and my Sunday school teacher from childhood. I was blown away by the evidence of Christ's love for me displayed by the crowd of people in my home. I was overwhelmed by love and a peace that transcended human understanding even as my heart was breaking within me.

I am also amazed, looking back, that these people showed such love for my children and me despite dealing with their own grief. Everyone, in one way or another, was also in deep mourning but came to my aid, displaying the hands and feet of Christ. They put their own pain on hold to comfort my kids and me; I am humbled and grateful.

As I lay down in bed one night that first week home, I fell asleep thinking of the songs I wanted played at the viewings. In my sleep, God whispered to my spirit what songs to choose. Before putting my feet on the floor after I awoke the next morning, I grabbed the pen and paper on my nightstand and quickly jotted down the seven songs God had laid on my heart to have played.

Another night, I took my phone to bed with me and repeatedly played voicemails Dave had left for me in recent weeks and months so I could hear his voice as I drifted off to sleep. As I was about to fall asleep one night, I heard a message that threatened to undo me but comforted me at the same time. It was a message Dave and the children had left me while I was on a cruise with my cousins in the fall of 2012, just months before the accident.

But that night as I lay down to sleep before continuing to plan the funeral of my husband and our sons, the message became their good-bye to me. As sure as I heard their voices coming through that phone, I knew my God had arranged this as their farewell. As sleep overtook me, I was sung into blissful rest by Dave, Dom, and Grant. Dave started the message by saying, "Bye, honey! Have fun! I love you!" Then Dom said, "Bye, Mom! Love you!" Grant followed, saying, "Bye, Mom! Love you!"

Dave spoke one more time, finishing the message by saying, "Bye, honey! Love you!"

The funeral loomed, and I knew I had to prepare to lay my husband and my sons to rest with honor. I had spent the days since returning to my house getting ready for the services. I picked out a suit for Dave to wear and selected shirts and pants for the boys. I went through photos and mementos—anything I could find to bring to the services to represent my boys and their lives, to tell the story of who they were.

The day I had to go to the funeral home to plan the services, I was surrounded by my parents, Dave's parents, Dave's uncle Larry, and my sister Deanna. As we sat in that small room, I had to make decisions no mother should have to make. I could not believe this was my reality. I could not believe I was being asked to choose the color of the caskets for my boys.

I answered every question matter of factly, almost robotically. God had placed a hedge of angelic protection around me, a shield deflecting the arrows of utter hopelessness, keeping me from succumbing to the horror I felt rising up inside of me. He gave me the strength I needed to do the unthinkable. He gave me the power to plan the funeral for Dave and our sons.

When the night of their wake arrived, I dressed in black dress slacks, a black turtleneck, and a gray scarf of Dave's. I didn't put on any makeup. I was dead inside; I couldn't have cared less what I looked like on the outside.

Dave's parents drove Kate and me to the funeral home. A friend of my sister Elizabeth watched Finn and Elise for me. They were ages four and two, and I had decided I did not want them to see their daddy and their brothers lying in those caskets so cold, so still. I would allow them to join me the next day for the funeral when the caskets were shut.

Arriving at the funeral home, I couldn't get inside fast enough. I had to see my boys. I felt a desperate need to be as close to them as I possibly could, knowing full well they were not there anymore. I wanted to seize the time I had left to lay my eyes on them. I would not see them again until reaching the other side. I knew full well that they were no longer in those bodies and that I would find only empty shells, but my need to be near them remained the same.

Only Kate and I were allowed to enter the viewing parlor. I saw my boys; I saw Dave. I walked closer. They we so still. They were so … empty. I went from one to the other, touching them, caressing their foreheads, their hands.

Dear Jesus, no mother should have to face this.

Kate was silent. I put my arm around her and asked if she was okay. She nodded that she was.

"They are so cold," she finally said.

I reminded her that these were simply shells and that her dad and her brothers were no longer there. They were warm, happy, and in bliss at that very moment. But even while I was saying this, my heart was breaking. As I watched my girl stand by the casket of her best friend, her brother Grant, I could only imagine the grief she was feeling.

Father, no child should have to face this.

The doors were opened for the visitation to begin. That evening was a testament to the legacy of love that Dave and my boys left on earth. The line of people who had come to greet me and Kate and my family and to pay respects to our guys snaked around the viewing parlor and out into the hall. As each grief-stricken person greeted me with tears, hugs, and condolences, I kept saying, "They are okay. We know where they are. They are okay."

I had to say it over and over to remind myself that they truly were okay.

At one particularly hard but stunningly beautiful moment that evening, several Cub Scout packs came to pay respects to my boys, row upon row lining up in formation in the parlor, I saw my boys as I looked at the little boys in their uniforms. As I watched their faces, so somber for such young souls, the boys lifted their hands to their heads in a group salute. My heart crumbled inside me and soared with pride at the same time.

At one point during the evening services my nephew's teacher came to me and said, "I never met your husband, but I wanted to come pay my respects. He must have been a great man, because Riddick talks about him all the time."

As the evening drew to a merciful close, my sister told me that one of her friends had extended her condolences. The woman had arrived at the funeral home but couldn't bring herself to come into the viewing parlor to see my boys laid out. I assured my sister that it was okay. Had I not been the mom and felt a duty to be there, I would not have wanted to see that, either.

The next morning I was awoken by Aunt Nancy. Having spent the night, Aunt Lee and Aunt Nancy got Finn and Elise dressed and awakened Kate and me to prepare for what we were about to face that day.

The drive to the funeral home was a long, quiet ride. There is nothing you can say when you know you are about to watch your sons and your husband be put in the ground.

Despite the circumstances, the parlor was beautiful. My sister Deanna had a family photo book made; she had also arranged pictures on poster board to be displayed at the parlor. We had hung the boys' Cub Scout shirts on display and had set out Dave's guitar for all to see. I saw my life, my past joy, and my boys' lives represented in the photos before me. Had I not been held by an unseen hand, I would have collapsed, never to rise again. That burden is too great for any woman to bear.

Kate had made a binder to honor her dad and her brothers. She had included a scrapbook of sorts with drawings and photos of her and her brothers and of her and her dad. She had written messages to Dave and to the boys and had encouraged others to leave messages in the pages of her binder.

As I entered the parlor, I could see that several guests had already arrived to pay their respects. A couple of Dave's friends had driven all night to be there, one from Tennessee, another from Louisiana.

I was greeted by a friend, Kathleen, from our days in Germany, who was in the St. Louis area. She grabbed me up in a hug. Pulling back, she held my hands and looked at me. We simply did not know what to say to each other. She explained, through tears, that she could not stay but that she wanted to give me something. Kathleen pulled a bracelet off of her wrist and put it on mine, explaining its meaning.

Having just survived an ordeal with breast cancer, she found much comfort in the bracelet. I could see many words of encouragement on it: peace, love, hope. But one word stood out above the rest: endure. Kathleen said she hoped the bracelet would bring me as much comfort as it had brought her. I stared at the word, and in that moment, it became my focal point, my purpose, my only motivator, and my motto for the rest of my life.

I will endure; I will simply endure. I will get through today; all I have to do is endure.

The services to honor my boys were beautiful. Dave's dear friend from boot camp days, Dustin, spoke about Dave's loyalty. My mom recalled my boys, their interests, and their intellects; she also spoke about Dave and his steadfast love as a father and a husband. Expecting her first baby, Dave's sister Brittany spoke about how she wanted her child to be just like Dave and our boys. She recalled many memories of her childhood with her brother.

In one particularly moving moment, Gloria, Dave's Cub Scout mentor from our days in Germany, addressed the attendees. Having transferred from Germany to Missouri, she was able to represent the Cub Scouts at the services. She called me to the front of the parlor and presented me with two framed certificates, one with a photo of Dom and the other with a photo of Grant. Gloria explained that my boys had been named honorary Eagle Scouts and that the certificates were signed by the top three men in the Boy Scouts of America.

And then I spoke. I had grand plans for all the ways I wanted to honor Dave, Dominic, and Grant with my words that morning, but when I stood at the podium, the caskets behind me containing the shells of my husband and my sons, no words came at first. When they finally did, I said, "I don't even know what I want to say. I just know I need to say something."

I read passages from Dave's Bible that he had marked with sticky notes years before in men's Bible study classes. I went on to talk about my boys and all the things I loved about them. As I was coming to a close, I looked toward each of my brothers and thanked them from the bottom of my heart for going to the trail days after the accident and gathering as much information as they could about my boys' last earthly moments. With what they were able to learn, we determined that my boys had fallen asleep in their daddy's arms before going to heaven. I wanted my brothers to know that I could have received no greater gift than that assurance.

Finally, Pastor Steve Neill spoke on the new heaven and the new earth. He reminded us as he read through Scripture that we would surely see my boys again. Even then I felt it; even then I knew it. My spirit knew I would get to hold my boys again one sweet day, but at that moment, I saw only the enormous loss before me.

As I sat listening to the pastor speak words of comfort and hope, even quoting from Dave's Bible as he held it in his hands, my mind briefly drifted to memories of Dave and trips with our children. Whether we were at a zoo, a museum, or a grocery store, Dave and I had a system. He would take a couple kids and I would take a few kids, or vice versa, and we would sometimes split up for a portion of the outing and regroup as the trip continued. While we each had a few kids, Dave and I would occasionally get each other's attention from a distance and hold up our fingers, indicating how many children we had under our care, assuring that all five were accounted for.

As Pastor Neill was coming to a close, offering a beautiful reminder of the glory we could all anticipate as believers in Christ, he addressed me directly. "And Sarah, just as you and Dave had your system while out on an outing with your children, each of you holding up your fingers to identify how many children you were each accountable for, I believe Dave has those boys. He has those boys, Sarah. And if you look, I believe you will see him tell you he's got those two." The pastor held up two fingers.

As he spoke, I looked to Kate, Finn, and Elise sitting next to me, and quietly I spoke for only Dave and me to hear.

"And I've got these three," I said, holding up three fingers.

My brothers David and Richard, Dave's friend Dustin, his childhood friend Mike, and his uncles Ted, Larry, and Bob acted as pallbearers. As they carried Dave and the boys from the funeral home, I prepared my spirit for the final leg of the journey we had to take that day. It was time to drive my guys to their final resting place on earth.

At Jefferson Barracks National Cemetery, Dave and the boys were laid to rest with full military honors. During the twenty-one-gun salute, my heart jumped as each round was fired. Dave's mother sat next to me, and next to her was my mother; Dave's grandmother was at the end of the row. Dave's mom and I held hands, and my aunt Mary stood behind me, her hand resting securely on my shoulder. My mother, Dave's mom, Dave's grandmother, and I were each presented with a folded flag. The serviceman presented me with the flag that had draped Dave's casket. As he knelt before me to hand me the flag, we locked eyes, and I could almost hear him through his spirit, through the look in his eyes, try his hardest to convey sympathy to me. But I knew that even if we were able to speak at that moment, no words would come.

In the weeks that followed, my guys were honored at Scott Air Force Base during a memorial held in one of the chapels there. I was honored as I listened to Dave's boss, his coworkers, and his supervisor recall the ways my husband influenced the workplace for the better in his short time at the base. I listened as one coworker told a funny story about Dave and his antics at work. I was grateful for the smile the tale brought to my face and to the faces of those around me. Watching the missing man ceremony in honor of Dave tore at my heart but also made me swell with pride. As boots, a helmet, and dog tags rested untouched at the front of the chapel, a serviceman called out his name, "David Paul Decareaux Jr."

With no response, the call came again, "David Paul Decareaux Jr."

My heart broke and bled with the silence.

My spirit cried out that Dave should be there to see the love and honor poured out for him at that moment. I was reminded deep in my spirit that he was there.

I was presented with a shadow box displaying all of the ranks, ribbons, medals, and awards Dave had earned during his eleven years in the air force. Each of my children and I were also given dog tags inscribed with the names Dave, Dominic, and Grant.

I was supported by many family members and friends at the memorial. Dave's parents, his sister, my parents, all of my siblings, my uncle Greg, my aunts Judy, Janet, and Mary, my cousin Hilary, and family friend Lynn all attended. The homeschool group from the base put on a beautiful reception afterward. These people were the hands and feet of Christ. I was touched and humbled by the acts of love by our air force family at the Defense Information Systems Agency and on Scott Air Force Base.

In early February, Kate and I flew down to Louisiana for a Mass held in the gymnasium at Dave's Catholic high school. Dave's mother, his aunts, and several of his mom's cousins organized the beautiful Mass, which honored my husband and my sons at Dave's alma mater. Three hundred family members, friends, and classmates gathered to honor a man they knew and remembered: their classmate, friend, brother, cousin, nephew, and son. Many who could not make it to the services in Illinois were able to attend the Mass in Louisiana. Among them were Dave's uncle George and his aunt Glenda, his cousin Heath, and many other relatives and friends. I was honored as I sat amazed, looking at the crowd lining the walls of the gymnasium. Dave was more than a stellar father and husband. He was loved immensely by so many people, and my spirit soared within me even as my heart broke.

Finally, Dave and my dear friends from our Germany days, Kim and Chris, had arranged with several clubs and groups on the base in Germany to honor Dave, Dominic, and Grant with a memorial service there in conjunction with the Cub Scouts.

Kim and Chris and their baby girl Sydney were family away from family for Dave and me and our children. We met on base in Germany when Finn was nine months old, and our families grew together. Kim and I were pregnant at the same time and had Elise and Sydney only four months apart. Kim and Chris were dear friends, "Auntie" and "Uncle" to my children. They knew and loved Dave, Dominic, and Grant like family. We got together for many holidays during our years in Germany. July Fourth and Halloween became annual celebrations together.

Since the tragedy, God has seen fit to move Kim and Chris closer to the children and me. Chris got stationed at Scott Air Force Base a year after the tragedy, and God has since blessed them with another beautiful baby girl. I am forever indebted to them for the bond they have shared (and share) with my family.

The memorial that Kim, Chris, and the Cub Scouts organized to honor Dave and the boys in Germany was videotaped by the Armed Forces Network, and I saw snippets of it online. I was greatly honored. I succumbed to tears as I saw three flaming arrows shot into the sky in honor of my guys. Dave loved leading the Scouts while in Germany; it was a calling for him, not a hobby, not a job. And to see that love reciprocated was overwhelming. No words can convey my gratitude for all the love shown my three precious guys.

As the ceremonies came to a close, I was looking at the memorial binder Kate had made for her dad and her brothers to be displayed at the funeral weeks before. I flipped through it, reading all the loving comments, all the precious memories of my family, when I saw an anonymous entry that took my breath away.

> Dave,
>
> Although I didn't really know you, I know you served your country, I know you served your community, I know you served your family, and I know you served your God. I know that is living a complete life.

Chapter 4
Angels on Earth

In February, I was contacted by one of the first responders who had worked on Dominic. I welcomed the conversation. I wanted to gather as much information as I possibly could in order to piece together a time line of events. I needed to have a better understanding of what happened on those January days. After we introduced ourselves, he asked, "So what do you want to know?"

"Anything," I said. "Anything you can tell me. I want to know as much as I can."

I didn't care how brutal the information might be. I wanted an accurate account of what had happened during the search, the discovery of the boys, and the rescue efforts to better process the tragedy. The man's next words made the breath catch in my throat.

"Your husband is a determined man."

My heart fell out of my chest. I was filled with an unexplainable pride, but also terror, at all I was about to hear.

"What do you mean?" I could hardly speak the words through a closing throat. I couldn't get the information out of him quickly enough.

"He was a determined man. He carried your boys. He carried your boys awhile. Then he laid them down, he covered them with his jacket, and crawled about twenty more feet."

My heart was soaring and breaking at the same time. The first thing that registered in my head was that he had changed his wording from "is a determined man" to "was a determined man." It comforted me to think of Dave in the present tense. Adrenaline coursed through me as I pictured the scene the first responder had described. I tried to sort out and piece together the information as he gave it.

When Dave couldn't carry our boys any longer, his body breaking down as he succumbed to hypothermia, he placed them beside the trail, side by side, face up; covered them with his jacket, and did an army crawl on his knees and elbows, dragging himself twenty feet down the trail until he could go no farther.

He was found face down, his arms still bent in the army crawl position, barefoot (as in the final stages of hypothermia, victims think they are hot and start shedding clothes and shoes), and with mud caked on his arms and at the waistline of his pants.

I was silent as I listened to the first responder, the entire scene playing out in my head. I felt horror but also a strange pride. As he spoke, I coupled all he said with the accounts I had gotten from my brothers weeks before.

Just a few days after the accident, my brothers returned to the trail and were led by searchers and lodge workers to all the highlighted sites on the time line. They were given information as they hiked. My brothers found a trekking pole. We believe Dave ditched the trekking poles to have both hands free to carry our boys. Judging from where the pole was found, Dave carried our boys about a mile before he could go no farther. Dom was seventy pounds, and Grant was about forty pounds.

My brothers also found Dave's glasses. The men guiding them said that the glasses were where our boys had been found.

"Were the arms of the glasses folded or not folded?" I asked my brothers.

That would indicate to me if the glasses had fallen or if Dave had taken them off. My brothers assured me the arms of the glasses were folded.

A strong theory held by many of us is that after Dave placed Dom and Grant next to the trail and covered them with his jacket, he took off his glasses, set them on the trail, and then laid on top of the boys, in an attempt to warm his sons before deciding to continue crawling on the trail.

Just days after the accident, I learned from my brothers that Dave had obviously lain down with our boys. Weeks after, I learned from my conversation with the first responder that Dave had carried our boys and crawled. All of this information was an invaluable gift to me because it cemented what I already knew in my spirit—that my boys had gone to heaven asleep in their daddy's arms.

The first responder said a searcher found my boys lying beside the trail side by side, face up, and Dave about twenty feet farther down the trail. He said Bear, our dog, "wasn't letting anyone near that little one."

The first responder said that Bear kept running from Dave to the boys. The searchers had to tie Bear to a tree to get to the boys and attempt a rescue. He said he and another EMT attended to Dom. Others ran to Grant, and still others went to assess Dave's condition and pronounced him passed away at the scene. But they were all determined to save those boys.

He said Grant was a little farther down the trail than Dom, as if something had dragged him a foot or so. His pants were ripped. Then everyone realized what had happened. Not only was Bear protecting my boy from strangers, but he had tried to pull him down the trail by gripping Grant's pants leg with his teeth. And because Grant was the warmest of the three, we believe Bear lay on top of him in an attempt to keep him warm. Our loyal companion was only five months old.

I always found that information about Bear's guardianship over Grant comforting and interesting. Dom was his master. Dave and Dom shared care and control of Bear. Grant was as hands off with Bear as

Kate, Finn, Elise, and I were. But it seems that Bear felt a need to protect the smallest and most vulnerable of the pack. And he did his best. I am forever indebted to that dog, our dear, loyal Bear.

My conversation with the first responder ended up spanning two days. We spoke for hours the first night and a few more hours the next day. The story he told me was horrific and heartbreaking, but also heroic and valiant. Dave and our sons had shown unbelievable tenacity and resolve as had all those trying so hard to find and save my boys. The first responder said he did CPR on Dominic. When his arms went numb and he couldn't use them, another EMT relieved him. The first responder was part of a multiagency search party of fifty-plus that looked for my boys all Saturday night until the search was called at 12:30 a.m.

He told me how disgusted he was that the search was halted. He had no option but to obey. After orders to stop, uniformed personnel no longer have insurance coverage for injury or death. He assured me that several civilians continued to search through the night.

The first responder gave me much information about the search efforts. He said the team was all over the trails that Saturday night on ATVs, searching any old barns or structures they came across, even calling for Bear. He said searchers finally started to think that my boys had been swept away by a swollen creek at an unsuccessful creek crossing, since there was no trace of them.

Our conversation during those two days covered many topics. We discussed the search to find my boys and the scene when they were finally located, the courageous attempts to rescue them, and the ride in the ambulance. Piecing together the evidence at the scene, Dave's heroism and his determination to get home were clear.

I wondered why EMTs worked on the boys so long, since I knew deep in my spirit that all three of my guys were gone before they were even found. The first responders I spoke to said they could not bring themselves to give up without making a heroic effort to save the boys' lives. They explained that once an EMT starts lifesaving efforts on a patient, only a doctor can order those efforts stopped and call a time of death.

They worked on my boys on the trail and in the ambulance, and the monumental effort continued at the hospital. Looking back, I still believe they were already gone. Some of the first responders and a nurse at the hospital that day confirmed this but said they were essentially trying to bring the boys back to life. With hypothermia, the body may go into a state resembling hibernation, and it's sometimes possible to bring victims out of it.

While I am eternally grateful to every person involved in the search and rescue efforts, I believe my boys' spirits were already with Jesus and their daddy. The medical personnel were essentially trying to revive empty shells. I formed a friendship with one of the people who had worked on my boys, and in a four-hour phone conversation we had in March of that year, this person told me, "Sarah, all I am going to say is that there is a fate worse than death, and even if we could have brought your boys back that day, they would no longer have been your boys."

They had already been gone for so long by the time they reached the hospital that they would likely have been left in a vegetative state if revival attempts had succeeded. But my boys are alive. They are whole and they are fine. And while the efforts to keep them alive and with me did not succeed, they are more alive now in heaven than they ever would have been on this fallen earth.

Chapter 5

Their Trail and Walking Them Out

After the services, the funeral, and the memorial observance at Scott Air Force Base, I needed to have my own ceremony for Dave, Dom, and Grant. It was time for me to hike out to see the spot where they had gone to heaven and had met Jesus.

Two weeks after the accident, on a cold but sunny February morning, with my sisters Deanna and Elizabeth babysitting the kids, I went with my brothers David and Richard to the trail that took my boys home.

I woke before sunset filled with determination to get to the trail. My grief was overcome by resolve, and I readied myself with a sureness of spirit. I was going to say good-bye to my boys my way. I dressed in warm clothing, including one of Dave's sweaters, and filled a backpack with all necessary gear for the short leg of the hike we had planned.

My brothers arrived, and we started the two-hour drive down to the lodge. They would take me to points from the time line of events that weekend two weeks before. Then we would park at the lodge and hike two miles to the place where my boys were found. Having been walked through the time line days after the accident by lodge personnel, my brothers knew that I needed to see the points along my boys' journey.

As we took the exit off the interstate, with the drive consisting mainly of smaller state roads from that point on, I got a knot in my stomach and became increasingly nervous. All the familiar sights were having an effect on me. But the landmarks and the buildings looked much different. Everything was gray. The buildings, the signs, all of it was the same, but my world was dark—in stark contrast with two weeks before. Then I had seen these things in bright colors, in sunshine. My mind briefly drifted to a memory.

Two weeks earlier, as Dave was driving down the road through a small town only forty-five minutes from our destination, all the kids had needed a potty break. We'd decided this was also a good opportunity to let the dogs stretch their legs. Dave pulled up to a mom-and-pop restaurant, and everyone eagerly exited the van, the kids running to the doors to try to be first in line. Grant, Dom, Kate, and I went inside to find the restrooms, while Dave walked the dogs near the van where the babies, Finn and Elise, remained sleeping.

Inside the restaurant, Dom and Grant were making typical little-boy comments about the decor and the clientele, saying that everyone and everything in the place was "old." They were not being mean-spirited, but they were being funny, and they were right. I looked like a teenager compared with the dear folks in the restaurant that afternoon.

As I waited outside the door with Kate, the boys continued joking and laughing in the restroom. They were being so loud that I had to knock on the door to tell them to be quiet. Much to my embarrassment as well as amusement, I noticed that many of the customers were now staring at the out-of-towners who had taken over their restaurant. When my knocks on the restroom door didn't work, I opened it to the boys' shock and loud protests and told them, "Be quiet! Everyone is staring at us!"

After their initial shock had subsided, the boys succumbed to even more laughter, and so did Kate and I. Their laughter was contagious. As one of us laughed, that made the rest of us laugh harder, and the looks we were getting from the old folks were not helping.

When we finished with the restroom, we thanked the workers behind the counter and piled back in the van. My smile remained. As we got back on the road for the last leg of our drive to the lodge, I turned to look at my brood, at the kids Dave and I had made, at the family we had created. And I was so grateful for those little lives that were not only my kids but my friends.

My mind returned to the present. We had entered the small town where Dave had pulled over for that rest break. As the restaurant came into view, I couldn't take my eyes off of it. I longed to go back in time, to return to the laughter, the smiles, the giggles, even the stares of two weeks earlier. As the restaurant passed from my view, I saw only my new reality. As we drove through the town that cold February morning, it dawned on me that there was no more laughter, and I wondered in that moment, if there ever would be.

Nearing the first spot on the time line of my guys' journey, I felt dread, but I remained determined to see the last earthly sights my boys beheld.

We arrived at Sutton Bluff, a beautiful overlook near where the trail meets a state road. The spot had many picnic tables and rest areas. Overlooking the Black River from atop a cliff, Sutton Bluff was just the place Dave and I would have chosen to picnic with the kids. I could see why Dave was in such good spirits when the man happened upon him and the boys, the last time they were seen alive on earth. As my brothers and I drove down the road leading to the river below the bluff, I couldn't help but notice the area's great beauty. My heart was light. "At this point on the hike, they were in good spirits," one of my brothers said, and I could feel that in my spirit.

We got out of the truck and walked around a bit. I went to the edge of the river, threw in a few rocks, and bent down to touch the water with my fingers. I wanted to absorb the area, the last place where Dave, Dominic, and Grant were happy.

My brothers and I spoke only a little at the river, but as we walked on the rocks along the edge, they offered theories.

"Dave and the boys may not have actually come down to the river that day; they may have stayed on the bluff. Dave was probably in a hurry to get back to the lodge after taking a break here. He could probably see the storm was coming in," one of my brothers offered.

"I don't know," the other said. "Maybe they did come down off of the bluff to the river to let Bear get a drink. I could just see Dom and Grant skipping rocks across the river."

As they spoke, I pictured all they were saying. I saw my boys running, laughing, smiling, playing. I saw them skip rocks across the river. I saw Dave follow behind them, saying, "Okay, boys, it's time to press on."

The time we spent on Sutton Bluff and at the Black River was calm and peaceful. This was the right way to start the arduous journey that lay in front of us. It was time to see the rest of the trail.

We drove along the forestry roads intersecting the trail to the next spot on the time line, the place where Dave had built rock cairns indicating to anyone searching where he and the boys could be found.

As we neared the spot, I was struck by tunnel vision and could see only directly in front of me. I could hardly move or breathe, and adrenaline coursed through my veins. I needed to see what Dave had built. I needed to stand where my boys had stood only two short weeks before. I needed to see the evidence of Dave's heroic acts. I needed to be where he and the boys had been.

We parked the truck and got out, and the two rock cairns were right in front of me. They stood opposite each other on the sides of the trail, and one was larger than the other. I pictured Dave building one of these pyramids in the pitch dark, his cell phone and his flashlight no longer working. I heard him call to the boys to build another on the other side of the trail. I saw Dom lead his brother across the trail to gather rocks as best they could in the dark. I saw Grant, afraid but determined to help his dad and his brother do all they could to help the searchers find them.

I walked over to the larger rock formation, knelt beside it, and ran my hands over the smooth stones, still almost perfectly in place two weeks after they had been assembled by Dave's strong hands. I touched the grooves on the rocks, wishing with everything in me that they had indicated to searchers that night where Dave, Dom, and Grant were.

And then on the ground in front of me I saw orange peels. They were dirty, dark, and starting to shrivel, but they were orange peels all the same. I had to avoid the urge to scream. I wanted to scream in anguish, in despair, in horror, in sorrow. I knew Grant had put oranges in his backpack for the hike, and now I saw that Dave and the boys had used orange peels, bright sides up, to indicate their location. My heart broke over and over again as I sat on the ground near the rock cairns, near the orange peels my guys had left. I felt their desperation but also their resolve. I felt their determination, their courage, and their strength.

Sitting on the trail and touching the rock pile, I felt something else. I felt overwhelming pride. A surge of love washed over me, and tears filled my eyes. They were not tears of sorrow but of immense love for my boys. I recognized that they were willing to do anything and everything to save their lives. I was honored to be the wife and the mother of those three beautiful souls who made their final earthly journey along this trail.

As we headed off down the forestry road, I watched the rock cairns until they were no longer visible, and I wished with everything in me that they had served their purpose, indicating to searchers where Dave and the boys were. Now I knew it was time to see the place on the trail where my guys had gone home to heaven.

As we drove slowly down the forestry road toward the lodge, my brother spotted something flying above his truck. Pulling over, we looked up to see two glorious bald eagles in the stunning blue skies. As we watched them soar ever higher, my spirit rose as well. I couldn't place why I felt such a connection to these creatures flying above me. I felt drawn to their beauty, to their gracefulness, and I could have watched them all day that way, in that peace.

"Your Eagle Scouts, Sarah," my brother said, breaking the silence.

Yes, my spirit recalled, *my Eagle Scouts.* My boys had been named honorary Eagle Scouts. All at once the connection I felt to those birds made sense. In a way, they were my boys, traveling along with me as I followed their trail, as I walked where they had walked, as I prepared to say my good-bye to them. They were there to support me and to encourage me.

As we pulled away, I watched until the eagles were out of view. And just as I could no longer see the eagles but knew they were there, I knew my boys, too, were just over the horizon, just beyond my view. And I knew they were as free and peaceful and glorious as those eagles were in that perfect sky that day.

Arriving at the lodge, we parked the truck, and my brothers and I took a lunch break in the parking lot before hiking to the spot where my guys had gone home.

Seeing the lodge again for the first time in two weeks was easier than I thought. But then I saw our cabin, and everything came flooding back. As my brothers ate their sandwiches, I walked toward the cabin. I passed the teeter totter my kids had broken only weeks prior and I stopped short. God whispered to me that there was no reason to walk to the cabin. There was no reason to return to that place in my spirit. There was no reason to disrupt that last pleasant memory I had of seeing my guys off on their hike.

I turned my back on the cabin and returned to my brothers to eat my lunch, knowing some memories are better left alone.

After refueling with sandwiches and drinks, we suited up with our daypacks and prepared for the short two-mile hike into the forest to the place where Dave, Dominic, and Grant had left this earth.

As we started up the trailhead—the one that Dave and the boys had walked as Finn and I watched from the back porch of our cabin—my head was spinning. I was trying to absorb all the sights and sounds and smells that my guys may have experienced as they started out on that path two weeks before. This was an easy path, a bit uphill but not too treacherous at first. My brother joked that my boys had put us to shame, since they probably ran up the path that we adults were walking at that point.

My brothers and I engaged in light conversation for about the first mile. But as we neared the second half, which would lead me to the spot I was seeking, the last place my boys were on earth, the conversation changed. My brothers tried to prepare me, describing the layout of the trees, the way the boys were found, and how Dave was discovered twenty feet down from them. I collected all the information and stored it away, but besides listening to them, I was preparing my spirit for what I had to do.

As I traveled that last mile into the woods, it dawned on me how close we were to the lodge, how close Dave and the boys were to coming back to me that night, and my heart broke all over again. But I regained my resolve. I was determined to honor my boys, and I quickly put that thought to the back of my head.

As we neared the place where my boys were found, my brothers described what to look for as we approached our destination. I watched for the landmarks and suddenly saw that we had arrived.

The bend in the path was just as my brothers had described it. The scene was different from what I had pictured, however. The place was hilly and narrow, and there were trees all around, almost creating a canopy even in their late-winter bareness. My brothers quietly pointed out where my boys were found and then allowed me to walk ahead.

As they talked, describing the scene as it was sketched out for them weeks before, I heard sounds but couldn't make out their voices. My world had gone narrow. I pictured what Dave must have seen that early morning as he was carrying our sons. The sun may have offered just a hint of light as he neared the end of his earthly journey. I saw him set down our boys. I saw him take off his glasses and lie down next to our sons. I saw him crawl twenty more feet. I turned my head to the section of the trail where Dave was found. I walked slowly to it. I sat in that spot. I looked above me and thought, *So this is the last thing you saw, Dave?*

There were no tears at first. I couldn't cry. I couldn't even feel. I was numb to emotion but trying to absorb the sights and smells and sounds around me, all at the same time. Walking back to where my boys were found, I knelt. I ran my hand along the ground where my brothers said my boys had lain. I wanted to lie down where they were found, hoping desperately to feel closer to them in whatever way I could. But I didn't. Instead, I took out a folded paper from my pocket and did what I was there to do. I was there to honor my boys. I was there to say good-bye.

I had written down some verses from Scripture on the piece of paper. As I prepared my spirit to read that passage, to pray over my boys' spot, to say my good-bye, my brothers gathered behind me in the distance, just off the trail.

I read aloud from 1 Thessalonians 4:13–18.

> Brothers and sisters, we do not want you to be uninformed about those who sleep in death, so that you do not grieve like the rest of mankind, who have no hope. For we believe that Jesus died and rose again, and so we believe that God will bring with Jesus those who have fallen asleep in him. According to the Lord's word, we tell you that we who are still alive, who are left until the coming of the Lord, will certainly not precede those who have fallen asleep. For the Lord himself will come down from heaven, with a loud command, with the voice of the archangel and with the trumpet call of God, and the dead in Christ will rise first. After that, we who are still alive and are left will be caught up together with them in the clouds to meet the Lord in the air. And so we will be with the Lord forever. Therefore encourage one another with these words.

As I read, the tears came, but my voice grew stronger. I was determined to honor my boys and their sacred spot, and I continued to read. As I folded the paper back into my pocket and closed my eyes to sit in the stillness of that moment, God whispered to my spirit, *Do not grieve as if you have no hope, daughter. This was not the end of their story. They are alive with Me here. This was not the end of them.*

After some time spent kneeling at my guys' spot, I decided it was time to go. It was time to move on. God had assured me that my boys were no longer in that place but were in bliss unseen. It was time for me to get up, to hike my way out of the forest, and to return home to my babies awaiting me there.

As we started back toward the lodge, a light snow began to fall. Walking in silence at first, we found ourselves in light conversation as we neared the halfway point to the lodge. We shared many memories of Dave and the boys. The air felt thick around me as I walked the two miles out of the forest. I felt as if a cloud of witnesses was with me (Hebrews 12:1) even as I walked the trail through the falling snow.

Deep in thought, my brothers had walked slightly ahead of me, and they suddenly stopped.

"Sarah, you have got to see this!" one of them called.

I hurried over to see what they were pointing at. It was Dave's trekking pole. Days after the accident, my brothers had found Dave's glasses and one trekking pole. The location of the first trekking pole indicated the place on the trail where Dave was believed to have started carrying our sons. Everyone assumed the second pole had been grabbed by a curious creature at some point.

The second trekking pole was lying under a bush, tangled in the brush. Freeing it, my brother held it up and saw that the rubber handle had indeed been chewed up by some forest animal. Handing the pole to me, he told me to use it for the rest of the hike.

As I started walking, trekking pole in hand, the snow still falling, I stumbled a bit. As I regained my balance with the pole, my brother turned to me with a smile and said, "See. Dave is helping you hike today."

I smiled back, but I was deep in thought. As I walked out of the woods that snowy day, I spoke to my boys inwardly, saying, *We found your trekking pole, guys, and I am going to walk it out of here for you.*

And in a strange way, with Dave's trekking pole in my hand, I felt as if I were hiking them out of there. I was finishing the short last leg of the journey that would have brought them home to me that night.

I am walking you out of here, guys, I thought.

When we saw the end of the trail ahead of us, I felt a satisfaction, an inkling of completion. While I had to pretend I had walked my guys out of the trail that snowy February day, I knew full well the way they really left the trail that January day weeks earlier. They were not hiked out by me but were carried out by the hands of the almighty Father. And I knew they wanted me to know that they were okay and that this trail was not the end of them.

Chapter 6

Dark Days but Rays of Light

The Lord your God is with you, the mighty warrior who saves.

—Zephaniah 3:17

After the funeral, after the memorial service at Scott Air Force Base, after the Mass in Louisiana, after I knew the memorial in Germany had taken place, and after I had hiked to the spot in the forest where my boys had gone home, I faced – Now, what?

I was proud to have honored my guys, and quite honestly, I was glad to have that part behind me. But once Dave's parents had gone home to Louisiana after more than two weeks in Illinois near the kids and me, after my siblings stopped spending the night at my house, and after my family's story was old news to the newspapers, I had an overwhelming sense of uncertainty and wondered, *What do I do now?*

One day, early in my grief journey, I was absolutely overwhelmed. I could not get out of bed. I could hardly breathe. My grief was sucking the life out of me, almost punching the air out of my lungs, and keeping me paralyzed in utter sorrow. My grief was physical. I was suffering greatly. But deep in my spirit, I had the conscious realization that I was undergoing a spiritual attack. Slowly, I pulled the covers off of me and got out of bed. I crawled, laboring with each movement, to my phone on the dresser across my bedroom. I had no idea what I was going to do with the phone in hand, but once I reached it, I heard a soft, small voice at the depth of my being tell me to text a dear sister in Christ—a young woman so anointed in the Holy Spirit that I knew she could call out to the Father for help on my behalf. I texted my friend Dori, "Help me. Pray for me right now. I am being attacked by the demons of despair, hopelessness, and sorrow right now. Please pray for me."

After I had made my way back to bed and thrown the covers over myself, I slept a sweet, merciful sleep. When I awoke, I noticed I had received a response from Dori.

"Sarah, I don't want to upset you," she wrote, "but I want to share something with you. I had a vision the other day. It was a vision of the moment your guys entered glory. I saw them standing in white, pure white. I saw them standing in awe at all they saw around them. And then I saw Jesus come to them, walk toward them. He motioned for them to follow Him. As all three followed, Dominic followed slowly, as if contemplating all he saw around him. Grant followed willingly, and Dave followed behind both of them, as if shepherding them toward Jesus. They arrived at a table of sorts. At this table, Jesus was talking with them about what to expect, about all the wonders that awaited them there. He assured them that they were safe and that all was going to be okay. Dave and Dom were listening intently, soaking up all the

Father had to say to them. But Grant seemed uneasy about something; he seemed preoccupied; he seemed worried. While Dave and Dominic listened to Jesus in silence, almost too much in awe of Him to speak, Grant quietly yet surely spoke up. He asked the Father, 'But who is going to take care of Mom?'

"Jesus looked to your sweet, precious boy and answered him strong and sure, 'I will.'"

I was bombarded with memories of my family—of what used to be. I was haunted by thoughts of despair. I battled with despondency and with sorrow. The Enemy of my soul (Psalm 143:3–7) was working overtime to take me down in those early grief days.

Weeks after the accident, I got a phone call from a doctor's office reminding me of Dominic and Grant's upcoming appointment. I had made the appointment for a routine checkup and had obviously not thought to cancel. As the woman spoke those words, I felt as if a knife had been plunged into my heart.

"They are not here! They are not here!" I screamed into the phone, nearly dropping it.

I hung up the phone and slumped into a mess of screams and tears on my basement floor. I had scheduled checkups for all five of my children before the accident. How could it have happened that I received a call reminding me about the appointment for Dom and Grant, the two who had just gone home to heaven? While the dear woman at the doctor's office couldn't have known that and was simply doing her job, that call hit my spirit hard. Even in my deep grief so early in my journey, I realized that the Enemy planned to play dirty (John 10:10), that he would try to destroy me as he thought he had destroyed my family. And while I didn't feel it then, looking back I see that this was one of the first moments when I resolved to fight the spiritual battle of grief with all that I had.

Beginning my grief journey, I was terrified at the thought of living without my family intact, but at the same time, I felt relief at finally starting my true mourning. I had lived in a bubble since the tragedy. God had provided a covering of family and friends over us, and our every need was met. And while that was exactly what I needed at the time, I also knew I needed to be alone to start mourning and going it alone.

In those early days, I considered giving up traditional living, uprooting the kids, selling our house, and becoming a missionary in Africa or somewhere else in the third world. I couldn't fathom trying to live normally when nothing in my life was normal any longer. I could not imagine how to go on living without my entire family intact. The thought of living among the suffering appealed to me. I reasoned I could help others in their grief while forgetting mine in the process. The notion of living among the hurting felt more comfortable than trying to live with my aching heart and my broken spirit among the intact families all around me.

But God whispered to my spirit that I would simply be running. I would not be entering the mission field to help others but to help forget my grief, and He needed me to stay right where I was. He needed me to face my grief head-on, not to run from it. I knew God would ask me to start walking the grief road, the long, arduous path of loss. He would ask me to stay put, to fight the battle and to do the hard work. He would ask me to heal His way and in His time.

My dear friend Amy came to stay with the kids and me for a week in the first several weeks into our loss. She and her husband, Steve, lived in Florida, and she flew up in the earliest part of my grief journey. Dave and I had known Amy and Steve since Kate was twenty days old. Steve was Dave's captain in the Azores, and he and Amy quickly took us under their wing. We looked up to them, continuing our long-distance friendship as we moved on with our lives and traveled the world. Dave and I often said we wanted to be "just like them when we grow up." They loved adventure, were always on the go, were young, active grandparents, and took friends in as family. I looked up to Amy.

In my newlywed years, she was one of the military wives who modeled for me how to be a successful military spouse.

I was grateful when Amy came to stay with us. She cleaned my house, folded the laundry, played with the kids, kept me company, and helped me organize the many flowers we had been given at the services. I found her company comforting. As she held my hand, we cried together.

When visiting their son, stationed a few hours from Dave and me in Germany, in March of 2012, Amy and Steve took a day to come see us. We had a blessed visit at a playground, and Amy and Steve got to know all five of our kids, to see Baby Kate (as Amy had dubbed her years before) for the first time in years, and to get reacquainted with Dave and me. During her time at my house, Amy and I talked of how grateful we were for that visit.

Amy's visit at the end of February 2013 was a brief reprieve from my brand-new grief journey. When she left, I knew it was time to ready myself for my new reality and to see what it would feel like to step out into the great unknown.

My readiness to step into the great unknown quickly turned to worry as I looked at our bank account balance online one afternoon. Sure, I could make the house payment with what was in the account, but that left us with almost nothing. I had not done the paperwork to start Dave's financial provision for sustaining the children and me.

The Cub Scout pack to which Dave and the boys had belonged started a Decareaux memorial fund, and the money kept us afloat for several weeks until I completed all the paperwork ensuring our livelihood through other means. I am forever indebted to the dear souls in that Cub Scout pack and throughout the community who contributed toward it.

One particularly trying day early in my grief journey, the plumbing in our unfinished basement backed up, and there were several inches of sewer water on the concrete laundry room floor. I was still finding it hard to do even small chores and wanted to lie on my couch or in bed all day to mourn. So the added stress was not what I needed that day. I called the plumber, explained the situation, and asked him to come out right away. As he was on his way, I thought, *I have no idea how I am going to pay this man. I have just enough to write him a check, but then I will not have the house payment.*

As I was waiting for the plumber, I decided to go outside and check the mailbox. It was a good thing I was sitting on my couch when I opened the mail. I found a letter from Dave's old college fraternity. Included in the letter was a check. Fraternity members had taken up a collection. The amount was enough to cover my next couple of house payments. I was overcome with gratitude, and I started weeping. I was amazed even then that despite everything else falling apart around me, my God was making sure our needs were met through the hands and feet of His people.

I started out slowly on my grief journey, taking only one step at a time. But as I walked, God walked right before me, making sure our needs were met.

The first night I gathered my kids into the van, just the four of us, was weeks after our tragedy when I drove to my parents' house for my brother's birthday. I can't adequately describe the feeling of getting into the van that had taken our family of seven all over Europe, that had transported our family of seven to Louisiana earlier that year, that had just taken the seven us to the lodge two weeks before—with only the four of us returning.

There we sat, just the four of us: Kate in "my seat" (the passenger seat), me in "Dave's seat" (the driver's seat), and Finn and Elise strapped in the back in their normal spots but with two empty seats where my boys should have been sitting. I was stunned at how something so seemingly small as seat placement and vacant seats in our van could have such a huge impact on me. I realized that those seemingly small things would threaten to undo me in the days ahead.

I have found that the pain does not allow me to move. So when I am paralyzed by that pain, if I take just one step in faith, God pulls me, lifts me, and pushes me the rest of the way. And sometimes He makes it interesting.

One night in February, we were invited to my sister's house for my nephew Michael's birthday. I didn't want to go. I didn't want to do anything, to see anyone, or to talk about anything. My parents, my siblings, and their kids were all invited. I knew there would be a big group, but while I loved everyone there, I wasn't feeling celebratory. But I realized that I needed, and the kids especially needed, a change of scenery from our four walls, so I decided to go.

As I got ready to go, I felt an old, seemingly far-gone feeling—getting ready to go out to a social outing. I wanted to be excited, to feel like a normal mom getting her kids ready for a blissfully routine family birthday party. Behind me and ahead of me, I could see a normal life, but it was out of my reach. I was not allowed to touch it.

As we pulled out of our circular gravel driveway, I lost control on the ice, and our van ended up in a ditch to the side. I tried to get us out. I threw the van in reverse. I threw it in drive. I slammed on the gas, and I turned the wheels. Nothing. In fact, I had made the problem worse. In trying to get us out, I had dug us further into the ditch.

Completely dejected, I got out of the van, slammed the door shut, and tried to push the van out of the ditch. I knew full well I wouldn't succeed, but I needed to hit something, to push something. Finally, I stood defeated, staring off into the dark woods all around me. I screamed, "This is when I need you, Dave!"

I missed my husband so badly at that moment, and I burst into tears. I cried for all the things I missed about him, for all the things we'd never do together again, for all the things I had to do alone for our family now. I cried for all the "man jobs" around the house that were all my responsibility now. Then my crying turned to whining and fit throwing and became less about grief and more about anger at all those "man jobs," like the stuck van, now mine to handle.

And then a resolve took hold: I was going to get that van out of the ditch one way or another. Kate asked why I did not call our neighbors, our only neighbors, up the lane to help tow us out. She and the babies looked at me as if I had completely lost my mind.

"No way," I responded.

I needed no one's help, and if I was forced to do "man jobs," then I was going to do them! I tried again, revving the van in drive, revving it in reverse. Finally, about forty-five minutes into the ordeal, I thought, *Okay, I do need outside help, but I won't be calling family or friends, I can still do this myself. I will pay for a truck to tow me out.*

I called the tow truck operator and said, "Hi, my name is Sarah, and I need a tow. I'm struck in my own driveway."

As soon as I spoke that last sentence, Kate and I were struck by how funny it sounded and we broke into wild laughter. We looked at each other, took turns repeating "stuck in my driveway," and laughed even harder.

Then we saw how we were sitting tilted because the van was stuck so deep in the ditch, and we laughed still harder.

We continued on that way, laughing to tears until we could laugh no more and the truck arrived to tow us out. After we were freed, the tow truck operator was paid, and we were on our way to my nephew's birthday party, I smiled to myself in the dark van because it hit me that no matter what lay ahead, no matter what lay behind, I had just laughed—uncontrollably laughed—for the first time in more than a month. And I felt a little lighter as I drove the van that night.

Chapter 7

Darkness and a Message

In early February, my cousin Randy and his wife, Valerie, came to dinner with their three beautiful children, lasagna and all the fixings in hand. I was grateful for the company. No one spent the night at my house any longer, and I appreciated the time alone, since I wanted to begin the grief journey on my own. However, I was grateful for the visits from many family members and friends in the days and evenings. Each visit made the day go by more quickly. The visits lightened my load and brought sunshine to my day and to the kids' day, filling the afternoons and evenings with conversation, tears, and prayers.

In the first several weeks after our tragedy, I had company every day, sometimes multiple guests. I did not feel overwhelmed; in fact, I woke each morning thinking about who I would see that day. Those visits proved to be yet another lifeline, yet another way God was using the hands and feet of His people to propel me ever further down the grief road.

I was blessed to talk with family and friends, acquaintances, and new friends whom I otherwise would not have had the opportunity to get to know. When life gets busy and we all have our own schedules, it can be hard to find time for anyone other than those in our immediate circles. I realized that God will bring blessings through sorrow. While I would have traded anything to have Dave, Dominic, and Grant still with me on earth, it did not escape me that God was allowing me to create soul ties with family and friends during this time of grief and mourning, connections that I otherwise would not have had the chance to make.

That evening I was surrounded by Randy, his dear wife, their children, and my children playing, having fun, talking, and even crying some. At one point, their three-year-old daughter had climbed up the stairs to my loft, though we adults were unaware of this while deep in conversation in the living room below. As we heard the little girl fall down the stairs, Valerie jumped up.

"Oh, God!" she screamed as she ran to the stairs to scoop up her baby girl, who was scared but uninjured.

I watched as my cousin's wife cradled her little girl, checking her for injuries, consoling her as she cried, comforting her in her fear. I was thankful she was okay, but I said inwardly, *God, I love my boys just the same. I wanted to find them, to rush in and save the day, to comfort them, to hold and console them. Father, why didn't You let me?*

I was overcome by the beauty of a mother's concern for her child and broken by it at the same time.

All through the evening, my faithful companion, our baby before we had babies, Cleo, our twelve-year-old husky, lay at my feet. Just as Dominic was Bear's master, I was Cleo's. She was another baby for me, and I loved her dearly.

Cleo had come along on just about every Decareaux adventure. Dave and I had gotten her and her brother Bo in the Azores when they were ten weeks old—before we knew we were pregnant with Kate. Bo passed at two years old while we were still in the Azores, but Cleo came with us to almost every duty station.

She also lived with us in Idaho. During our two years in England, she lived with Dave's parents in New Orleans, but upon our return stateside, she lived with us in Illinois. We shipped her to Italy upon our move there, and she came with us to Germany. My dad liked to call our new house in Illinois Cleo's retirement home after a lifetime of adventure. She and Dominic were even birthday buddies. He was born January 4, 2003, and Cleo was born on that date in 2001. I found much comfort in my familiar friend in the days and weeks after my family's tragedy.

That evening, as was routine, Cleo stood at the door, indicating she had to go potty. I let her out, knowing when she was ready to return, she would give a quick howl at the front door. After a beautiful visit, my cousin and his wife had decided it was time to be on their way. We said our good-byes and I saw them to the door. After thanking them for a nice evening, I closed the door and sat down. I went over the events of the evening in my head. I was grateful for the visit and was ready to go to bed.

I had been sitting for only a few moments when there was a knock at the door. Kate and I arrived at the door at the same time, and when we opened it, we found my cousin standing on the front porch. His face had a look of dread that I recognized could not accompany good news.

"Is everything okay?" I quickly asked.

"I don't want to have to tell you this," he began, "but your dog is on the other side of the street. It's been hit."

"What? Bear's dead? What?"

I immediately panicked, assuming Dominic's dog, Bear, who had bravely tried to save Grant a month before, who had been Dominic's faithful companion, and who had been the only one to survive the ordeal on the trail, was dead.

"No," he said. "It's the other one."

"No!" I immediately screamed and broke into sobs.

But above my own sobs, I could hear something else. My Kate dissolved into a heap on the floor, screaming, wailing, and sobbing. Everything she had held in after her dad and brothers' passing seemed to have broken loose at that moment, and she couldn't take anything more. I scooped her up, and we stood in the foyer, with my cousin at the open door. Kate and I were screaming, and crying into each other's shoulders. My cousin's wife came in and hugged me. I screamed into her shoulder, "What is happening? Why is this happening? God, why are you punishing us? What have I done? Why are you taking everything away from me?"

I broke away from Valerie and went to Kate, who had retreated to the couch. She and I slumped to the floor, the couch supporting us from behind, and she screamed, "Mom, why is God punishing us?"

I would like to say that I was able to give my daughter some wise answer, some sage advice, some encouraging words, but all I could muster through my own shock and sorrow was, "I don't know, Kate. I don't know."

And I did not know why a God who loved us would continue to take everything away from us. I felt cursed and punished. I also felt terrified. I felt scared of God. If He could allow continued tragedy, if He could allow Cleo—a companion who was bringing me so much comfort after I had just lost my husband and my sons—to be taken away from me while I was barely hanging on to my sanity, then nothing was sacred; nothing was safe.

Composing myself just enough, I called my brother David and asked him to come over to help my cousin gather Cleo off of the road. Mercifully, she was intact, and my cousin was able to pick her up himself. Once my brother arrived, Randy and his wife were on their way home, and David buried my dear companion in the backyard.

As my brother dug the hole to lay Cleo to rest, I discovered that he knew about her before I called him. When my cousin came to the door to tell me about having found Cleo on the road, I let out such a deafening scream, such a pathetic cry of grief and shock, that my relatives heard me on the other end of Valerie's phone as she contacted them from her car.

As I lay down to sleep that night, utterly spent, utterly exhausted, utterly done, I decided I could not go on in that way. I could not live my life in such pain any longer. I had known too much joy to live another second with everything having been ripped away from me. And I also wondered, *What next?*

That night, I dreamed that I was picking up Dave, Dominic, and Grant from Cub Scout camp. I was sitting on a bench outside a rustic-looking building, waiting for them to come out. One by one, they did. First came Grant. He walked slowly toward me, but instead of having that huge Grant smile on his face with light shining through his eyes, he wore a contemplative, sympathetic grin. He came over to me and hugged me. He had never hugged me that hard in life, and it felt as if he were really there with me. Then came Dominic. Like Grant, he walked slowly toward me, as if contemplating each step. He also wore a concerned, sympathetic smile. Concern and care showed through his eyes. He, too, hugged me so hard that I wondered, *Wow, guys. I'm just picking you up from camp; it's been only a week. Why the long faces? Why the intense hugs?*

Then out walked Dave. He gazed into my eyes with such a look of love, yet concern and compassion, that I started to wonder in my dream, *What is going on?*

Dave walked toward me and grabbed me up in a peculiar hug. This was not the passionate embrace of a husband and wife or even the frontal hug of family members or close friends. He put his arms around me from the side and pulled me beside him. He squeezed me so tightly that I thought, *Guys, what is going on? It was just camp. It's been only a week since we've seen one another.*

And then with a start, I woke up. My eyes popped open and I sat up in my bed. I knew immediately what had happened. I had just had an encounter with my boys. I had just had an encounter with my man. Everything made immediate sense when I awoke though it made no sense while I was dreaming. My boys were allowed to comfort me that night. They knew, and my heavenly Father knew, that I was done.

The night I buried Cleo, I was done with life. I couldn't take one more step on my grief journey; I couldn't endure any more pain. Cleo's death was the last straw. But in my deep sorrow, I was comforted by Grant, Dominic, and Dave. The hugs, the sympathetic looks, and the concerned faces made sense. They were concerned about me, they were comforting me, and in that way, they were encouraging me. Though I did not feel encouragement at the time, I felt comfort. I felt known. I felt they were aware. I felt God was aware.

When I awoke, I decided to continue on the road before me, because I knew—even in the deep darkness, even in my continued grief, even with the loss all around me—that my boys were aware. And if they were aware, then God was certainly aware. And I was then encouraged.

As I awoke that morning to face another day, I could still feel the hugs, I could still feel the tiny arms wrapped tightly around my shoulders, I could still feel the strong arms pulling me to his side, and I was able to get out of bed.

Chapter 8

Reflections

In February of 2013, I started to journal. I had been gifted with a beautiful journal by my dear friend Ami, but it sat empty for weeks following our tragedy. However, one February day, I found myself so overwhelmed with emotion as I stared at Kate that I had to write it down.

From Journal No. 1:

"It is a humbling place but a beautiful place when you realize you admire your own child. My Kate has the heart of a bear, like her daddy. My strong, wise, compassionate, protecting, sweet young woman. My Kate."

That day, I made the first of what has turned out to be many journal entries. To date, two years after our tragedy, I have filled ten journals and have typed many more entries into my computer, surely equaling another two printed journals. I started to write with veracity anything and everything that was on my spirit at the time: I wrote angry entries, desperate entries, reflective entries. I wrote lists of honors my family had received since our accident. I wrote letters to Dave, to Dominic, to Grant. I recorded dreams I had. I recorded dreams others had. I wrote song lyrics that spoke to my heart. I wrote conversations I had with God, prayers to Him. Journaling became a life-sustaining outlet for me, especially in the early days of my grief journey. I wouldn't hesitate to make several entries in one day. Writing became an integral part of my mourning. It was a blessing.

From Journal No. 1:

"Boys, I saw the most beautiful sunrise today. I felt I got a glimpse of the glory you are in. I woke to the most beautiful sunrise. It replaced the hole in my chest I normally wake to. I woke just long enough to see it, and then fell back asleep a bit. I feel like God woke me just long enough for me to see it."

Writing down my dreams became an almost a daily occurrence in those early days after the accident. I was dreaming a lot.

From Journal No. 1:

"I can't remember the details, but I know I just dreamt a glorious dream! Dave got a second chance. We were at some function together, and he was wearing a white dress shirt. I remember explaining to him what had happened and saying that he got a 'do over.' I remember the relief I felt at having him back. I remember whispering, 'Just stay with me.'

"I dreamt of Dave again tonight. I see him ready for work, and he says he has to go. He rushes off to work without so much as a kiss good-bye. And he's gone. And I feel so empty. Then I wake feeling truly empty, knowing he is not coming back and what his leaving for work represents. I feel so empty. I miss my husband so badly that my heart feels broken, crushed, torn—like it will never heal—and that life has ceased for me here. I dream very seldom of my boys, as if my mind can't handle it yet."

I also recorded the time line of the weekend my boys passed to heaven. I replayed their journey, the story of that weekend, over and over in different ways in my journal. In the very early days, each weekend after our accident, I commemorated the time line.

From Journal No. 1:

"Week of the sixth anniversary of losing them. I woke in the middle of the night; they are gone. I wake again at 7:00 a.m.; they are gone. They would have passed by this time six weeks ago. My babies. My love. Empty. I feel empty. Sorrow is thick."

I wrote down anything that struck me. I reflected on how the services went for my family. I recorded the time line of the memorial service held at Scott Air Force Base following the funeral as best as memory would serve. I wrote the details of the Louisiana memorial Mass held in early February, and I wrote all I was told about the American military community's memorial honoring my family, held in Stuttgart, Germany.

From Journal No. 1:

"The thought of them in Stuttgart silently racing two unmanned cars down the Pinewood Derby track in honor of my boys is enough to rip my heart out. I am honored to be sure, but oh the thought that their little hands were not there to do it. Lord Jesus, please have mercy."

I wrote much about nature and about how God was speaking to me through His creation. I wrote on many varied topics; anything that came to me I tried to put down on paper. Sometimes a day's entry became a flow of random thoughts, all equally important for me to get out but nonetheless seemingly unconnected.

From Journal No. 1:

"Beautiful sky as sun breaks through the clouds in the late-afternoon sky today …

"I know pastor told me that a good, healthy marriage creates a cord between husband and wife and that the death on earth of one of them does not break it. We are connected, maybe even more connected now, than we've ever been. But I want him here. I want to touch him, to kiss him, to laugh with him, to smell him, to hug him, to cook with him, to tell him he is playing his video game too much. I want my friend here ...

"The kids are so used to me crying now to praise music, when I turn it on in the van they ask, 'Are you going to cry, Mom?'

"Or Elise will come up to me and say, 'It's okay, Mommy. You no cry. You all right, Mom. You want to hug Daddy?' ...

"My thoughts are no longer earthly. I find no pleasure, joy, calm in anything of earth, short of my babies and loved ones here. My heart is no longer here. My heart is in heaven ...

"I found down in the basement an Awana poster that Kate had made years before that said, 'I have gone to prepare a place for you' (John 14:3 KJV). I felt it was a message from my baby boys ...

"A friend told me grief is a fight. I am trying to battle, Father. It is so hard; I want to surrender at times. I feel defeated at times. Mighty warrior, fight with me."

Journaling became lifesaving for me in so many ways. Looking back at my journals, I can see how my handwriting reflected my mood. Hurried, messy handwriting usually indicated a feverishly written, desperate entry, whereas my more sorrowful entries are written slowly and neatly. Early on I wrote a statement that has stuck with me through my journey. God laid it on my heart in the days after the accident, and I have clung to it as a truth.

From Journal No. 1:

"Profound loss has got to have a profound purpose. Let it be so, Lord, please."

Part II

Learning to Function Again, One Breath at a Time

CHAPTER 9

Hopelessness—but Something More

From Journal No. 1:

"Despair is what I feel this morning. Today, seven weeks ago, in about an hour, is the last time I saw my three boys alive. I intended to listen to praise music and to make this a morning of praise. Started to. Led to songs of Dave and me. Missing him. Missing them. Don't give in to the despair, Sarah. Feel it, allow it, wallow, cry, let it rip your heart, then come on out. Hope. Promise. Beauty. Love. Come back. Come back to that. Fight the good and honorable fight."

At least twice during those first several weeks after Dave and the boys went home, I considered committing suicide. I had written the "good-bye; here are the instructions to take care of my affairs" letter and then destroyed it, only to write it again weeks later. Even Christians can succumb to the false allure of suicide when suffering deep grief. I didn't look at it as ending my life; I looked at it as facilitating my entrance into heaven.

I spun suicide as a positive, as an escape, when I was enduring the deep grief and despair that had overtaken me.

Through the first year of mourning, tidal waves of grief hit me. Around week seven, I fell into a pit of despair. I was done. I was finished with the sick emptiness in my chest that traveled to my stomach, leaving a chasm in my body. I awoke to that sensation every morning for months. I awoke feeling physically ill every day. I managed to get out of bed in the mornings, only to find the kids in terrible moods (probably feeding off of my vibe), and I couldn't handle it any longer.

From Journal No. 1:

"Today is a day I want to give up. I am tired. I am lonely. I feel hopeless. I feel I am fooling myself about trying to overcome such loss. I feel useless, despondent. It is eight weeks since I had to say good-bye to my family. My family is shattered. My family is destroyed. My family is ripped apart. My family is no longer whole. I feel punished. I feel Dave was punished. I feel I will never have joy again. I feel like a walking zombie. I feel dead. I feel there is life all around me, but that mine is over, forever broken. Why, Lord? What did I do to deserve this? Why don't You love me? I know You do, but I feel unloved, forgotten, bruised, broken, shattered, my heart broken, battered, bleeding. Will I ever heal or feel whole? I can't fathom my next breath with this loss, my next steps, my next day, much less a lifetime.

"I don't want to do it, Lord. I want to be done. I am angry that my life is forever altered, that I have to live with this, and that I have to go the rest of my life with loss. I have to live in the spiritual realm for comfort while still on earth. I cannot be a normal person with a normal life. I want the life I had back right now. I feel pathetic, trying to overcome. Why? For what? To continue to live life with utter loss? Suffocating loss. Anger. Sadness. Why did You do this to me? To us? To them? Anger rises, boils. Sadness overtakes. There is life all around me. I am alone in sorrow, alone in suffering. So many whys, Lord.

I want to be alone, secluded, left alone. So much demanded of me. Kids, life. I want to have honor. Too hard. I want to quit, to live in the past or not to live at all. So much suffering in this horribly broken world. Yet I feel alone in my suffering. People talk about me, pity me. I hate it. I want my family back."

One day in March, the kids were on their worst behavior, and the house was a disaster. I thought, *What is the point? My family is over. The kids don't need me. I am not even raising them well; their behavior today reflects that. I can't handle all the responsibilities in front of me. I'm done.*

I went outside to take the trash can to the curb. It was another of those "man jobs" I resented having to do, because it personified Dave no longer being there. We lived on a country lane, so taking out the trash was not as easy a task as one may think. It required hauling a trash can weighing almost fifty pounds down my rocky driveway and slightly up the lane—not that big a deal. But in my state—broken, defeated, exhausted, hopeless, angry, resentful of another task I had to take on since Dave's passing—it seemed like I had to move a mountain. As I pulled the can behind me, I made a decision. *This is it. I am done. It's okay. I'll do these jobs today, because I will never have to do them again.*

The thought that I could control my situation—that I could leave my path of grief and hopelessness forever—gave me a surge of power. I took the trash can the rest of the way to the curb, all the while considering how to put my plan into motion. First step: writing the note.

I sat in my bed and wrote a lengthy note explaining why I had chosen suicide, even reasoning why my sister would be better at raising my kids. I listed all the passwords to my accounts and my hopeful wishes for the kids' futures. I felt so empty writing those words, but I also felt that I was finally taking control of my situation. I was making a decision about my fate. No one else was involved. This was a power grab. I needed to regain control, and if this was the way, then so be it.

After writing the note, I took the next step: I started thinking about the method by which I would facilitate my entrance into heaven.

Plan A: I thought so many, many times about walking out onto Route 163 right outside the country lane by my house and letting a big truck end all the pain and take me to heaven. Death would be instantaneous, and my family was but a breath away. But logistics kicked in and I thought, *Sure, but I don't want it to be messy, I don't want my kids to find me. I don't want to hurt anyone else, and the driver who hits me may be physically injured or at least be emotionally scarred.*

Plan B: I had some pills from a recent oral surgery in my bathroom cabinet, and the bottle was nearly full. But after some research on the Internet, I decided this might not do the trick, and I didn't want to end up a vegetable for the rest of my life. If I was going to do this, I had to go all the way.

Plan C: I decided I would wait until nightfall. I would take a shower while wearing a T-shirt and shorts and get soaking wet. Then, when the kids were asleep, I would walk out to my woods on a cold, late-winter evening, sit with my back against a tree, and wait for hypothermia to overtake me. I wanted to fall asleep as my boys had. I thought it completely fitting to go home the same way they had.

So it seemed I had a plan. But then got to thinking. I didn't want my kids to wake and wonder where Mom was and to be alone. So I thought, *Okay, I will call my sister when I feel death is imminent* (as if I would have that much control over the situation), *and when she arrives at my house, she will see my note with instructions on where to find me.* So my children would not be the ones who found my body, and they would never be left alone.

Two years later, it pains me to write these words and to see where my mind was, but I want to be brutally honest. I want to share all the details to show where even a Christian can go while in grief.

I wasn't thinking of my children. I was thinking only of myself. If I were thinking of my children, I wouldn't even have considered leaving them after the pain they had already suffered. To argue that they would be better off raised by someone else was an attempt to justify my selfish behavior. I needed out of my pain. I needed out of my life. I needed out of my grief. I needed to be reunited with my husband and my boys. *I* needed.

I couldn't wake another day with the overwhelming pain. I couldn't wake another day with the weight and the suffocation of our loss. I couldn't wake another day with the responsibility of raising my kids, running a home, and carrying the emotional burden all alone.

My struggle with suicidal thoughts shortly after our tragedy opened my eyes and pierced my heart with compassion for those who feel suicidal and for family members and friends of those who have committed suicide. I know firsthand the desperation of feeling like there is no more life to live. My heart goes out to all those struggling. I encourage anyone feeling suicidal to take one step in faith, one labored step out of the tunnel of pain, and to call out to God. He will come alongside you and guide you the rest of the way until you are firmly out of the shadow of death. I offer prayers for comfort and peace for those who have experienced a loss through suicide.

So what changed my mind? Why am I still here? Well, several things, and none of them involved sudden changes or lightning bolts from heaven. I was brought out of a suicidal mind-set through gradual changes.

The night I had planned to walk into the woods soaking wet, my brother Richard was due over for dinner, so I had to put my plan aside to make sure the house was ready for company and to prepare a meal. (I was still able simply to thaw and serve one of the many donated meals I had stacked in the freezer, from the many big hearts in the community.) I wondered if I should cancel our visit, given my mood, but I did not, and my brother arrived. We sat and chatted for a few hours. The conversation involved nothing big, nothing life-changing.

But when Richard left, my desire to walk out into my woods soaking wet had vanished. I grabbed my good-bye letter, ripped it into pieces, and soaked it under a running faucet before throwing it away. Destroying the letter was one more way of utterly destroying the idea of ending my life. Had I been able to locate matches, I probably would have burned the letter instead.

God intervened that night. He did not send an angel to tell me in a vision, "Daughter, don't do this."

He didn't reveal Himself to me in a dream and announce His grand plan for keeping me on earth.

He sent my brother for dinner. And that made all the difference.

While I sat with my brother, my Father slowly, quietly spoke to my spirit. I thought the idea not to end my life was mine. We take credit for things that we have no part in.

At about week seven and again at about week fifteen after the accident, I thought seriously about facilitating my entrance into heaven. I had my letter written twice, I had a plan ready, and I had saved the pills from my oral surgery but decided, instead, to fall asleep in the woods as my boys had done.

It was all quite logical to me. I was without emotion through most of the planning. I saw suicide as nothing more than a matter-of-fact solution to my utter despair. I felt in control of something for the first time since Dave and our boys had passed to heaven. My decision to end my earthly life was a little coin in my pocket that I could pull out at any time. I felt noble in choosing to endure even another day when at any time the pain I felt every morning could be over.

Choosing to live another day and to endure the pain made me feel in control. For me, everything was about control—control over ending my pain, control of my destiny, control of my circumstances and my path, even control of my death and my entrance to heaven.

One day I was looking at photos of my boys meeting Elise in the hospital for the first time after her birth, their faces glowing as they saw their baby sister. Instead of bringing me joy, the pictures brought me to my knees. I reasoned with God, thinking, *Lord, You cannot expect me to endure this loss. You cannot expect me to endure this severing, this void where joy used to reside. Look at the photos, Lord. I can't live without that joy.*

One afternoon I watched a video of a family birthday celebration. Dave held baby Finn on his lap and fed him cake on his birthday. Dave laughed, and Grant and Dom sang "Happy Birthday." We were a family of seven sitting around the dining room table, peaceful, singing, and joyful. I couldn't fathom living without that for another second, for another breath, much less for days, weeks, months, or years. But I thought, *It's okay. I will see them soon anyway. I am done. I can withstand this for now because it will all be over soon enough.*

That memory and the surge of grief left me on my couch for almost two days. Kate, bless her, fed my babies and put them to bed. She should never have had to do that.

I could not get off of the couch. I was curled into a fetal position and seemed paralyzed. I felt a demon was perched on my back, claws sunk into me, holding me in that position, in that spot. I stayed that way from a Saturday morning to Sunday. I did not get up to eat, to shower, or to brush my teeth.

My brother's visit had brought about a previous intervention, and an unexpected visit from family friends produced another one.

That Sunday morning I finally got up, though not for positive reasons. I got up so I could see the clock on my stove. Every Sunday for weeks after the accident, I commemorated the time the search party located Dave, Dom, and Grant. I would pour over photos of them when the clock struck the time they were found. With the kids still asleep in the other rooms, I would look at the photos and wail, the breath nearly knocked out of me by grief and despair.

The time was approaching. I watched the clock from the living room floor. What would I do when the clock struck the time the boys were found? I didn't know, but I had an intense need to commemorate that time every Sunday. I sat on the floor, my eyes darting from the photos to the clock, when the doorbell rang.

What? Was that the doorbell?

Again, the doorbell. I looked up and sure enough, through the frosted glass window on the front door, I could see someone standing outside. I was dressed only in a T-shirt and underwear, had not bathed in days, and had not brushed my teeth in two days. I had to get past the front door to reach the stairs and head up to my room to put on pants. I watched through a side window until I saw the arm of whoever was at my door turn slightly. Guessing that the person was no longer facing the door, I capitalized on that moment and ran upstairs to my bedroom. I threw on some pants, ran back down, and answered the door.

My parents' longtime family friends, Julie and Doug, and Doug's brother, Dave, had come over to build shelves for my basement. They had tried to call to let me know they were on their way. They did not know that I hadn't moved off of my couch for almost two days, much less answered my phone, so they came over anyway as we had planned. (In my grief, I had forgotten.) I quickly explained my appearance as "the baby keeping me up all night," shoved the photo spread of my family under a living room table, and invited the three of them inside.

While they got the materials and tools to make the shelves, I ran upstairs again. I brushed my teeth, put on proper clothes, and got the babies cleaned up and ready for the day. I would like to say that this intervention changed the course of that weekend, but it didn't. Not yet, anyway. I put my despair on hold though, making sure the people working in my basement were fed and had anything they needed to get the shelves up.

My parents arrived about twenty minutes later, and I told my mother some of what had happened to me that weekend. My mother ministered to me. She let me talk, cry, sob, and vent, listening with patient ears and a compassionate heart. I could see from the look on her face that she wished she could take away her daughter's pain, but all she could do was listen and hold my hand.

God had sent another intervention. Weeks before, He had sent my brother for dinner, and that weekend, He sent family friends in the midst of my despair, and my mother to minister to me while my dad and his friends worked in my basement.

I would like to say that when the shelves were finished and my company had left, my calmer spirit remained, but sadly, the demons of despair and emptiness threatened to take control of me again. I walked down to the basement to see my family friends' beautiful handiwork. They had lined an entire wall with floor-to-ceiling shelves to get my many boxes off of the ground. I cried with gratitude. As I was standing there, taking in the smell of the wood, I asked out loud, "What now, God? What do I do now? Where do I go? What do I do? What now, God?"

I walked upstairs, stood in my living room and repeated the questions through tears. And God answered me. Not audibly but strong and sure to my spirit, He said, *You need milk.*

I thought, *God, I cannot even decide which room in my home to walk into next. I cannot go to the store right now.*

He simply repeated to me, *You need milk.*

So I got the kids ready and we headed into town for milk.

For a girl who had traversed the globe, lived in Europe, and driven all over the United States, going to get milk three miles down the road seemed almost a task too big for me to perform. But I did it. With God knocking those demons off of my back, holding me in His hands, and propelling me forward, I did it. I drove to the store and got milk, and on the way home, my spirits started to lift.

Back home, I asked Kate to sit with the kids for fifteen minutes while they watched cartoons so I could head out to the woods for a breath of fresh air.

We have a beautiful plot of land, a few acres; our home backs up to woods that lead to a meadow, which leads to woods again and to a creek. I find much solace there. So I walked into the woods, intending to find peace and quiet and to get my head back on straight.

But as I traversed the paths in the woods, I got angry. My boys loved those woods. If I closed my eyes and listened, I could still hear them talking and yelling and laughing excitedly in the distance as they ran on the trails. Dave loved those woods. He loved clearing brush with his machete; he loved putting his Indiana Jones hat on and building a bonfire with the brush in his special clearing. Dave had plans for those woods; he took pride in being a good provider and in owning that plot. I got so angry that they were not there to enjoy those woods anymore, and I screamed, "I want my boys, God! I want my boys *right now*, God! Bring them back to me right now!"

I walked back through the woods toward my home, crying, sobbing, and whispering, "My boys, God. I want my boys. Where are my boys, God?"

As I entered a clearing in the woods, pine trees on either side of me, the setting sun providing just enough light for me to see my way to the meadow and to find my way home, my boy, my Finn burst through the woods.

"Hi, Mom!"

My heart immediately sent forth such a surge of love and thankfulness through my soul that I jumped into a run to grab up my boy. My God had answered me again. There was my boy. Finn had learned from Kate that I was out in the woods, and he ran to meet me.

I asked God where my boys were, and He showed me. The boy who still needed me on earth was right there in my arms.

So what stopped me from considering my earthly demise? Well, every time I thought of it, God whispered to me how very fruitless it would be for me to leave this earth. He had left kids here on earth in my care. God also used my love for Dave to convince me to remain with them. I felt an unquenchable need to make Dave proud, to look after our babies as he had watched out for our boys until their last earthly moments. I had to make Dave proud. I needed to care for our kids the same way I would have expected him to care for them if the tables had been turned and he was the sole caregiver. I did not want to let him down. My kids deserved the best I could offer them, just what Dave and I had given them together. They deserved the same love, the same adventure, the same experiences.

God also told my spirit that I needed to rely on Him to fight my battles. Relying simply on my own strength to fight the spiritual battle with grief would not be enough. I needed Him and His strength.

He also told my spirit that I was still needed down here. I have always felt I was needed on earth for a mission, as I feel we all are. God has told me since I was a little girl that we are all here for a reason.

God said to my spirit, *Daughter, your mission is not over yet. Dave's mission on earth was completed, and I need Him to further my coming kingdom up here now. Your boys—as hard as it is to believe, their mission on earth was through, too. They were Mine before they were yours, and I entrusted them to you and your husband. I need them back now. They may have been your baby boys on earth, but up here they are exactly who I need them to be to further My advancing kingdom.*

The afternoon I felt that revelation to my spirit about Dom and Grant having a mission, I was going through the motions of trying to keep my house in order.

Finn and Elise were napping, and Kate was with a friend; the house was quiet.

I needed to stay busy. So I started sorting toy boxes. It seemed like such a tedious task, but the tedious tasks were what I needed, something totally mindless—busy work. As I worked, God said straight to my soul, *Daughter, they may have been your baby boys on earth, but up here they are exactly who I need them to be for My purposes, to advance My kingdom.*

I stopped sorting, sat with a toy in midair in my hand, and my breath caught in my throat.

What, God? I thought.

He repeated the sentiment to my heart. *They are needed up here. They are not just your baby boys anymore.*

The revelation hit me and immediately sank into my heart, mind, and soul. My boys were more. They always had been and always would be. I was simply a part of their grand design. I got to play a role in their existence, which continued after they were my babies. They were now part of God's advancing kingdom.

I believe work is being done in heaven. Scripture tells us God will return and make all things new (Revelations 21). This world will be over, heaven and earth will be joined, and Christ's followers will enjoy forever the ultimate victory of life over death, good over evil. Love wins.

I believe God is preparing that kingdom, preparing for that final battle, preparing for that new heaven and new earth—and that my boys are a part of that.

I was at once honored and relieved. I was willing just a little bit more that day to release them to God.

Dave had an earthly mission, and he fulfilled it. He now has his eternal mission and, like my boys and all the other saints, is helping our Father to advance the kingdom of God, our new heaven and new earth.

Dave's earthly mission was obvious in some ways. He was an outstanding leader, father, husband, and friend. He was a community leader, a take-charge personality, and a man full of integrity, hope, love. My husband was a man of change. He wanted to change hearts. He wanted to raise a family of changed hearts.

While we were dating, Dave and I were having steak in a restaurant one night, and a thought hit me so hard I had to say it out loud. "I feel like we have a mission together," I told him.

Dave stopped short and looked at me. "What?" he said.

I repeated, "I feel like we have a mission we are supposed to complete together."

He stared at me, started to tear up, and through the emotion shown all over his face, he said, "Me, too."

Dave grabbed my hand from across the table, and that was it. The deal was sealed. We had a mission together. Now we had to wait to find out what it was. Over the years that mission has become clearer to me. We had five kids. We created five beings on this earth. They needed a little bit of him and a little bit of me. God only knows the difference they will make in this world and in His kingdom, but they needed to be here and we made them.

And those are only the parts of the mission revealed to me. Only God knows His grand design, the parts of the tapestry of life and eternity not revealed to me yet and how my family fits into that grand design. We are all part it, every one of us ever created.

To that end God erased the desire in me to facilitate my entrance into heaven.

Daughter, your mission is not complete, God said to my spirit. *Kate's is not complete. That's why she brought the 'wrong shoes' and didn't go hiking that day; Finn's isn't complete. That's why Dave decided at the last moment not to take him hiking. Elise's is not complete.*

I do not want to enter heaven and hear God say, "Sure, I am glad you're here, but daughter, there was so much more I needed you to do. Life will forever be altered because you did not do the part set aside for you."

I do not want to enter heaven under those terms. I want to earn my reward. I want to fulfill my mission.

God cemented that revelation one day when my dear friend Becky was over to hold my hand and to talk with me. I have known Becky since childhood, and she is more like a sister to me than a friend. Godmother to Kate and treasured friend, she has been a constant support and has walked alongside me at every turn on my journey.

That day, as she was holding my hand and letting me cry, she said something to me that completely changed my outlook on my journey.

"Sarah, I do believe you are going to have to crawl through the rest of this life emotionally just the way Dave crawled through the last part of his life physically. You are both going to crawl to the ends of your earthy lives. But when you get there, Sarah—oh, when you get there—oh, the homecoming you are going to receive. Jesus will be standing there, and He will say, 'Well, done, My child. Look at the life Kate, Finn, and Elise were able to have because you stayed and were faithful to fulfill your mission.'"

Her words took my breath away.

As she spoke, I pictured Dave and my baby boys, Dominic and Grant David, standing off to the side. My Father welcomed me into His presence. I had fallen to my knees in worship, and He lifted me back to my feet, He pointed toward my boys, and I turned my attention toward them. He said, "They have been waiting for you."

Chapter 10

Anger

From Journal No. 1:

"I am angry that other people still have their husbands and kids and go on with their lives. I am angry that people point out to me in cards and messages that they 'cannot imagine what I am going through.' Thank you for reminding me that your worst nightmare is my reality."

Around early March, my despair gave way to intense anger. I was like a wounded animal that would strike if anyone came near. I was broken, I was desperate, and I was angry. I wasn't angry at all times; my fury came in waves. And I would lash out at anyone whom I felt needed it.

As a Christian, I knew the truths of the faith, had the Holy Spirit in my heart guiding my words and actions, and tried to display the fruits of the Spirit (Galatians 5:22–23). When grief took over, though, everything I knew by faith wound up on the back burner, and instead of relying on my Father to avenge, to reward, and to justify, I felt the need to do those things for Him.

There were some instances that needed to be called out. I would defend my family when people pushed the envelope, stepped over boundaries, and helped when I didn't want help. However, given what I had to endure, I expected a free pass for the rest of my life. I didn't get one. Family squabbles and hurt feelings still reigned, since we are a fallen people. The good in folks outweighed the bad, but the bad was there. And it felt overwhelming.

My problem boiled down to the fact that hurt people cause hurt. Grief brings anger, and mourning manifests itself in different ways in different people. When those forms of grieving collide, no good can come of it.

All the anger and the occasional family squabbles in those early months were an important lesson for me, however. I learned that God was not going to go easy on me just because I had suffered a tragedy. I had lost my husband and two sons; I had lost my companion of twelve years, my dog, not even a month later, and only months before Dave and the boys went to heaven, my father had discovered that he had pancreatic cancer, and the disease was slowly overtaking him.

When we suffer grief and loss, the vast majority of people will show compassion, care, and concern and will offer help and comfort. However, a small number of people will not. Those suffering their own hurt will hurt others. I had to learn that the hard way. I thought that I was somehow exempt from further pain and that everyone would have compassion on a widow and a mother of passed children. That was not the case.

Fortunately, we serve a God of second chances, third chances, and fourth chances. He is the God of forgiveness. He can forgive, so we should forgive and ask to be forgiven. Our heavenly Father helps us pick up the pieces and move on.

Those instances of family strife early on my grief journey left me stronger. Instead of despair, I felt a new fire burning inside of me. I needed to stand my ground and to protect my family. I was like a lioness defending her young. It is hard to feel hopeless when you are on such a mission. Those are not the emotions of hopelessness and death but of hope and life. Those squabbles helped me regain a bit of my life, a bit of my fire, and a bit of my desire to live.

To deal with anger in grief, forgive much, ask forgiveness, remember that life's losses do not exempt you from future hurt, and press on. God used even that anger to mold me into the person He needed me to be so that I could endure the grief process. He is further refining me with many fires. He is molding my spirit and my character so that I will be the person He wants me to be, for His purposes.

Chapter 11

Protecting My Young

One late winter day in 2013, we had a major snowstorm. Not one to watch the news, I was in town to drop off some mail and to pick up milk and heard folks there say that we were in for a bad winter storm. I came home with the urgency of a momma bear determined to get her young in order. I couldn't protect my boys from the cold, Dave couldn't do anything more to save our sons than he did, but I could protect in every way possible the babies I still had at home.

The sleet had already started to fall during my three-mile drive back home. I checked the fridge and the pantry to make sure we had all the food we needed. I checked to see that the heater worked well, and I checked the propane tank outside to ensure we would have enough hot water and heat if we were snowed in for a few days. The propane tank was down to about 6 percent capacity. I immediately called in an emergency order to the gas company. A truck came out and I paid a same-day fee to get the tank filled.

I did everything I could possibly do to make sure my babies were safe, and we weathered that storm.

My brother Richard once described Dave as having the spirit of the bear. Bears were his life totem; he admired them, was fascinated by them, and identified with them.

Perhaps I had a little of Dave's spirit of the bear in me that day. I was a mother bear protecting her young.

God worked through my love for Dave, and my drive to please God and Dave in the care of our kids on earth, to drive me in many things.

Again, not one to watch the news, I was sitting on my couch one evening in late spring/early summer writing thank-you notes. I did one batch each month, since the job was emotionally taxing and there were hundreds to write. That evening, Kate had her cousin Hailey over, and they were quietly playing in her room. The babies were upstairs in the loft, building with Legos and playing with dolls. The house was quiet and peaceful. As I wrote, I reflected on how grateful I was for all the good will people had shown us.

I could tell the weather was getting bad. We were in for the kind of awesome summer storm that I used to watch from the front door as a little girl. I have never been afraid of storms. In fact, I love them. I got up to watch the brewing storm from my open front door. The wind started whipping a bit, and even in the darkness, I could see by the fading moonlight how quickly the clouds were moving. The temperature dropped slightly, but it was still a warm evening.

Then I heard it—a buzz like the notice on a cell phone. I kept my phone silent, one of my coping mechanisms. I rarely answered my phone, preferring to let messages go to voicemail and deciding later whom to call back and when. I applied the same method to texts; I kept my phone silent and checked periodically for any missed messages.

I heard the buzz of a cell phone notice, forgetting I had recently charged Dave's phone and had it sitting on a shelf next to my phone.

I had received Dave's phone from the coroner after the accident. On it were precious photos Dave had taken of our sons on that hike while things were still good and everyone was smiling and happy. I have three precious photos of my boys on that final trek, so I kept Dave's phone close to me.

Again, I heard the buzz. I went to check the phone and saw a notice: "Severe storms projected for your area. Take cover now."

My heart fell to my feet. I immediately leaped into action and got the kids into the living room so I could call out orders.

"Get to the basement. I'll grab a flashlight. I'll get Bear out of his kennel and bring him to the basement with us. Go!"

My sisters and my mom called to make sure I had seen the news predicting the bad storm and possible tornado.

I hadn't. I would not have known anything severe was forecast unless Dave's phone had alerted me.

At some point, Dave had apparently put Weather Channel notifications on his phone. That night, God allowed Dave to warn us through his phone. I had been oblivious to the danger. I did not have the television on to hear any warnings of the forecast as I sat peacefully on my couch writing thank-you notes and walked to the front door to watch the wind pick up.

By the grace of God, those storms passed just north of us and ended up being less severe than predicted. But God, using Dave's phone, had warned us of possible danger, allowing me to make sure our children were safe and sound.

My Dave watching out for his family, always.

Chapter 12

Loss

From Journal No. 1:

"Dave was there when his boys entered this earth, and he was there when they left this earth. All together. Strangely comforting. A sacredness to that."

One of the hardest parts of my grief journey was the loss of so many parts of my identity. I was identified as a mother, as a wife, as a homeschooling mom, and as part of a military family. As this journey continued, I also discovered that the afternoon was the hardest part of the day to endure. I was about to be reminded why.

Afternoons were a bustling time after we moved into our house in the fall of 2012. Dave worked the swing shift, and we were homeschooling, so we had family time in the mornings and the early afternoons. We had lunch together many days, and then I took Dave to work around 2:30 p.m. so I could have the car for the children's extracurricular evening commitments. After Dave had gone to work, the kids and I buckled down on their studies. We had a very unconventional schedule, but we were used to that, having been a military family.

Family time was important to us, so the hours Dave was home were devoted to family. School, chores, and errands waited until he was at work. At the end of Dave's shift each evening, I would pick him, usually with a kid or two along for the ride.

One particularly hard afternoon after our tragedy, I needed to get out of the house and I decided to go for a drive. Especially in the early days, I found much calm driving the country back roads near my house while listening to contemporary praise music on our local Christian radio station. When I could not find the words to form a prayer, praise music did it for me. Even now, so many prayers from my heart are sent to the Father in the form of a Christian song.

As I was driving that afternoon, my heart aching, my spirit crushed, my eyes so blinded with tears I could hardly see the road, I noticed I had already gotten halfway to Dave's workplace. As if by instinct or rote memorization, my drive on the back roads had brought me halfway to the gates of Scott Air Force Base. I looked at the clock in my van. It was around 2:30 p.m., the time I would have been driving Dave to work on those roads just months before.

Something took control of me at that point—a sorrow so dark, a hole so deep, a void so vast that nothing was going to fill it. Even with praise music filling the air around me and with prayers from my heart rising in the form of those songs, I had only one mission—to drive Dave to work. I continued on our usual route. I drove as if he were right beside me and we were on our way to Scott Air Force Base.

I absolutely broke as I drove. I wailed, moaned, and uttered sounds of primal grief I had never heard before. I was fully aware of my desperate situation as I pretended I was driving my husband to work months after he had passed to heaven. The sense of normalcy, of routine, of familiarity felt good but so terribly bitter at the same time. But this was something I had to do.

Nearing the base, I drove up the road leading to the gates and got to the point I was not allowed to pass. The guards at the gates stood ready to check IDs, and they would allow only those drivers with military ID cards to go any farther. I turned around in a nearby parking lot and started back home.

This was one of the darkest, most desperate moments on my early grief journey. Not only had I gone through the motions of driving Dave to work, but I was no longer allowed on base without Dave, who had the military ID card.

After having been an active-duty military wife for seven years, living on bases from Portugal to Idaho to England, and enjoying the camaraderie of the military community in Italy and Germany while Dave was a civilian working for the Department of Defense, I had come to that moment. I was no longer allowed to enter the base to which I had taken Dave only months before.

I looked in my rearview mirror as I drove away from base, watching as cars passed through the gates and went on their way in blissful normalcy.

The gates got smaller and smaller as I left the base behind. I realized that yet another part of my life was gone. My time as a military wife became as far away from me being able to touch as those gates were becoming in my rearview mirror. I had suffered another loss. Another part of my identity had been stripped from me.

There were moments on my early grief journey when I did not think I could get any lower. That day I was proved wrong. I had hit a new low.

Chapter 13

The Sun Starts to Shine

In mid-March, the days started to get brighter, and so did my spirits. While fall is my favorite season, spring places a close second. Everything about spring is hopeful: the sun shining more brightly, the new buds on the trees, the flowers, the bushes, the birds singing again. The breezes become warmer, the days grow longer, and hope fills the air.

At that point in our early grief journey, we still had not developed any kind of routine. We were just surviving, taking each day as it came and welcoming visitors to our home. I spent many hours writing, contemplating, praying, and meditating. The kids played. Kate spent a lot of time crafting, reading, and doing schoolwork. On that March day, the weather was absolutely gorgeous. It was a day filled with hope and expectancy, as if something grand could happen at any moment.

But there was a constant cloud over me, reminding me that no matter how glorious the day, there would be no escape from my new reality. I captured the day in a journal entry dated Friday, March 15, 2013.

From Journal No. 1:

"I am playing outside with the babies this early afternoon. We are in shorts and short sleeves. There is lots on my mind and my heart: our anniversary was nine weeks ago. I watched a beautiful sunrise this morning. I had a productive morning around the house. I have plans for today: teach Kate some school lessons, straighten up some more, enjoy this time outdoors, since the weather is supposed to turn cold again. Enjoy this, God willing. I want to walk in the woods with my children today. I had a peaceful night last night. I have had movie night with Kate here at home two nights in a row; it helps us to feel normal.

"Yet I miss my three guys so much, even on—especially on—this glorious day. But I do feel them. They have this beauty and so much more where they are. But I wish I could share this beautiful day with them, too. Dave had so many plans for our home, and this is just the kind of day when he would have done something to the yard, something outdoors. If they were here, I would plan a day trip on a day like this …

"Dave, we can't waste a beautiful day like today …

"I see my boys running in our woods, climbing our trees, swinging on the limbs. I can see all my children, our brood, playing outside, going to the creek in our woods, coming home dirty and sweaty.

"I picture a feeling of hope, promise, and productivity that spring brings. I see Dave and I mapping out this gorgeous day—how to spend it as a family. I see it culminating in a relaxing evening. I see us playing outside, working outside, and then maybe grilling up some dinner.

"But reality hits me, and it stings.

"But my eyes truly open to my reality, and I see this: I see my Finn and Elise running, playing, talking, laughing. I see their joy. I see the fun they are having; I hear Elise call out to me, 'Mommy, I love you!'

"I see Finn digging in the dirt, playing with his cars. I see Kate join us on the porch. And I feel a different hope, a promise. I am grateful for this day, for the sun, for this home, for this moment, for God's promises of what is to come, and I am grateful for my Kate, my Finn, and my Elise."

Spring brought more light little by little.

A stray cat kept coming around our house. In September of 2012, Dom and I had named her Ce Ce, and when Dave left for work each night, Dom and I would sneak her into the house. But soon after the accident, Ce Ce stopped coming around. However, in March of 2013, she reappeared in our yard. And later that month, she had five kittens. Those precious kittens brought Kate much joy. I saw a familiar flicker of happiness and peace in Kate's eyes as I watched her care for those tiny kittens. I watched her, ever so responsible, ever maternal, help the momma cat, Ce Ce, care for her babies and love on them. I listened as Kate cooed her sweet coos to those adorable brand-new lives, and I knew in my spirit that God had allowed just such a project to keep my girl busy and happy.

That spring, family and friends continued to visit with the kids and me now and then. On one particularly light day, my entire family came over for an impromptu St. Patrick's Day barbecue.

My brother Richard had planned to barbecue and visit with the kids and me that afternoon. In conversation, my sisters learned of that plan, as did my parents and other brother, and decided to come over, too. Before I knew it, my entire family was at my house. It was an unexpected blessing that rainy early spring day. I captured St. Patrick's Day 2013 in my journal.

From Journal No. 1:

"Rainy day, but we barbecued anyway. My whole family is over here. I listened to sermons this morning, then journaled. My family came over. Dee

is here doing dishes, Rich is barbecuing, and Mom and I are helping with dishes. Mom talks about heaven. Many kids play—nieces and nephews, my kids. Dad and David are here. David is playing with Bear. Elizabeth and her kids are here. We ladies are all talking more about heaven. I showed the new kittens to all. I showed David some photos from Dave's Taum Sauk hike in November of 2012. We had great dessert. My sisters and I made plans to start a Bible study together. It started to storm outside just as we wrapped up the day. Blessed day; thank you, Lord."

During that barbecue, surrounded by my family, a slight glimmer of hope snuck its way back into my soul.

As I watched my sister Deanna wash my dishes that day, I was overwhelmed by her love for me and my children. At a moment's notice, she was always there to help me.

I recalled how just weeks before I had called her in a panic, feeling as if I were losing my mind to suffocating sorrow, and told her to come get my kids immediately, because I was overwhelmed and needed to be alone. Standing in line at the store at the time, she left the goods she was about to purchase and came straight my house.

As I scanned the people surrounding me, I saw my sister Elizabeth. She was always willing to babysit, and I watched as she kept the kids occupied, making them laugh and telling them stories. I looked at the artwork I had hanging on the refrigerator, artwork she had helped my kids make for me one day when she was babysitting them. Their precious handprints appeared on the piece of paper with a poem written under them. As I watched my family all around me, the pain remained overwhelming, but a strange sensation rose up in me—comfort. And I was grateful.

The days started to get brighter for Kate as well. I journaled about some of the happier moments she was having during those spring months.

From Journal No. 1:

"Red star days for Kate lately: going to the mall with Aunt Dee Dee; makeover day with cousins and Aunt Elizabeth; City Museum field trip with Nola and Heather; our impromptu St. Patrick's Day barbecue here with all the family; to the creek lately with Nick, Nola, and Uncle David; cookie baking day with our neighbors; movie nights with me. The kittens are getting bigger every day. Kate stays busy keeping Ce Ce's 'nest' clean and safe for the kittens. We've named them Paris, Robinson Crusoe, Jenny, Ally, and Panda Bear."

While the days in March got lighter, there were still plenty of dark days, unfortunately. Looking back on my journals, the ups and downs I experienced in those early days of my grief journey are apparent.

From Journal No. 1:

"I feel overwhelmed this week. Too much structure, too many changes, too much 'moving on.' I need focus back. I need alone back. I want meditation back. I want Scripture, prayer, journaling mornings back. I feel an utter loss of control over my life. I feel better on less busy days, staying at home, taking it one day at a time. Feeling so much pressure. Wanting to mourn full time. I can't do it all! Life is forever altered and will never be the same. I don't feel I will ever fully live again. I will do what I can for my Kate, Finn, and Elise. But I don't want to numb this. I want to feel. To feel the loss is at least to feel them. I don't want to 'move on.' I don't want to 'live again.' I don't want to 'find my joy again.' Just trying to survive. Family, friends, counseling—I cannot do it all! I am only one person. I am a mother, but I am also a mourning wife and mother and an individual! I want to mourn. Let me! Stop trying to make me 'move on,' 'not give up,' 'structure,' 'look ahead.' I just want to do my best for Kate, Finn, and Elise and then look toward heaven. Come now, Lord, please! …

"People, stop telling me I will heal! Time will heal! I will never heal after such a massive loss! To do so would utterly dishonor my family. My husband

and my boys were not a phase of life I must heal from. Our family was my life. I will not heal. I will simply survive, get through each moment/day, and wait for our rescue. Our Savior's coming. I will be the best I can for my kids and complete my mission. Be honorable …

"I feel like I died that day, too …

"It has already been eight weeks since our wedding anniversary Friday. Mom reminded me last night that time here on earth flies. I am happy about that. It is scriptural, too, that life is fleeting, but a breath (Psalm 39:5). I am glad. I will be reunited all the sooner with you, my boys. Of course, I wish we could have had a long, full earthly life together, but we didn't. It was certainly full but not long. I wish I didn't want to rush earthly life away. I do have my little girl and my sweet babies, my dear family, my unbelievable friends, bringing me joy here. But I just wanted us to be reunited and to be whole again …

"Many things I have had to do since you've been gone, Dave: put propane in the tank, pay bills, tow the van, get a plumber for the basement twice, get the van to the shop, get a rental, a new windshield. Thank you, Lord, for providing …

"Grief is heavy, heavy tonight. I am lonely. I am bored. I am distraught, hopeless, scared, sad. Just sad, despairing, full of sorrow. It's too much tonight. Eight weeks ago tonight, we were eating our 'magical' meal, babe. How do I do this? I can't. I don't want to. I want you. I want our sons. Do you still see your beautiful babies here? They are thriving, beautiful little people, hon. They love you; they miss you. We ache. I need you. I need you all here. Now …

"Bear is a miracle; he is blessed to be alive. He was the last to see my boys alive. He saw them pass to heaven. He stayed with them. Boys/Dave, I have your dog. Vet says he's amazed Bear is alive. He says he was meant to come back here. Ironic we got him to be your dog, and now he's mine."

In early March, I took my second trip to the trail where Dave and the boys entered heaven. I went with my brother David to hang wooden signs pointing to the lodge that he had carved to prevent other hikers from losing their way. I journaled the highlights of the day.

From Journal No. 1:

"Very, very good hike day. Left at 7:30 a.m. with David to put up lodge signs. I am so grateful he carved those signs. They are beautiful. Wonderful workmanship from a compassionate heart.

"Great drive down. I felt light. It was a beautiful day. It felt great to hike. Sixty-plus degrees in March. It's been eight weeks since Dave and the boys' feet were on the same trail. I crossed a creek without my shoes to keep them dry—one of many hike tips David taught me as we traversed. We hiked and talked; blessed time with my brother. Two miles in, we arrived at their spot. David and Bear hiked on, giving me alone time. I prayed there, meditated, cleared my mind, thought about what I had lost, talked to my boys, had memories of them, and then let my mind be free. Beautiful sun, beautiful breeze. Peace as I sat. I almost fell asleep. Peace and calm there at my boys' spot.

"Bear and David found me again. We hiked on for another mile. We got to the intersection where Dave and the boys missed their turn. David hung up four lodge signs he had carved into wood with the letters in yellow paint. An honor to my boys from their uncle, an honor to my man from his friend.

"As we were nearing the end of our hike, the end of the trail, David told me I looked like Dominic. I smiled inwardly, honored that my boy looked like his momma. It was such a productive day, a peaceful, fulfilling feeling. We hiked six miles of their journey that day."

Chapter 14
Not Alone

I awoke on a May morning to a memory. Our family of seven was in Louisiana in January of 2013, visiting Dave's family for a late Christmas celebration and to mark Dom's birthday. We were all piling into Dave's dad's boat, set to head out onto a lake for an afternoon of fun. Dave stood with one foot on the boat and the other on the dock, helping our kids into the boat. As he bent down to help Elise, she pulled her hand away from her daddy's and with her two-year-old's sense of independence, insisted she could do it herself. Dave looked to me, standing at the back of the line behind our kids, and shot me a look of feigned hurt. With a smile, he asked, "So when's the next one?"

He was sad that our baby, our youngest, was getting "too old" to need Daddy's help, and he was ready for another baby to join our family.

"You let me know," I responded, returning his smile, equally open to the idea of another baby joining our brood.

As my mind returned to the present, I recalled silently, almost reverently, the names Dave and I had decided upon if we were ever blessed with another girl or boy. And in that moment, I mourned a child who had never been made, had never been born. I felt the weight of unfulfilled dreams, of hopes cut short, never to be. But I was also overcome with something more. I was overwhelmed with gratitude at being married to a man who loved children so much that he wanted our family filled to overflowing. I was grateful for five little lives, five souls who came into being because Dave and I found each other that cold December night many years before. Despite my heavy heart, I knew that nothing could ever take away the fact that Dave and I had made five kids. And even though two of our babies had already gone from my arms, they had come. They had been, and nothing, *nothing* could ever change that. Nothing would ever erase the memories, the experiences, the love, the existence of all five of the lives Dave and I had created.

In May of 2013, I was tested for the BRCA gene, a genetic mutation that makes one highly susceptible to breast cancer (more than 90 percent susceptible) and ovarian cancer (more than 40 percent susceptible).

My mother was a carrier of the gene and had suffered breast cancer and ovarian cancer since 2009. Because many other women in my family had tested positive for the mutated gene, I decided to have myself tested. In the winter of 2012, I scheduled a genetic test for February of 2013, but when tragedy struck our family, I canceled the test.

When I scheduled the test, Dave and I had discussed the potential of my carrying the mutated gene. We decided that if I tested positive, we would try for one or even two more babies before I had to have a preemptive hysterectomy to remove my ovaries so I could avoid the danger of ovarian cancer developing. We even had names picked out for babies if we ever had another girl or another boy.

In May of 2013, I decided it was time to reschedule the genetic test.

The day I went in for my results, I knew in my spirit they would be positive. God had prepared me to accept that I had the mutated gene and another obstacle on my journey. And sure enough, as I sat at the desk in the doctor's office, she approached me and said matter of factly, "Well, it's positive."

I told her I had figured it was. "Well, how soon can I schedule my surgeries?" I asked.

Once I tested positive for the gene mutation, the doctor strongly suggested that I have a preemptive hysterectomy and also a double mastectomy. My mother had had a double mastectomy with reconstruction after being diagnosed with breast cancer. She and my sister were my examples. When my sister found out only a few years before that she was positive for the gene mutation, she had a preemptive hysterectomy and double mastectomy with reconstruction. She did this within months of her gene diagnosis while only in her early forties.

There I sat, at thirty-five years old, my husband and sons just having passed to heaven four months prior, being told that I was a carrier of the mutated gene and that the best and most responsible course of action for me was two radical surgeries.

The doctor spelled out my options and her suggestions, even informing me of my children's risks of having the gene since I was a carrier. She said they should be tested in the far future.

My decision was clear—surgery as soon as possible. *Let's get this out of the way,* I thought. *The only person I want to have babies with is not here anymore, so let's do this.*

My doctor suggested I "give the kids a summer" first and then have my surgeries in the winter of 2013 or early 2014. As I was leaving her office, she looked at me with compassion all over her face and said, "I really wish you weren't here alone today to have to hear this news."

I looked at her and with sureness in my voice told her, "Oh, I wasn't alone."

I felt Dave so strongly all around me. I felt his spirit. I felt the Holy Spirit. I felt strength. And while I was facing another loss—the loss of my opportunity to have any more children with the upcoming loss of my fertility—I knew I needed the surgeries to stay well for the children I still had on earth with me.

I went into the restroom nearest the doctor's office and pulled Dave's driver's license out of my purse. I had started carrying the license with me so I could see his face as I spoke to him. I said, "Well, babe, we were sure I had it. Surgery it is. But I don't get to have those babies with you first."

As I prepared to leave the restroom and to face the rest of the day knowing that serious surgery lay ahead for me, I felt Dave speak strong and sure in my spirit.

Sarah, doc says give the kids a summer. Give our kids the same sense of family and adventure we were giving them together.

One week later, I booked plane tickets for the kids and me to take a trip to the Grand Canyon in June. I could almost hear Dave laughing at my impulsiveness, but at the same time, I felt him say, *That's my girl. We are still the Decareaux family; we do not tiptoe lightly into things. You give those kids a summer.*

I was told by the doctor and by Dave to give our kids a summer, and I planned to listen.

Chapter 15

Light Up the Sky

In May of 2013, I had the opportunity to go to the Agape Christian Music Fest at my alma mater, Greenville College, with my sisters and some of my nieces and nephews.

This was somewhat of a tradition. In 1997, my sisters and I had attended the music fest with our church youth group for the first time. That trip ignited my desire to attend Greenville College. I attended the event with friends in the years I attended Greenville, and I welcomed the opportunity to go again after many years when my sisters suggested it.

I was a little nervous because this would be my first outing after our tragedy, and I wasn't sure if I was emotionally ready. But I thought that Kate needed it and that it could be an uplifting time for me as well, since many of the top Christian artists were set to perform for two days on the Bond County fairgrounds in Greenville, Illinois. So I arranged for Faye, my dear friend and babysitter, to stay overnight with Finn and Elise.

I met Faye right before the tragedy took my guys to heaven. She has walked closely with me throughout my grief journey. Like a constant undercurrent of support, Faye has always been there when I needed her. She has been an absolute blessing, providing encouragement and support.

Knowing the kids were in good hands with Faye, I packed an overnight bag for Kate and me and bought our tickets. Armed with goodies made by my sister-in-law Roxanne, we piled into my minivan with my sister Deanna; her kids, Meg and Nick; my sister Elizabeth, and her daughter, Hailey.

It was only an hour-and-a-half drive to the weekend getaway in my old college town, but we filled it with it laughter, stories, jokes, and snacks—exactly what my spirit needed after hearing the news of my gene diagnosis only days before.

I had high hopes for the festival, but they were tinged with guilt. It felt unnatural to be laughing and to feel jovial. I didn't think I was allowed to have fun. But the rainy weekend turned out to be a reprieve for my aching soul. Standing in our ponchos and rain boots under our umbrellas, we enjoyed funnel cake, hot cocoa, and good music.

I was particularly looking forward to hearing the Afters, a Christian band that played one of my favorite songs, "Light Up the Sky." That song had ministered to me and had become a prayer for me in the early days of my tragedy when I could find no words of my own. As the band played the song, my heart was aching but soaring. I sang along in my spirit, my soul calling out the words directly to my Father's ears. As the band neared the triumphant climax of the song, I looked up and saw three hawks flying over the stage in a circle. They soared – gliding, flying ever higher as the band sang out the final lines of the song.

I could hardly believe what I was seeing. I looked at my sister next to me and was about to say, "Do you see what I see?"

But before I could get the words out, she said, "I know. I am filming it."

Neither of us could believe our eyes. Those three hawks had come out of nowhere and were flying directly above the stage.

There are almost no words to describe what happened in my spirit at that moment. I closed my eyes. My soul was drawn higher. Tears streamed through my closed eyelids and down my cheeks. I felt my heavenly Father had spoken to me. I knew this was a message for me. I reveled in that moment, absorbing every second of it.

And as the song ended, I looked up to see the hawks slowly fly out of sight.

My heart opened just a little more that day.

That was a pivotal moment on my early journey. That moment took me to a new level. I was willing to open my heart just a little bit more. I was not alone. God was right there with me, I was assured.

And any time I can't believe what I saw that day, I go back and watch, because I've got the video to prove it.

Chapter 16

Summer Days

The summer of 2013 was a roller coaster of many bright days but also of many more challenging days on my early grief journey.

As the summer started, the kids and I made day trips to places in the St. Louis area and continued to welcome visitors to our house. We had several groups of out-of-town company—Renee and her husband, friends from our days in England; my dear college friend Kim from Texas and her three beautiful children; my dear friend Kim from our Germany days and her daughter, Sydney, and my friend Trinity, along with her four gorgeous children, from our time in England. The days were bright as the summer started.

The first day trip the kids and I took after our tragedy came in early June. I decided it was time to return to the adventures our family used to enjoy together, just as Dave had whispered to my spirit that afternoon I received my BRCA gene diagnosis one month earlier. I had booked a big trip to the Grand Canyon to counteract the bad news about my gene diagnosis, but I was having a hard time with the idea of small local excursions. *What if I see someone I know?* I thought.

I had become somewhat of a hermit during the initial months of my grief journey, preferring my home, my yard, my land, my woods to visiting anyone else's home. Looking back, I see it was difficult for me to deal with normal homes and normal lives; it was easier and safer for me to stay in my haven.

Dave and I embraced the places where the military stationed us. We tended to get assignments people did not usually want, most preferring larger bases to the smaller bases where we were assigned. But interestingly enough, those turned out to be the assignments Dave and I enjoyed the most. We hunted for day trips and adventures wherever we happened to be. We made lists of places to visit, things to do, and even regional foods we wanted to eat.

So, in the spirit of continuing to instill a sense of adventure in our kids, I made a list of all the places in the St. Louis area I wanted to take them. I jotted down all the typical sights: the Arch, the St. Louis Zoo, Grant's Farm, Forest Park, the Magic House, the St. Louis Science Center. I felt a sense of fulfillment, a familiar, seemingly far-gone happiness, as I made the list.

Our first outing was to Grant's Farm. A zoo of sorts, Grant's Farm, named after Ulysses S. Grant, had a collection of animals, from goats to camels, along with a German-style biergarten, a carousel, and an elephant show. This was just the place the kids and I needed for a nice afternoon. My brother Richard, his wife Roxanne, and their baby girl, Maggie, accompanied us.

At one point, I reached for my camera and told Kate to pose with Finn for a picture. She gave me a perplexed look. An avid photographer, I had not taken photos since our family's accident; as with many other things, the love of photography had been sucked out of me after the tragedy. But I wanted a photo to capture that beautiful early summer day with my family.

"So we're taking pictures again now?" Kate asked me.

"Why not, Kate? I guess now is as good a time as any," I answered.

As we continued taking in all the sights, the sounds, and the sunshine the day had to offer, something shifted within me. A light started to shine deep down in my spirit, and I was grateful for the change I felt.

As the summer continued, my sister Elizabeth, a friend of hers, and I continued a Bible study we had begun in my home the prior spring, meeting on Wednesday evenings. I started feeling strong enough to go to my friends' homes for play dates as well. I left my house more often—my home, my sanctuary, my ark, as I had started to call it. I became a little stronger that summer. I was now willing to step outside the confines of my haven and to tread lightly into the brave unknown of the world again.

I know of no other people on earth with whom I laugh more than my cousins Colleen and Hilary. They are my preferred travel companions, more like friends than cousins. We have many adventures together under our belts. Colleen and Hilary visited Dave and my family in England and Germany. We traveled all over England, all throughout Germany, and even to Paris during those visits.

And that summer, as our Grand Canyon trip drew ever closer, I was thrilled when Colleen said she could come along with the kids and me. The group traveling to Arizona also included my nephew Jake.

As I packed for the trip, however, my spirit felt uneasy and my heart felt heavy. I was unsure about taking such a grand trip without Dave and our boys. This would be my first step into the great unknown without them, and I didn't know how to process that.

But God whispered to my spirit, *Daughter, they have that and so much more where they are now. Enjoy your Grand Canyon. You have no idea what your boys get to see here. Remember, even the most beautiful sights on earth are but a shadow of what I have in store here.*

And with that confidence in my spirit, we embarked on our first travel adventure as a family of four. Our trip to the Grand Canyon had its ups and downs, with sibling spats and moody toddlers, but overall this adventure was just what my spirit needed. In fact, those sibling spats and moody kids reminded me of the many times Dave and I had hauled small children all over two continents. That trip—the good, the bad, and the ugly—helped me feel just a little bit more like my old self.

July brought with it my birthday. Dave was so good at recognizing important days in our family. Whether it was our anniversary, birthdays, or holidays, Dave knew how to make them special. We worked as a team to make holidays special for the children, and when days were specific to one or both of us, Dave filled them with fun, festive memories.

Because Dave and I had been little more than strangers when we got married, I thought it wise to make some expectations known to him upfront, and he did the same. As my birthday was approaching that first year of our marriage, I said in a playfully serious tone, "By the way, birthdays and holidays were always a big deal in my house when I was growing up, and I don't expect that to change." I got my point across.

I recalled dear childhood memories of birthdays—sleepovers with my girlfriends in our family tent in the backyard, spending the day at the swimming pool in town, riding my bike all day with my friends in the neighborhood and then coming home to a fun party with my family. My parents knew how to make my siblings and me feel like the only kid in the world on our birthdays. It was a Hartrum family tradition for us to pick the flavor of the cake and the color of the icing. We also got to pick the kind of ice cream served and what we had for dinner that evening. My mom would make the cake, and when my dad came home from work, we'd sit down to a family meal. After heading into the living room to open presents, we would return to the kitchen to sing "Happy Birthday" and eat cake.

As in any household with a bunch of kids, life growing up in the Hartrum house wasn't picture perfect. I had a typical upbringing. There were plenty of sibling spats, crabby teens, and rough days in a house with so many people, but special days were made special without fail every year. And while I didn't expect Dave to treat me to a sleepover in my backyard or to bake me a cake, I wanted him to know that my family always made those days special when I was a kid and that I wanted the tradition to continue for us and our children.

He rose to the challenge with flying colors. I discovered that Dave also wanted our lives filled with celebration and excitement and was happy to make big deals out of special days, family memories, and tradition.

In 2009, we were living in Germany and I was turning thirty-two. Dave worked all day, and when he came home, he was carrying bags from a local store and told me, "Go upstairs and don't come down until we call you." I went up to my bedroom and could hear a busy commotion and hushed voices in the dining room below. When I was called downstairs and reached the bottom of the staircase, I saw Dave and the kids standing proudly before me. They had hung streamers from all corners of the dining room, had balloons taped to every chair, had gifts wrapped and placed in the center of the dining room table, and had strawberry shortcake plates, napkins, cups, and party hats on the table.

The kids dissolved into giddy laughter and excitement as I exclaimed how great everything looked. Fighting back tears of joy, I looked at Dave. He stood proudly next to his handiwork at the dining room table with a grin almost as big as the ones the kids were wearing. He was gifted at making all of us feel special, and at that moment, I was so grateful that I had made that impulsive decision eight years before to marry a man I hardly knew.

Days later as I was showing a friend photos from my birthday, she asked, "Wow, all that for thirty-two?"

"Yep," I responded. "That's Dave."

For various birthdays Dave would have flowers delivered to the house and present me with homemade gifts. He gave me framed collages of family photos and plaques with the precious footprints and handprints of our babies. He would take off from work so we could visit Stonehenge, a cathedral, or a museum. Sometimes he would put the kids to bed and we would snuggle on the couch as we watched a movie.

Dave always made me and the kids feel special on our birthdays, and we couldn't wait until his special day to reciprocate.

By Kate's eleventh birthday in December of 2012, we were living in our home in Millstadt, Illinois. Dave had to work that evening, so the family celebrated Kate that afternoon. While I was preparing the cake, Dave said he had to run out to the store. He returned with a mystery present in a bag and wanted us all to wait to see what he was giving to Kate. As she was opening her gifts, Dave handed her the mystery bag. Kate excitedly opened it but was confused when she started pulling out items that didn't match what an eleven-year-old girl would want: a whoopee cushion, a pop gun with several rolls of poppers, a can of slime. "It's your barter bag, Kate," Dave explained.

"My barter bag?" she asked.

"Yep, your barter bag. When you don't want to do your chores, you now have something to barter with your brothers with. For example, you ask Dom to do your dishes after dinner tomorrow night, and offer to barter the pop gun for his doing the dishes for you."

Kate's eyes immediately lit up and a huge smile formed on her face, knowing the gift her daddy had just given her could get her out of several chores in the next several weeks. She started throwing out examples, much to the chagrin and the envy of the boys, who called out in playful protest, "Not fair! That's so not fair!" But they fooled no one, since they said this with smiles on their faces, knowing they would also get something out of the deal.

On Dominic's sixth birthday, Dave thought it was time to pay back the trickster in our house. Even at such a young age, Dom was always up for playing pranks on all of us. Dave bought him a huge Lego set and secretly worked for several nights to put it together after Dom had gone to bed. During Dom's birthday celebration days later, Dave handed him a wrapped box filled with rocks to make it seem as if the Legos were inside. Dom opened the gift and dumped out the contents of the box in utter confusion.

"Oh, no!" Dave exclaimed, feigning concern, "What happened here? There's got to be some kind of mistake. Why are there rocks in this box and not Legos?"

"Where are the Legos?" Dom asked in a defeated tone.

"You know what? There's been some kind of mistake," Dave said.

Dave asked Dom to "go into the other room while your mother and I discuss what to do about this." When Dom opened the door to the foyer, he immediately saw his completed Lego set right in front of him on a shelf.

I got the entire trick on video, and even above Dom's shrieks of delight and the kids' giggles of approval at the joke played on their brother, Dave can be heard laughing. He knew he had made his boy's night. As I videotaped the event, I tried with everything in me not to cry tears of joy that I had the family I had. Dave indeed knew how to make us all feel special.

When my birthday arrived in 2013 that first year without Dave and the boys, I had no idea how I would get through it. I had no idea how to do that day without Dave and the joy he brought. But God provided a day of peace, a day filled with hugs and memories made with Kate, Finn, and Elise. We spent the day looking through old family photos and watching videos of birthdays past. After that, Kate insisted on doing my "birthday makeup." All dolled up, Kate and I decided we better go out somewhere, so I piled the kids in the van and we headed to Lone Elk Park. Later, the kids and I had a nice Italian meal at one of my favorite restaurants.

On the way home, Kate asked me to stop at the store. She asked for some money and went into the store alone. She came out several minutes later with bags and a cake. She insisted I not look in the bags, and when we got home, she asked me to go upstairs and not to come down "until we call you down." Several minutes later, Kate, Finn, and baby Elise called me downstairs, and what I saw took my breath away.

Kate had decorated the dining room with balloons; she had placed a pink table cloth on the table and had made place settings with pink-and-white polka dot plates, napkins, and cups. She had even placed party favors at each place setting. I walked slowly to the table, trying my hardest not to cry, and hugged and thanked my babies from the deepest part of my heart. As I sat at the table, Kate instructed the babies to start singing "Happy Birthday" to me as she carried in the cake.

She had decorated it with sprinkles, and "Happy Birthday, Mom" was written in icing. As my babies, all three, sang birthday wishes to their mommy, I couldn't hold it in any longer. I succumbed to tears of utter gratitude for my precious babies left with me and for my young lady, who had outdone herself.

Kate handed me the first of many gifts she had bought, wrapped, and placed on the dining room table. After I had opened the gifts—lotions, earrings, makeup, and a sunhat—Kate had one more to give me. She handed me a bag. I put my hand inside and pulled out items that were not what a thirty-six-year-old mommy would normally receive: princess hair ties, a can of slime, various kinds of candy, army men figurines. I looked up at Kate. She had a huge grin of satisfaction all over her young face.

"It's your barter bag, Mom."

I sat in absolute awe. I was amazed that Kate, only eleven years old, had such composure, such wisdom, and such a compassionate heart. She had done her very best, going above and beyond, to make her mom's day special. I was overcome with love and gratitude for my girl. And as I held her and thanked her from the depths of my spirit, I told her how proud her daddy was of her. I thought, *Dave knew how to make birthdays special indeed, and his legacy of unabashed love, thoughtfulness, creativity, and giving will live on.* And in that moment, it lived on in my baby girl, turned young lady, right there in my arms.

The birth of my niece, Eleanor Jean, offered a welcome reprieve in the middle of that summer. My brother Richard and his wife Roxanne learned they were expecting baby Ellie when the tragedy struck my family.

Days after Ellie was born, I braced myself to meet her. Only five short months after my boys had gone to heaven, I feared the emotion holding that brand-new life might stir in me. I feared that greeting this precious new life might be my undoing as I recalled my boys at just such an age.

As I prepared to visit my brother's house to say hello to baby Ellie for the first time, I recalled Grant and Kate playing one afternoon in late 2012. From the other room, I heard Grant declare to Kate that when he grew up, if he had daughters, he would name them Ellie and Jenny.

Returning to the present, I left the house feeling a little securer. My brother and his wife had no idea that Grant had intended to name a future daughter Ellie, and therefore they did not choose that name for that reason. But as I started my car and pulled out of the driveway, I saw this as a sign that just as on so many other points in my journey, my boys were with me that day.

On my drive over, I had resolved that when I entered my brother's house, I would put aside myself and my loss and would be happy for him and his wife.

As I was handed baby Ellie for the first time, my breath caught in my throat. I looked at the brand-new life in front of me and started to cry. But I didn't cry out of sorrow for my losses. I cried tears celebrating the new life in my arms. I cried as I acknowledged all the joys and the struggles, the mountain tops and valleys, awaiting the precious baby in my arms as she grew.

I felt like I was holding a piece of my boys. The same blood that flowed through Ellie flowed through Dom and Grant, her cousins, and for that, I cried tears of joy.

I handed Ellie back to her momma, my sister-in-law Roxanne, a dear sister to me, a calm, patient mother who set the bar for all other mothers. I said a silent prayer, thanking God for this brand-new life. And as I smiled through tears at that precious face, I asked Him to provide her many mountaintops and overflowing joys.

As is often the case on this fallen earth, the new life we had just welcomed was balanced with the loss of another. We received word from family in Louisiana that Dave's aunt Glenda had passed after a battle with cancer.

Dave's cousin Heath, Glenda's son, was more like a brother to Dave, and Dave loved him very much. It broke my heart that Heath had to lose his mother so soon after Dave— his cousin, his friend, his brother—had gone to heaven.

Due to the generosity of friends, Kate and I had been able to fly down to attend the Louisiana memorial Mass for Dave in his hometown months before. I recalled a conversation I had with Aunt Glenda at the meal following the Mass. In a weakened state and sitting in a wheelchair, she looked at me and said, "He came to see me. When he was in town last, he came to see me." Her voice was filled with emotion.

Aunt Glenda was recalling the fall of 2012 when Dave drove down to see his family. While I went on a cruise with my cousins Colleen and Hilary, he took the opportunity to go see his parents, his aunts and uncles, his cousins, and his friends. Never one to shy away from a challenge, Dave packed, piled our five kids in the minivan, along with both of our dogs, and headed for the New Orleans area.

That Dave would drive ten hours to Louisiana with our kids and our dogs showed what kind of a father he was. Dave decided he didn't want to sit and wait until I returned from the Caribbean, so he set out on his brave adventure. He never shirked his responsibilities as a father. In fact, he relished them. He was born to be a husband, a father, and a family man. And on that trip to Louisiana, he looked forward to being a son, a nephew, a cousin, and a friend as well.

While he was in the area, he visited Aunt Glenda. She was in precarious health, and Dave wanted to spend time with her and make memories with her before she was called home. As he sat with his aunt, Dave couldn't know that he would be entering heaven several months before she did.

As I visited with her that February day in 2013, weeks after Dave had passed, I could see on Aunt Glenda's face just what Dave's visit months before had meant to her.

As I got the news of Aunt Glenda's passing that summer, I was saddened for all who loved her, but I was also comforted. Dave was with family who had gone on before. His Papa (his grandfather), whom Dave loved dearly, had passed when Dave was a little boy. He often told the children and me stories about this man he remembered so fondly. Dave frequently said he wanted to be called Papa when he became a grandpa, in honor of his grandfather and the bond they shared.

Dave's cousin Anthony had passed as a young man ten years before Dave and our sons. Dave and Anthony were very close, and it brought me comfort to know that while I missed my husband, he was surrounded by love. He had not only the love of our Father in heaven and of our sons but the love of family, and now Aunt Glenda had joined him.

As I left the porch to go inside and continue my day, I remembered a picture Dave had in his photo album of him and his aunt.

Back in the house, I grabbed the album off of a shelf and found the photo I was looking for—a shot of Dave, at nineteen years old, holding his guitar, with Aunt Glenda beside him. She was leaning toward her nephew with a beautiful smile on her face. The photo captured a precious moment between aunt and nephew.

I was comforted as I pictured Dave and his aunt sitting in a similar way at that moment, with Dave playing his guitar and with both of them in glory, at peace, free of worry, strife, and pain. As I gently placed that precious photo back in the album, I could almost hear Dave strumming that guitar.

As the summer progressed, the *St. Louis Post-Dispatch* carried an article about our family.

I was approached by a reporter asking if he could interview me to write a story for the paper's religion section. Hesitant at first, I reasoned that I could use the opportunity to shine a light on God's provision through the early part of our journey, and I agreed to do the interview. The interview was difficult from an emotional standpoint, since I had to recall many moments from our tragic weekend so soon after these events. But I was pleased with the article. In fact, the paper decided to put it on the front page of the Sunday edition instead of in the religion section.

I was honored that a wider audience would read my family's story, and I hoped and prayed many would recognize God's provision from the details.

The article was also posted on the newspaper's website, and I read many of the comments posted by readers. While some were out of place and cruel, most were positive. After God spoke to my spirit, I reasoned that even the hurtful comments served a purpose. They sparked an online discussion about religion in the comments section under the story. And I thought, *Isn't it just like God to get a religious discussion started in an otherwise secular forum?*

That summer, Kate was able to attend Camp Courage, a camp for bereaved children, through Annie's Hope, a nonprofit group designed to support children through the loss of a loved one. She spent a week swimming, crafting, making friends, and more, all while participating in breakout sessions designed to guide children through their loss. She had a wonderful time, and I could see Kate turn a corner on her grief journey. She was not alone in her grief, and the camp helped her to recognize that.

Also that summer, we were blessed to meet Debbie, a trainer down the road from our house, and Kate started taking weekly horse riding lessons from her. Kate trained on Honey and had to learn how to groom, saddle, communicate with, and guide the horse, tasks that required patience and a sense of responsibility. This was exactly the therapy for her aching spirit that I had hoped it would be. Dave had always loved horses. He had visited family in Oklahoma as a boy and had ridden horses there, and it was a skill he had hoped to pass on to our children. I was calmed in my spirit as I watched Kate fulfilling a dream her daddy had for her while bringing a blessed reprieve to her restless soul.

As the summer continued, my aunt Marsha, my cousin Shanika, and her beautiful kids came to help me plant a beautiful weeping willow in my yard. While she offered no details, my aunt told me she had a dream showing that in the years to come I would make big decisions under the shade of that tree. She said I should call it the "decision tree." We wrote those words on a stone and placed it under the newly planted tree.

My aunt Cindy, my cousin Melissa, and her beautiful son and niece also came to spend an afternoon with the kids and me. Aunt Cindy's husband, my uncle Rich, one of my dad's brothers, had passed to heaven only a few years before Dave and my sons. She and I shared stories about our widowhood. I wanted to learn any lesson I could from this beautiful woman, who had already walked the road for years. As a young widow, I felt grateful for her wisdom during those early days on my grief journey. One thing my aunt said that day has stuck with me, bringing an entirely new perspective to my journey.

Because Aunt Cindy is a nurse, I posed questions to her about my boys' last earthly trek. At that early stage, I was still troubled by some issues. I could not shake the fact that Dave had crawled those last twenty feet. I was not at peace with the way his last moments may have played out, and I was having a hard time putting my imagination to rest. With the most brutal stages behind them, those in the last stage of hyperthermia are supposed to be euphoric, since their brains have tricked their bodies into believing they are warm. Their passing from earth imminent, many simply drift off to sleep. "I just don't understand," I told Aunt Cindy. "If Dave was supposed to be disoriented and his body tricked into thinking he was warm at that point, why didn't he just drift off to sleep? Why was he still fighting? Why was he still so desperate to get home? Because that shows me that he was still very aware of what was going on."

My aunt answered me almost without hesitation, and what she said took my breath away.

"Sarah, what makes you think he wasn't crawling to Jesus? What if he saw what lay just before him? What if Jesus was waiting to take him home, and he was crawling to Jesus?"

Immediately, my heart leapt in my chest and my breath caught in my throat. *Crawling to Jesus!*

Many days later, as I thought about what my aunt had said, I pictured the skies opening up, Jesus coming down, and Dave crawling to meet Him. Dave could see the One he had worshiped, served, taught our children to adore, and praised in song for so many years, and now he was crawling toward Him, knowing he was going home. I thought about the story of Stephen in the Bible and how there was a precedent in Scripture for believers in Christ seeing what lies just before them as they make their transitions home (Acts 7:55–56). I decided that no matter how my boys' homecoming had transpired, I at least knew where they had gone and that I would view Dave's crawling those last twenty feet as his coming home to Jesus. I was reminded to see with my spiritual eyes and not just with my earthly ones. I was also reminded that God's ways are not our ways; they are far greater than anything we can imagine (Isaiah 55:8–9). And that has made all the difference.

As my aunt left my home that afternoon, I felt inspired to be a widow of dignity, just as Aunt Cindy so beautifully demonstrated. I was grateful beyond measure for her words of wisdom.

That summer, my parents' dear friends—Doug, Julie, and her sister Stacy—who built the shelves in my basement months before, came to help me weed my gardens and to plant in my yard. I was in awe of Julie and Stacy's knowledge of gardening. I even went to my journal after they left, and wrote down all I learned from them during our afternoon together.

My uncle Darrin and his girlfriend Stephanie also helped me work in my yard, and my dear friend Becky, her husband, and their family friend came to plant a beautiful tree there in honor of my three guys. I called it the memorial magnolia. My cousin April came bearing gifts for the children; her daughter Zoe and Finn became fast friends.

In those early grief days, Kate's American Heritage Girls Troop out of Missouri came to show support, bringing gifts, messages of love, and even a monetary donation for the children and me. I became friends with Michelle, the wife of Dave's commander at the Defense Information Systems Agency. She came over every few weeks to talk and to play with the kids, bringing goodies. Colleen, a dear woman from the boys' Cub Scout pack, whom Dave viewed as a mentor in the short time they led Scouts together, visited me often, sending texts and messages. The children and I were sustained by generous monetary provisions from the community, from the memorial fund started by Colleen, and from the boys' Cub Scout pack during those early grief days.

Also that summer, members of the homeschool group from Scott Air Force Base came out in droves to help me around the house in any way they could. They did yard work, washed my dishes, cooked for me, visited with the children and me, and brought ready-made meals. One day several ladies went so far as to gather the mounds of dirty laundry that had piled up in the laundry room of my basement and to take a dozen or more bags to the Laundromat for me. I usually kept my house clean and organized, but depression was manifesting itself in chaos, clutter, dirty dishes, and piles of laundry. The homeschool group even arranged with the sergeants club at the base to buy the kids and me a new dishwasher, since ours had stopped working weeks after the boys had gone to heaven. Every week for months after our tragedy, I had a visitor and/or a meal from the homeschool group. My heart is full of gratitude for those dear families that loved my children and me.

My cousins Colleen and Hilary were regular visitors, making me smile and laugh. My friend Heather was a constant presence, encouraging me (making me?) to clean and organize my bedroom, since it had become a cluttered mess, one night, until four in the morning. My dear friend Becky continued to be the rock she had always been for me since childhood, and my siblings were constant supporters in any way I needed. David took Bear to training classes, Richard did handyman jobs around my house, Deanna continued to visit and to hold my hand, and Elizabeth babysat Finn and Elise when Kate and I started Christian grief counseling.

My aunt Mary, one of my dad's sisters, was also a steady visitor. Aunt Mary was a constant support to me from the earliest point on my grief journey. She was always willing to offer an encouraging text, a hopeful letter, or a comforting visit or to help with a project at my home. We found that we had a common love of planting, of getting our hands in the dirt, and of growing new life in the earth. We spent summer afternoons repotting plants and weeding gardens. We grew close during the early days of my grief journey.

Unfortunately, Aunt Mary and I were about to share something else in common—a burden no mother should ever have to shoulder. My aunt was about to join the mothers who have had to usher a child from this earth.

I received a phone call one afternoon saying that my cousin Eric, Aunt Mary's oldest son, only in his forties, had been in an accident at his job. No one was sure of his status. When I arrived at my parents' house, my mom told me that Eric had passed. Shocked, I prayed that God would immediately surround my aunt with the same love and shield of protection He had provided me at the outset of my grief journey.

When I visited her the next day to offer whatever support I could, my aunt talked, cried, and shared her story. And as I sat and listened, I realized I was about to embark on another phase of my own journey. God was asking me to share some of what He had taught me, even early on my grief journey, to help my aunt get through hers.

As I listened to Aunt Mary talk, a thought entered my head, a phrase I had written in my journal months before: "Profound loss has got to have a profound purpose."

At that moment, I had an inkling of how I could use my tragedy to help others. I resolved that my family's suffering would not be in vain. I vowed to find purpose in Dave, Dom, and Grant's passage to heaven that cold January morning.

After making great progress on my grief journey, I took a downward turn as the summer wore on. Anger returned to my spirit. While my anger in February and March was directed toward people, my anger that summer was directed more toward God. In one surge of anger brought on by grief, I paced the country lane outside my home for hours while the kids were inside watching cartoons. I shouted aloud to God as I held a can of Off to battle the intense onslaught of horseflies and mosquitoes, which only worsened my mood. I was ready to fight everything and everyone—bugs and God. Chaos reigned in my heart. Dave was gone, my boys were gone, my dad was very ill with pancreatic cancer, my kids on earth were without their father, my aunt had suffered the tragedy of losing a child, and I blew.

I walked up and down the lane, screaming aloud to God, questioning Him, His methods, His love, and His existence. It was a good thing that I was living in the country and that it was the summer and everything was in bloom. No neighbors were within view. Anyone seeing me would have thought I was a schizophrenic as I paced the lane, yelling, gesturing, and screaming to myself. I was battling with God. And it felt good. God could take it.

After about two-and-a-half hours, I came inside, spent and exhausted. I reasoned that there was a draw. No one had won. But my heart felt lighter.

On another night that summer, I was sitting in the house after a long, emotional day. I had tried to be productive outside, but productivity would not come and I found myself sitting on my couch, feeling like I had wasted a day. I was angry. I had given in to grief. I had allowed myself to wallow in it, but instead of feeling the cheap satisfaction of letting myself stay in my pit, I felt sick to my stomach for permitting sorrow to pull me down. I was angry that grief was seemingly winning and stealing so much from me. Not only had my family been stolen from me, but now the grief that crept into every corner of my being threatened to steal even more—my sanity, my motivation, my productivity, my joy. I found anger rising up in me again.

So at the tail end of the day, I threw on some old clothes and went out to my garden with a shovel, as if I were headed into battle with a sword. I was distraught, but mostly I was angry, and I wanted to hit something. I wanted to beat the ground. I wanted to battle. So, weapon in hand, I started digging and breaking up dirt for my family's memorial garden. As I dug, I talked aloud to God. I fell to my knees. I screamed, I yelled, I cried, I threw dirt, I slammed the shovel into the ground, and I ripped the grass off of the earth—the whole while wiping the sweat from my brow as I worked.

I continued that way for several hours. I tilled the ground until darkness fell and I could no longer see to work. I gathered my supplies, walked through my front door, and was met by Kate.

"Mom, you look like you have been in battle," she said. "You're filthy."

She had no idea how right she was. I had wrestled with God that night out in the garden. I walked to my bathroom and saw I was covered from head to toe in dirt from kneeling, sweating, wiping my brow, crying, and brushing away tears. The tear stains had cleared a path through the dirt on my face. I was indeed in battle that night. But at least, I reasoned, I went down fighting, not sitting on my couch, taking it. And my heart felt a little lighter as I lay down to sleep.

As the summer drew to a close, my anger subsided and my desire to be productive returned. I began tackling house projects that Dave and I had planned to do together. After moving into the house in the fall of 2012, we made a list of things we wanted to do. I decided it was time to start some of those projects to honor my husband and his plans for the home his hard work had enabled us to buy.

Over the summer, I hired contractors to do many renovations to the house. In late summer, I started having our basement turned into a family room with a fireplace.

I was so proud to put the house plans in motion. Dave had grand dreams for our home. He couldn't wait to make his mark on our new space; he couldn't wait to call our new house a home. The first weekend we were in the house, he excitedly drove to a nursery and bought two trees for the backyard. He and Grant eagerly planted the pin oak and the sugar maple that fall day. I have the most precious photos of Dave, standing between the trees, shovel and bucket in hand, so proud of the plot of land that he could call his own. Only God could have known that we would live in the house for just three-and-a-half short months as a family of seven.

Not only were the projects designed to honor Dave's wishes, but looking back, I see how God used the decisions I made in getting those projects done to help me build a sense of ownership and accomplishment in the house that was now my complete responsibility. This was another step in learning how to do life without the partnership, guidance, and support of my husband. I see how God turned my desire to honor my husband into an opportunity for growth. The home projects became yet another step forward on my grief journey. With each decision I made, with each bit of progress on the projects, I felt more in control of my life and of my situation as a newly single woman. I felt a confidence. I felt an ownership. I felt capable.

Our house became a safe haven for the children and me as we walked the new road on which our family had been placed.

I am eternally grateful for God's use of every little detail to fulfill His grand design. I am grateful for a God who has every facet of our lives completely under control even if we can't see that.

The summer closed with two blessed trips, one to Missouri and one to Florida.

That first week home after our tragedy, I made a phone call to the breeder who gave Dave and Dom our dear Bear. I felt a need to call that woman to let her know what her dog tried to do for my boys on that trail. I had never met Glenda, but I knew she and Dave had established a nice rapport after Dave and Dom bought Bear from her when we moved into our home.

After our first conversation, she and I became friends. In June of 2013, Glenda and her daughter came to my home with Bear's parents, Abby and Samson. We had arranged for them to have a doggy play date in the backyard. We had a wonderful visit that afternoon as the dogs and the kids played. Glenda, her daughter, and I talked about Dave, Dom, Grant, faith, and, of course, dogs.

As the visit came to a close at the ice cream shop in town, we said our good-byes, but Glenda had one more thing to tell me. Abby was pregnant with her last litter before her retirement, and Glenda said she would like to name that litter the Decareaux memorial litter in honor of Dave, Dom, and Grant. She also said that any proceeds from selling the puppies would go toward the Decareaux Memorial Fund started by the boys' Cub Scout pack earlier that year.

I was honored and thankful. God again showed me His love and continued provision through the hands and feet of His people. Almost speechless, with happy tears welling in my eyes, I thanked Glenda, and we made a plan for the kids and me to go to her home to meet the puppies when they were born.

In August, Kate, Finn, Elise, and I drove an hour to Glenda's beautiful home and plot of land to meet the Decareaux memorial litter. As Glenda welcomed us into the yard, what I saw behind her almost took my breath away—a litter of beautiful yellow puppies just weeks old. Glenda released them from behind a fence, and they ran in every direction. The squeals and giggles of delight those puppies produced in my children were priceless. Finn, Elise, and Kate got on the ground and were quickly overtaken by a pile of puppies. I could hear laughter and happy screams.

I wanted to cry in gratitude for that moment when my kids forgot anything about their lives, anything about their losses, and focused only on those puppies licking their faces and gnawing their shoes.

Kate's beautiful face was free of worry, pain, fear, and stress too great for her young features. All I saw was bliss. All I saw were smiles. I was eternally grateful for that dear woman Glenda, for those precious puppies, and for the God who orchestrated just such a friendship.

God allowed a peaceful close to our summer in 2013. Always up for an adventure, my cousins Colleen and Hilary, my travel buddies, had organized a trip to the beaches of the Florida panhandle. I gratefully accepted the offer, and in September, the kids and I and my niece Hailey made a road trip down to sunny Florida.

The trip was just what my spirit needed to round out that season. The summer months had been filled with growth but also continued losses on the family's grief journey. But I had resolved to find the pockets of joy that still surrounded the children and me.

Shortly after our tragedy, God had asked me to keep my kids' lives as normal as possible. I felt Dave speak to my spirit that day in May, telling me to give our kids the same sense of family and adventure we were giving them together, and I was determined to do so.

Going on those vacations without Dave, Dominic, and Grant felt unnatural at first. But with each smile I saw on my kids' faces, with each laugh that rose up in me as I was surrounded by my cousins, with each memory I knew I was making for my kids, I realized our trips were a gift. Those moments were a gift. And that every opportunity I had to add blessed experiences to my kids' store of memories thus far in their young lives, I was going to do it.

As I stood on the beach one evening in late summer watching the waves come in and the sky offer a brilliant show of colors as the sun retreated, I felt a peace beyond my understanding. I felt secure and loved. I watched the glowing sky and thought, *My Father, how beautiful is Your creation. I cannot even imagine what You have done up there if this is but a mere shadow of that.*

I was overcome by the beauty surrounding me as the waves crashed, the sun set, the seagulls sounded, and salt scented the air. I was in awe that the God who had made all that surrounded me, also held my hand as I walked on my grief journey. I was humbled that such a mighty God would come to my level, would seek me out, would speak His words of wisdom to my spirit, and would lead me every step of the way down this road. And while the journey was not easy, I knew it would be bearable, because I was held up by a God who had made all I could see. I was comforted beyond words at that moment.

As I turned to leave the beach, I was reminded of Dave's words to my spirit earlier that year: *We are still the Decareaux family; we do not tiptoe into things. You give those kids a summer.*

I smiled and was happy to have obliged.

Chapter 17

A Summary of Provision

In October 2013, nine months into our grief journey, I wrote a letter in response to a dear friend who had asked how I was doing. The letter summed up what the first several months of the journey had looked like.

"How is my immediate family doing? My little family—my kids and I? Well, we are doing okay. God is sustaining and carrying us every single day. We have been on quite a journey. It was very, very dark in the beginning. My life was over. I saw no joy, no peace, no love; I saw nothing but darkness, sorrow, hopelessness. God had numbed me and covered me with supernatural peace to get through all the services and memorials, but when all was said and done and reality set in, so did many clouds. My guys were so honored in every way. My babies were named honorary Eagle Scouts, and the list goes on. I actually did list all our family's honors one day, and it took me two typed pages to list everything.

"Dave, Dominic, and Grant touched many, many hearts and lives. But when that was all over and life was supposed to pick back up, things were very dark for a long time. In fact, much of January through March is a blur. Had I not started to journal in February, I might not be able to recall much of it.

"I do know that in January I went to the place where my boys met Jesus. I went to their trail. Then in March I went again with my brother. I hiked six miles of their journey and helped my brother hang lodge signs he had carved to prevent other hikers from losing their way. Dave was never lost. But at one point, in his hypothermic state, he missed one right turn that would have brought him back to the lodge in the time it took him to walk in the wrong direction to the place where they passed to heaven. If I were not a Christian, that fact alone would have done me in. But you know God takes my questions like that and settles them this way. There are things I will not know until I am in heaven … He reminded me (not audibly) at the trail, *This was not the end of them. There are very much alive here with Me. This was not the end of them.*

"Despite all the reassurance and so many signs and revelations from the Holy Spirit, in weeks seven and fifteen, I was suicidal. (We are now in week forty-one.) The grief was overwhelming and it took control of me. I woke every day with a chasm in my chest. I felt suffocated, and at a moment's notice my chest would tighten and I would either stare as if comatose or cry uncontrollably, screaming, wailing, raging at times, and throwing myself onto the ground. And the only thing that fixed it was sleep. I was hopeless and my life was over. So I constructed a way to facilitate my entrance into heaven. My family was but a breath away.

"But God saw to it that this thought process was stopped. He sent subtle revelations and made changes to my spirit to erase that from my heart. There were little things like Finn constantly saying in the beginning, 'Mom, I want to keep you,' and Elise saying, 'Mommy, I don't ever want to miss you. I want to keep you.' And I was watching Kate struggle with trying to be a normal preteen with such baggage to carry. He made me sympathetic to the hurt she was already going through and made me aware that I could not add to her pain.

"But honestly, my kids notwithstanding, the biggest thing that kept me here was this: God said to my spirit, *You have no idea what you will mess up if you do this your way. It was Dave's time to come home. I need him here for My advancing kingdom, for My purposes. I need Dom and Grant here. They were Mine before they were yours; down there they were your baby boys, but here they are what I need them to be for My purposes. I have a kingdom coming. You work from your end, they'll work from My end, and you'll meet again in the middle.*

"I felt a pending kingdom work, and He needed them there. Period. He needs me here. Period. That took away that dark desire to no longer be alive.

"So that brings us to about April. Things started to get brighter in my spirit. The sun started shining, and we started working in our yard. Finn and I planted a garden, I got the kids a swing set, and we spent much time outside. This home, this land, this yard, is our sanctuary. I am still able to homeschool the kids, so we have many days together to heal, mourn, cope, endure, grow, and learn. We do so much outside: planting, weeding, mulching, and mowing. In June, I planted a memorial garden for my family in our backyard.

"People say time will heal. No, it will not. I will not ever fully heal. So I do not heal, but I endure, I move forward, and I survive. I fight this spiritual battle against sorrow, hopelessness, anger, and bitterness every single day. There is so much more to our existence than we can see with our eyes. And I feel with this tragedy I have a bit of a peek into the unseen. I see it with my spirit and with my soul. There is so much more than this. And with that said, I feel there is a grand purpose. I am reminded of what I have said before, 'Profound loss has got to have a profound purpose.'

"I feel it in my spirit so thick. I feel the hopelessness is a demon on my back, and when I wanted to end my life, those demons were perched on me, making me stone still at times, curled up in my bed or on my couch, and God said, 'Enough. I did not leave you down there for that. Get up.'

"So spring was the start of light coming back into our home. I took Kate to Agape at Greenville College. I had a God encounter there that cannot be denied. God is so very real. To deny that after seeing all the signs, revelations, solace, peace, and angels on earth in the hands and feet of His people would be foolish.

"So that puts us at May. And I started thinking, *Okay, if God is holding us, setting a hedge of protection around us through His people, and I know nothing can pass into my life without having been permitted by Him, then He must really have a reason for this.*

"Summer was very busy. We started to try to be Decareauxes again. I felt like getting back out for day trips we did as a family of seven. So tenderly, slowly, we started with very small outings again—the park—then branched out to the Arch in St. Louis and Grant's Farm. Throughout spring and summer, I read snippets of *Heaven* by Randy Alcorn. I also read *One Minute after You Die* by Erwin W. Lutzer. I listened to audio sermons by John MacArthur on heaven. Spiritually, God is evolving me from wanting to know all I can about heaven to the new heaven/new earth, to prophecy, and to end-time events.

"We continued the summer by going to the Grand Canyon and to the beach in September. Locally, we went to the museum, the park, out to eat. Over the summertime, we were trying to get used to our new family dynamic and getting back out for adventures as a family. Since February, Kate and I have been seeing a Christian counselor once a week. In March, I put Finn in karate, and the end of summer brought another chapter on this new journey—we started school again, homeschooling full force, at the beginning of September.

"When fall came, Kate got involved in horse riding lessons and gymnastics. Finn is in karate and gymnastics as well. I teach the kids, take care of the home, and I am in the process of doing projects for our house that Dave and I dreamed of together. I am fulfilling those dreams in honor of him. We try to keep a fairly normal schedule along with these added commitments and look for pockets of joy along the way.

"God has carried me from suicidal to sustained and peaceful, to productive, to making my kids' lives as normal as possible. He gives me a sense of mission that goes beyond this earthly realm. I sense Dave and our sons all the time. I see them in sunsets, in Elise's eyes, in Finn's smile, in hawks as they soar above my home. I feel them in the sun shining on me as we play or plant outside, in the warm breeze that passes me now and then, in the earth in my hands as I dig to plant new life. I hear them in the sound of the wind blowing through the trees in our woods, in the crunch of the fallen leaves in this new season of chill in the air, as I traipse through our trails, in Kate's laugh.

"I see Grant in Finn's smile, Dave in Finn's jaw line, Dom in Finn's mannerisms. I see Daddy in Elise's eyes, Grant in her smile, and Dom in her kind heart. I see Daddy in Kate's face and in her artistic ability, Dom in her intellect, and I see Grant's gentle spirit in her as she plays with and loves on her baby brother and sister. God has made it very, very clear to me that this is a temporary separation, and that makes all the difference. It is how I am able to live, how I am able to have movie night with my sweet girl, how I am able to smile and to laugh with my babies, because we will all be restored one fine day."

Chapter 18

The Firsts

Fall came and with it beautiful crisp days. The trees were turning brilliant shades of orange, red, and yellow, the acorns were falling, and the air was crisp and cool. Autumn was in the air. One glorious fall day, the kids and I raked leaves, and I took pictures as they played in the backyard. Then the babies and I went on an acorn hunt, a pine cone hunt, and a fall leaves hunt in our yard, gathering any and all beautiful fall foliage into our buckets. It was a lovely day. My spirit felt light. I wouldn't have wanted to spend that day any other way.

But with the beauty of fall also came the start of days that once brought joy but that I feared might now bring about my undoing. We had arrived at what Dave and I had dubbed the Decareaux birthday season. It kicked off with Finn's birthday on October 17. Grant's birthday followed on November 3 and Kate's on December 2. The season continued with Dave's birthday on December 22 and Dominic's birthday on January 4. In between we had many other holidays. Dave and I celebrated our meeting anniversary on December 8, the start of our whirlwind courtship. Our wedding anniversary was on January 11. We got two anniversaries a year! Elise and I were the odd ones out with summer birthdays.

That fall I was despondent at the thought that I had to add the days my boys entered heaven to the list—January 12 and 13.

I was terrified. I had no idea how I was going to withstand the season that had once brought so much joy and celebration. I feared it might now bring much darkness. I shuddered under the weight of growing dread and despair. I had gotten into a comfortable place on my grief journey, and I was afraid the days ahead would undo any progress I had made.

I soon learned that God would not leave me comfortable for long. There is no progress in comfortable. I knew there was no way to go but forward, so I prepared myself to run the next gauntlet. It was time to face all the firsts.

As Grant's birthday approached, I wrote a good friend who had lost a son a few years before I lost my boys. I texted her, "Please tell me how to do this. How am I supposed to celebrate the birthday of a boy who is no longer here? I don't think I can do this."

The weekend before Grant's birthday, I went out to my guys' resting place, hoping to brace myself for what lay ahead. I wanted to do a dry run and to figure out in my head and my heart how I would approach the days to come. I walked to the cold, starch-white stone with my babies' names etched on it. The monument was too serious, too formal, too permanent. I knelt on the ground, saw my son's name, Grant D. Decareaux, staring back at me, and broke down. I lay on the ground and wailed right in front of the boys' resting place in the cemetery. I felt like my heart was bleeding out onto the grass. All progress to that point, all revelations God had given me on my journey up until then, meant nothing. There was no past, no future, only present sorrow.

And then I felt it—a tap on my shoulder. Annoyed at first, since the kids were supposed to be waiting in the car for me, I looked up. Completely spent, I expected to see Kate's compassionate face. Instead, I found a woman staring at me with a sincere look of compassion.

"Are you okay?" asked the stranger as she handed me a tissue.

I was embarrassed for a split second. I had thought the kids and I were alone in that section of the cemetery, and I had seen no one around as I lay on the ground in my despair. But in my grief and my brokenness, I had no strength to compose myself. "No, I am not okay," I quietly answered as I sat on the ground.

This compassionate woman held a tissue as she placed her hand on my shoulder.

"It is my baby's birthday next week, and I don't know how I am going to do this," I told her.

Through sobs, I gave her a brief summary of our story, that my husband and two babies lay under us. Her eyes widened as I described the extent of my loss.

When I finished speaking, she calmly said, "I am so sorry."

The woman tried to change the tenor of the conversation and to offer a practical response to my question about how I would get through the next weekend, "You know," she said, "when I come out here to see my mom, I bring apples for the deer. It is something different from flowers, and it makes me feel good to do that. I know when I leave that her spot is visited by deer."

She couldn't have known Grant was an animal lover and how appropriate that idea would be for my boy as well. I thanked her for talking with me and for comforting me, and she was off. I looked back briefly at the stone with my boy's name on it, and I continued to sob. Then I looked up and tried to get my bearings before heading back to my children in the car. The woman was gone without a trace.

I gathered my will to stand and to press on, armed with the idea of bringing apples to Grant on his birthday. The sorrow still weighed heavily on me, but a ray of light shined ever so slightly. I felt sure that God had sent that angel of a woman. Was she an actual angel or a woman used as the hands and feet of Christ? Only God knows, but she had given me the idea I had been searching for, and that encounter helped start a tradition. On all my guys' birthdays from that point on, we would go out with apples for the deer and cupcakes or cookies for the birds.

While the pain hadn't disappeared, a new plan had pushed it to the side.

Grant's birthday had arrived, and I journaled the day.

"Grant's birthday journal, November 3, 2013: Today was shielded and covered. There was sorrow, but we were not consumed. There were tears, but we were not overcome. God is faithful. It all started late last night. I couldn't sleep, so I journaled, and as I was writing a letter to my Grant David, I asked him to intercede for me and to ask the Father for peace. And instantly, I could almost feel a covering melt over me from head to arms to torso to toes—a calm and a revelation—Grant's gift to me and God's gift to me.

"Daughter, God told my spirit, *you celebrate tomorrow not a life that existed eight years and is over. Quite the contrary, daughter; you celebrate the creation of an existence that continues into eternity! Tomorrow, you don't celebrate a beginning and an end; you commemorate Me breathing air into his lungs and a life that continues even now—a beginning and a continuation. You celebrate his beginning, My creation of his being, which transcends his time on earth. We celebrate the creation, the spirit, which in its shell you named Grant David Decareaux. We continue to celebrate him for eternity—here, not there.*

"So we woke. I was so calm and peaceful. We got ready quickly and headed out with apples and cupcakes in hand, grateful for the sunshine. I understood simply enduring the day. It's as if you are facing a gauntlet of some sort, a rocky, hilly path, and you don't contemplate your route. You simply start walking—getting poked in the feet, tripping a bit, but walking steadily forward despite that.

"So that is how I started my day, dragging the load of grief with me, beside me, but walking. We went to the store for balloons and for Wildlife Rescue donations. (In honor of Grant, we donated supplies to the Wildlife Rescue, since Grant was and is an animal lover, a lover of God's creation.) Our next stop was the resting place. I sat and talked to my boy. I sang to him the special song I made up for him as a baby: 'Sweet beautiful baby boy...'

"The kids and I spoke of our favorite things about him: his huge smile, his twinkling eyes, his love and compassion for all living things. I talked to the children about God's revelation to me the night before and about how our guys' bodies will be restored one day when Jesus' second coming makes all things new.

"Then we took out cupcakes, and the kids ate theirs with their brother (leaving one each for Dave, Dom, and Grant and for birds to enjoy). We laid apples out at the resting place so deer could visit the spot and enjoy a treat—a perfect idea for my animal lover that I got from what I believe was an angelic encounter last weekend. Then we walked to the edge of the woods to watch some deer.

"Then we were on to our next stop—the Wildlife Rescue in High Ridge, Missouri, to drop off donations. Then it was on to Shaw's Nature Reserve to walk paths and trails and around a lake in true Decareaux fashion—lovers of the outdoors and God's creation always. Finally, a quick drive-through bite to eat and back to the resting spot for a goodnight to the birthday boy. Then home, where just as the sun was setting, we released nine (for my nine-year-old) balloons into the sky after singing 'Happy Birthday.'

"I am exhausted and emotionally spent. I am so grateful for all prayers said for us today. God opened those vials storing any prayers for this day and rained them down on me. I am grateful.

"I love you, my Grant David, my beautiful, charitable, peaceful, loving, compassionate soul. I can only imagine the ways in which our Father is

using you for His kingdom. You'll have to show me around when I get there, my son, as you did in my dream. I love you, my joy, and I carry that love for you in my heart as motivation every day for doing the best I can to further Christ's kingdom down here and to make you, your brother, and your daddy proud. I will see that sweet smile again! Praise God for His promises! Until that day, my joy."

We had survived Grant's birthday.

God did not allow me to sit long in grief after Grant's day. He knew that there was more to come and that I needed to be active, moving, growing, and learning in between each of the days in the Decareaux birthday season.

November was an interesting month; it brought a few more challenges that I had finally recognized were God's way of keeping my feet on the ground and my head in the game, engaged in life in all its ugliness and all its glory.

On November 8, Finn and I were in a car accident. It was a minor one, but due to the location of the damage, the van was considered totaled. Thankfully, we were not injured. I rented a car until I could secure a new vehicle, and I knew exactly what I was going to buy.

Dave had a Jeep Wrangler when we met. We moved it to the Azores with us and had it until Kate was born. When she was a few months old, we decided we needed a more family- friendly vehicle, and Dave reluctantly sold the Jeep. He had always pined for another one. We could never afford a second vehicle, however, and with our ever-expanding family, our one car had to be large.

When I learned our van was totaled, my first thought was, *God, this van got my family all over Europe. We brought Finn home from the hospital in it. We brought Elise home from the hospital in it. And now here You are, asking me to say good-bye to yet another thing in my life.*

But almost as if God were answering, my next thought was, *I know exactly what this next vehicle is going to be. Dave, I'm getting you that Jeep.*

But I have to get the family-friendly version, since I have kids to shuttle around.

I bought a brand-new Jeep Cherokee weeks later.

One evening I drove to my parents' house in our new vehicle. Proud of Dave's financial foresight, I wanted to show off what he was able to provide for our family even after his passing. My mom and dad and I sat in the Jeep, and as I was showing them all the bells and whistles, a song I had played at the funeral for Dave and the boys came blaring over the radio. Startled, I said, "I never listen to this song; it brings back too many hard memories."

I quickly turned off the radio, since the song was difficult to hear. But my dad, a contemplative look on his face, said something that took my breath away and made me swell with pride.

"Well," he said, "I think that is Dave saying he's happy with your vehicle choice."

December brought bright days and hard days. But they were getting easier to navigate. Kate's twelfth birthday was December 2, and we had a big family celebration on December 8, her parents' thirteenth meeting anniversary. What better way, I reasoned, to celebrate the night I met Dave, that magical night so many years ago, than to spend it celebrating our first baby girl?

For the first time since the tragedy, I had a house full of people for a good reason—for a celebration. I had invited forty-plus family members and friends. I had always liked to entertain, and Kate's party was my first go after the tragedy. Leading up to the party, I had a great sense of achievement while decorating, setting up, cooking, and making the house hospitable.

At one point during the party, I looked out of my living room window at our snow-covered driveway to see car upon car parked in front of my home. I was so grateful at the thought that all the people who had come in those cars were at my house for a celebration, the first in a very long time.

We gingerly celebrated the Christmas season. Festive activities felt unnatural, fake, and forced as the season began. But God took over and reminded my spirit, *Daughter, you still have three beautiful babies with you who need to grow up with the same wonderful memories that you and Dave provided for Dominic and Grant. Kate remembers the past joy, but her spirit needs that joy to continue even now. Finn and Elise were too young to remember when you and Dave made those memories together; they will never know that joy your family can provide if you do not do that for them right now.*

I decided to fully embrace the Christmas season and all the festivities that came with it: we went to see Santa, we bought and put up a real tree, as was tradition, and we listened to Christmas music.

And as Christmas Day approached, I was reminded that another special day in our Decareaux birthday season was on its way.

Dave's birthday had arrived, and I captured the day in my journal.

"Dave's birthday journal, December 22, 2013: How do you say good-bye to your partner, your mate, your friend, your confidant, your supporter, your husband?

"The answer: you don't. You simply say, 'Until we meet again, my friend, my love.'

"Dave's birthday was so quiet. I woke and asked God, 'Father, what do You want me to do to honor Dave on his day?'

"We were supposed to deliver Christmas cards to the vets at the veterans hospital in honor of Dave. The cards were made by Kate, Finn, Elise, me, and Dave's mother. But when I called the hospital to arrange the delivery, I was warned that due to my kids' young ages, they were susceptible to many infections at the hospital. So I decided Kate and I would drop off the notes at the hospital the next day when our babysitter had the babies, which is what we did.

"But that left Dave's birthday open. So I asked the Lord what to do that day. When I woke that morning, I heard so clearly spoken to my spirit, Be a family.

"I felt God telling me to just be a family on Dave's day. So, with that answer in hand and before our outing for the day, I spent the morning writing a letter to Dave in my journal. I recounted some of our favorite memories. I wrote to him what was on my heart—my admiration and love for him, my gratitude for our covenant, our marriage vows, and the unbroken cord between us that surpasses earth and extends into eternity, and my thankfulness to him for what he tried do for our sons. I wrote several pages to Dave; my heart spilled onto paper.

"After that, it was time to honor him on his day. So, as was becoming a new tradition, the kids and I visited the resting place, with apples for the deer and cupcakes for the birds, to celebrate Daddy as we did for Grant and plan to do for Dom. We felt it only fitting, since Dave gave Kate flowers for many of her birthdays, that Kate bring flowers for her daddy. We spent time at the resting place. I talked to Dave and told him how grateful I am for him. I recounted some of the deeds he did for our boys on that trail and made sure he knew how very grateful I am that he gave his everything for our sons.

"Dave made the ultimate sacrifice. He was called to be a father, a husband, a family man—a calling not many men take seriously at all anymore. Dave was known for it. He was a father to the fatherless, a man among men.'

"He was signed up to take not only Kate but her cousin Hailey to the father-daughter American Heritage Girls dance. Hailey's daddy is in heaven, and Dave didn't want her to feel left out, so he was going to have two daughters there that night.

"That night never happened; the dance was scheduled on January 19, 2013. The American Heritage Girls Troop canceled that dance in honor of Dave and the gift he was willing to make for a fatherless girl. He was a community leader, a man of integrity, a man of God.

"I am so grateful God allowed him and me to become partners on this journey. We are still partners in a way; I feel him guide me on so many days. The reunion I seek with him spurs me on. The restoration of what we created here on earth—this partnership, these five lives—will come one day by the grace of God.

"So, after visiting the resting place, we came home to be a family. I turned off the phone, and we ate, played Christmas music, and watched Christmas movies. Finn and I walked our woods out to Daddy's special spot—his burn pile, where he was chopping logs and had his bonfires. He was so proud of his piece of earth, God's creation, he could call his very own. We celebrated his thirty-seven years of existence thus far—thirty-six on earth, one in eternity.

"'I will restore to you the years that the locust hath eaten' (Joel 2:25 KJV).

"I feel God will restore to us these years of separation. I am so grateful for that knowledge and promise. Until then, friend, you've got those two, and I've got these three. I'll press on. You do God's work there, and we'll meet again in the middle. I can only hope to make you anywhere near as proud of me here as I am of you. By the grace and power of our Father, I will. So until then, it's you and me."

Just as with Grant's birthday, God saw us through Dave's. I welcomed the next few days leading up to Christmas to propel me forward on the grief (or perhaps the healing) road.

During that first Christmas season without Dave and our boys, God sent a healing balm over my cracked and bleeding heart and spoke to my spirit. I realized I still had three babies with me whom I could shower with all my maternal love—love I so desperately needed to pour over my boys but could not. The sudden inability to act on that love is fiercely inhuman, brutal, and unnatural. The maternal instinct to hold and to nurture your young is stifled; it's suffocating.

But God is good, and that Christmas season, I found myself grateful beyond words for the three beautiful babies I was still able to love, to nurture, and to hold. I was able to act on those primal instincts, that need to gather, to comfort, and to care for the babies whom God had left with me. I was grateful each time I watched my babies play, heard Kate sing along with a Christmas carol, wrapped gifts for my babies, held them in my arms as we read a story, or laughed as I tickled their precious little bellies. I filled my lungs and my spirit with long, slow breaths to counter the suffocation of the earlier months. The emptiness I felt when I could not hold Grant David or Dominic Christian was filled each time I pulled Finn Nathaniel to my lap, held the hand of Kathryn Elizabeth, or snuggled Elise Marianna. I am forever grateful for a heavenly Father who fills emptiness with a fullness beyond understanding.

God further reminded me of the beauty of the holiday season and how it related to the hope He had cemented in my spirit for an eventual reunion with my family. The whole reason for that hope was Jesus Christ. His birth and His sacrifice on the cross would make our eternal reunion in heaven possible.

From my Christmas 2013 journal:

"God absolutely shielded us from the flaming arrows of the Enemy—despair, sorrow, and loneliness—this Christmas. These arrows threatened to penetrate, but God's armor of love, righteousness, hope, and truth prevailed. All praise to God our Father.

> *Finally, be strong in the Lord and in his mighty power. Put on the full armor of God, so that you can take your stand against the devil's schemes. For our struggle is not against flesh and blood, but against the rulers, against the authorities, against the powers of this dark world and against the spiritual forces of evil in the heavenly realms. Therefore put on the full armor of God, so that when the day of evil comes, you may be able to stand your ground, and after you have done everything, to stand. Stand firm then, with the belt of truth buckled around your waist, with the breastplate of righteousness in place, and with your feet fitted with the readiness that comes from the gospel of peace. In addition to all this, take up the shield of faith, with which you can extinguish all the flaming arrows of the evil one. Take the helmet of salvation and the sword of the Spirit, which is the word of God. And pray in the Spirit on all occasions with all kinds of prayers and requests. With this in mind, be alert and always keep on praying for all the Lord's people. (Ephesians 6:10–18)*

"This Christmas season we stayed very busy. But it was a calm busy, if that makes sense, as opposed to the stressful busy of Christmases past. This season, God's all-surpassing greatness and His gift to us in sending His Son to earth were so very real to me. Dave and I always prided ourselves on making sure our kids knew the true meaning of Christmas each year, but

never has it gone from my head to my heart and seeped into my soul more than this year. Suffering brings unbelievable clarity.

"I know the story of Jesus' birth—we taught it to our kids—but I never really applied the redemptive glory of what that means to my life until now. God tried to have a relationship with mankind, and we ruined it, so He banished man from the Garden of Eden—His intention for life on earth for us. He tried again, but we ruined it again, so He sent the flood of Noah's day. Finally, He tried yet again, and this time He sent us a piece of Himself in human form, in Jesus, to show us how to live and how to love. That is love, unbelievable love. We celebrate that love at Christmas.

"The kids and I had much company, many visitors; we were secret Santa-ed by the homeschool group from the base; we had friends and family send cards, gifts, notes, and messages. We were surrounded by love. We had our babysitter Faye and her boys over for a gift exchange and dinner; we had dear friend Becky and her daughter—my goddaughter Grace—over for a gift exchange; we had my cousins Colleen and Hilary over for a gift exchange and dinner, and we drove through the Way of Lights nativity display at Our Lady of the Snows together. Dave and I did that with our kids last year.

"We had Dave's parents to our home for a three-day visit and Christmas celebration. In addition, the kids and I shopped and wrapped; we listened to Christmas music; we baked and relived memories. Finn and I picked out and drove home our tree. Kate and I unwrapped it and tried to put it up. Daddy knew we needed some comedic relief, so we completely failed at our first attempt to put up our tree without him here with us. But appropriately, it was his dad—Popsie—who was able to get it stood up for us during Nana and Popsie's visit days later.

"Christmas Eve we kept to Decareaux tradition: Chinese food (a family tradition started in 2005) for dinner, wrapping gifts, watching Christmas movies.

"Christmas Day: While there is much more concerning the emotions I felt during those quiet hours alone Christmas Eve night, wrapping gifts while my babies lay asleep, I will keep to the positive, the redemptive, the hopeful, because I was truly not alone. My Father, the Holy Spirit, and Dave and our boys were so thick in the air with me. I felt like I could reach out and touch any one of them. They are nearer than we could ever imagine.

"That morning, Christmas morning, I watched my babies' faces so full of joy. Kate's eyes shone with childlike excitement again as the too-adult look of deep sadness was erased from them in those precious moments. We were a family, the Decareaux family, and it was beautiful.

"Then later that day, we went to spend time with my family—my father, my mother, my sisters and brothers— who have been absolute rocks and pillars of strength for my family this last year. My kids played with their cousins; I visited with my dad.

"We all made memories, knowing Dad is on his own journey, and we must make the most of every single moment with him. Was there sadness? Yes. Did my heart feel like it was falling out of my chest as the cousin gift exchange took place and my boys were not there? Yes. Did my breath catch in my throat as I looked at the tags that read 'To Sarah' instead of 'To Sarah and Dave' for the first time in thirteen years? Yes. But my Father is bigger than that pain. He provided a calm, a covering, a protection that reassured me of the ultimate hope, telling my spirit, My daughter, your Dave, your Dominic, your Grant David are in My presence this Christmas and forever more. There is no greater gift, My child.

"God was there, sending his Holy Spirit to hold me up every moment of that blessed Christmas Day. I serve a mighty God full of supernatural peace. I am grateful.

"So when people said to me this season, 'Merry Christmas,' I could honestly, wholeheartedly agree, 'Yes, Merry Christmas.'

The Christmas season was over. It had been a shielded time of beauty, calm, and peace. What a good and compassionate God we serve. While Christmas was behind me, I knew I still had quite a stack of firsts to overcome. My reserve of endurance was running a bit low, having survived Grant's birthday, Dave's birthday, and Christmas. Knowing I still had Dominic's birthday and the anniversary dates of the tragedy to go, I began the new year with a heavy heart. I recorded my feelings in my journal.

"New Year's journal, 2013–14: New Year's Eve was rough. I had no plans, and even plans for a friend to come by to visit fell through. I was lonely. I was sad. Sure, I played a game with the kids, Kate did my nails, the babies played and watched TV, but my heart was absolutely breaking. I put a smile on my face for my kids, but my heart and soul were in battle against deep sorrow and were not winning. I missed my friend, my Dave; I missed my family, our traditions: New Year's Eve watching movies, having snacks, ringing in the new year together. Even last year, Dave had to work and then came home with a migraine, but Dom and I rang in the new year together, drinking hot tea and watching a documentary on the Mayans. I missed my family, what used to be, more than I have the words to describe. Sorrow was thick, almost suffocating.

"But it is just like my God to provide a fresh start the next day. I woke on New Year's Day and thought, I cannot carry this burden any further today. I have to lay it aside.

I turned on my phone to check messages, and here is what was staring me in the face in a window on the phone.

> *The Spirit of the Sovereign Lord is on me, because the Lord has anointed me to proclaim good news to the poor. He has sent me to bind up the brokenhearted, to proclaim freedom for the captives and release from darkness for the prisoners, to proclaim the year of the Lord's favor and the day of vengeance of our God, to comfort all who mourn, and provide for those who grieve in Zion—to bestow on them a crown of beauty instead of ashes, the oil of joy instead of mourning, and a garment of praise instead of a spirit of despair. They will be called oaks of righteousness, a planting of the Lord for the display of his splendor. (Isaiah 61:1–3)*

"My Father had done it again. He will never leave me stranded in my grief. He always comes to save me as my healer, my provider, and my mighty protector. It was as if He said to the Enemy and the demons of sorrow that day, 'You cannot have My daughter. She is spoken for. She is meant for more than this!'

"So He brought me up out of that darkness and allowed a beautiful, redeemed New Year's Day—a quiet day, calm and peaceful. Finn and I walked through our woods; my kids and I watched movies. Calm.

"Beauty for ashes. Gladness for mourning. Praise for despair. Amen."

While New Year's was not ideal, I had overcome it and was able to eke out a peaceful day. I was grateful to have the year 2013 behind me. I was pleased to put space between me and the day I lost my family—and happy to be moving closer to the day of our reunion.

Then Dominic's birthday was staring me in the face. I readied myself much as I did for Grant's birthday, but with a sureness in my step and a peace in my spirit I did not have before. Grant's birthday had set the bar for all the other birthdays to come. His was the first among the firsts. I had the luxury of hindsight, of having gotten through one of my boys' birthdays, so I approached Dominic's birthday better armed.

"Dominic's birthday journal, January 4, 2014: There is only one way to describe it: calm, absolutely calm.

"We woke that that beautiful sunny, yet cool day and planned to go celebrate our Dom—son, brother, friend. I woke hours before the kids and had a very quiet morning to journal, to reflect, to write pages of memories of birthdays past with my boy. I didn't have any major revelations for Dave or Dom's birthday, as I did for Grant's, because I believe that first revelation was for all my guys, to be applied to each of their birthdays. (We celebrate the day of their coming into existence, an existence that lasts into eternity. Life continues!)

"The kids woke, and we set out with our plans for the day. In much the same fashion as Daddy and Grant, we set out first for their resting place.

"We laid out apples for the deer and cupcakes for our guys, and the babies enjoyed cupcakes right there with them. We talked about what we love about Dom (his humor, his smarts, his smile, his laugh)—not what we remember about Dom or miss about Dom but what we love about Dom, present tense! Our Dom is still very much alive, a very present being. Amen! Then the kids let me have some quiet time to talk to my boy. I sang him the song I made up for him when he was a baby; I can still see him at a year old, swaying to it in my lap, eyes looking into mine, a smile on that sweet, chunky face, as I sang, 'You're my sweet, sweet boy...'

"What a beautiful memory. I cherish it in my heart. I depend upon these memories like the air I breathe; they are medicine for my aching soul, balm for my broken, utterly splintered heart. Memories like that, and the hope and the knowledge of our reunion to come, fill in the holes and the cracks in my soul and my heart. I am grateful. They are sacred, those memories.

There is an eternal sacredness in those sweet moments I was allowed with my family—with my little man, Dominic Christian, my kindred spirit, my friend. What an honor to be that creation's mother. What an honor.

"God created him, as He did his brother, knowing how many days they'd spend on this earth, and allowed me and their daddy to be the ones to make them, to nurture them, to love them, to guide them, to enjoy them, and to find joy in them on earth. I am honored and humbled. Thank you, my God, for such a gift as this.

"After visiting the resting place, we went to the Missouri History Museum in Forest Park, St. Louis, to explore and to do something to honor Dom, something he would love to do with us on earth. While there, it dawned on Kate and me how Dominic knows all the answers to all the mysteries now. He doesn't have to go to a museum but can go directly to the people who lived what we can only learn about. I'm amazed and grateful for that knowledge and for the promise of eternity. I am honored and humbled that my children and my husband—my partner and best friend— are there before me.

"As we were leaving the history museum, we overheard people talking of the blizzard set to hit St. Louis later that evening. Back in the car, I looked up the details of the weather report and decided we had just enough time to honor Dominic with one more outing before the bad weather started.

"We set out for Lone Elk Park, where we had gone for my birthday that past summer. It was such a neat contrast to see that drive-through wildlife park in the winter after seeing it in the summer. We saw seven buffalo and several elk, geese, and deer. That place reminds me so much of Idaho. Dear memories.

"After visiting the park, it was time to head home to beat the pending storm. We drove to a restaurant for a quick early dinner, went back to the resting place to say goodnight to the birthday boy, and then home.

"In honor of Dom, we are donating gifts to the kids who live at Missouri Baptist Children's Home, an orphanage. He had such a heart for children and was so touched and affected by things he saw on the news. I know he would be honored by this gift on his behalf. Calm—calm is the word for my Dom's birthday.

"It's been eleven years since your creation, ten on earth and one so far in eternity. I love you, my son. Until we meet again, my beautiful soul, I will press on in honor of your brother, your daddy, and you. Kate, Finn, Elise, and I will one day kneel with you three before our Father's throne. Anticipating that gives me chills, my son. I love you—such inadequate words. Thankfully, now you can feel my heart to fully understand the meaning behind them. Until then, my boy."

We had survived all birthdays during the Decareaux birthday season. Thankfully, the firsts were coming to a close. But we still had major dates to overcome. With the days inching ever closer, I immersed myself in Scripture, in sermons, in anything offering hope, as if preparing for battle.

The weekend of January 11–13 arrived, and the days proved to be unlike anything I had experienced up to that point. I did not know that emotions could cause such a physical reaction. I was reminded that weekend that sorrow had a taste.

The sorrow from the weekend a year before threatened to return and to undo all the redemptive work God had done in my life that past year, sucking me back into the darkness. I did not give those days the weight they deserved. I thought, *If I can get through birthdays, I can get through anything.*

I was wrong.

I recorded the brutal gauntlet I ran those three days.

"January 11, 2014, journal: Dave and I would have celebrated our thirteenth wedding anniversary. We were blessed to celebrate twelve years together on earth. This year was spent with us temporarily separated. While in heaven, we will not be known as man and wife, but Dave is my best friend. That bond will not change even if our titles for each other do. God gives us marriage as a picture of His love for us, showing how He longs to draw us in to a commitment, a covenant with Him. He wishes for us to stay faithful (to stay out of sin or to ask for forgiveness when we do sin), to get to know Him (to read His Word, the Bible, and to pray), to have a real relationship with Him.

"Dave was my dream come true. Going through some of the texts he exchanged with an old friend the fall before our tragedy, I came across his response when this friend asked what he was up to these days. Dave wrote, 'Living the dream, man, just living the dream.'

"And we were. It made my heart swell to read those words. We were blessed.

"God had brought us on quite a journey; we lived a thirty-year marriage in twelve short ones full of adventure, ups, downs, lessons, valleys, and mountaintops.

"We brought out the best and the worst in each other. We had an authentic relationship. We were always very honest with each other, for better and for worse. What we had was real. He saw me for who I was—the good, the bad, the ugly, and the in between, and I saw him the same way. We were each other's best friend, confidant, and support. He was just that person for me. When something happened, he was the first I wanted to share it with.

"On our anniversary, my heart was so very heavy. It was breaking. I was broken. I knew I needed to get out of the house and to enjoy my children. So, on that cold but sunny day, we drove an hour to Grafton, Illinois, to go bald eagle viewing along the Great River Road and the Mississippi River. We went to Pere Marquette State Park, hiked the trail there, and visited

the museum and the visitors center—a typical Decareaux outing with my kids. We saw about a dozen eagles throughout the day. While we were walking the nature trail, Elise was really holding her own. I said to her, 'Elise, you are doing so great!'

"She responded, 'Yeah, my daddy taught me how to hike on the trail.'

"I was so broken inwardly the entire day, but God didn't allow me to sit in that grief. He demanded I get out, live my day, and celebrate the day I made an eternal covenant with Dave. He wanted me to do this by enjoying our children. And I did. The sorrow was thick, but God helped me navigate through it. Celebrating a wedding anniversary with a mate who no longer shares the earth with you is an unnatural thing. Who do you wish a happy anniversary?

"But God reminded me, 'I am bigger than your sorrow today! There is more to My plan than this day! Survive it, My child. Endure it. You will be forever reunited with your love one day. For now, endure, press on, fulfill My mission for you through the grief you carry. The best is yet to come.'

"God has a beautiful forever in store for all who love Him. These days of sorrow will not last forever.

"On our anniversary, God spoke to me through the song "Strong Tower" by Kutless. As we pulled into the park, there was an adorable little family—a man, a woman, and two small kids—walking through the parking lot. I saw my past. I saw Dave, me, our small Kate, and our small Dom. As he threw snowballs at his wife, she grabbed a child and ran to the car. He caught up to her, and they collapsed on each other in laughter. He took the child from her arms and buckled that child in, while she grabbed the other and did the same. I saw my family—those simple exchanges, those simple moments. Just watching that young family threatened to break down any defenses I had built up for that day. But ever faithful, God said, 'No. You

will not crumble. You still have that family, and you will all be restored one day. Go enjoy your children; Dave is walking right beside you today.'

"January 12, 2014, journal: I got through our anniversary. Now time to face their journey. On January 12, I had no idea that the time line would come back to me, that I would start reliving every moment, every feeling. The sky was dark; yes, the sun was shining, but there was darkness all around me. I sat on my couch, frozen in grief. Not knowing which way to go, I felt like running out of my front door and never stopping. I wanted to run until I could leave those memories, that time line, those emotions, those images of my boys and of Dave, behind me. I wanted to run until I couldn't feel the pain, couldn't feel the fear, the confusion, the aching. I needed to do something to try to erase those things. I wanted to run, yet I couldn't move. My kids were milling all around me, but I felt like the only person on earth. I felt so very alone with no joy at all around me. I didn't see anything but a tunnel of grief going backward to that day.

"That day—the last day I saw them alive. The last day I held my boys, hugged my man. I felt their warmth, their bodies, smelled them, heard them, looked into their eyes and saw them looking back at me. That day—the day I would give anything to have back so I could beg them to stay, beg them not to go, beg them to stay a family. The day Dave made coffee and stood in the doorway of our cabin for a good photo of a vacation pose. The day Dom quietly got ready for the hike with his dad and his brother. The day Grant got ready quickly so he could play with Finn before the hike. The day we all ate Cheerios and I made Dave and the boys pose for photos before starting off on the trail.

"The day the boys ran ahead and started on the trailhead while Finn ran after his daddy, wanting so desperately to go along. The day I ran after him, Dave scooped him up, hugged him, and reassured him they'd be back soon.

The day I took my son as my husband handed him to me, a typical exchange for parents, and started back up the hill to our cabin, with Finn calling out for his daddy and reaching behind me for him. The day I went to the back porch of our cabin to watch them start up the trailhead, to let Finn watch them, to reassure him they'd be back soon. The day I took photos from the cabin porch of them walking the start of the trail. The day I watched them hike out of sight.

"The day I never saw them again alive on earth."

I sat on my couch that day and started writing the time line of events in my journal. I recorded everything—from the morning they left, to what I knew of their hike, to the search, to the next day. That next day. And God said, "Stop!"

He demanded that I put down the pen, and I distinctly heard Him whisper to my spirit, *You have no idea what that journey was like. You have no idea what went on as they trekked. There was more beauty to it than you know, and your imagination is only going to make it worse. There was sacredness to their journey, and I won't let you cheapen it with your imagination.*

God had reprimanded me, so I obeyed. There are things I will not know until I am in eternity. And God has asked me to keep it that way.

I also felt God tell me to stop reliving that day over and over. I felt Him tell me that I could never go back to that day, that I could never undo what had been done, and that all I could do was move slowly, steadily forward. Each day forward is another day closer to them. They had a path, and I have a path. I have things left to accomplish, and I can't do those things in the past. I must march forward with strength, dignity, and hope.

I continued to journal.

"This year has been a physical, emotional, mental, and spiritual battle. Grief is physically exhausting. I can do nothing going back. Going back is death. Going forward is life. God not only wants to sustain me; He wants me to overflow with hope and joy until that final moment of time here when

I will have joy forever—no more sadness, the cloud of grief forever lifted. The light will return to my eyes, never to dim again. God reminds me of all we have to look forward to."

And I got up from my couch.

I decided to take my kids out to get some fresh air. We went to the Pierre Menard historic home in southern Illinois and then to the Fort Kaskaskia ruins nearby. The forty-five minute drive was quiet. Kate slept, and the babies were quiet.

"It's hard to explain what despair and contentment feel like when both occupy my heart at the same time," I journaled.

I felt as if I were on a cloud, like my little car of four people was all that existed on earth. Appropriately, we were the only ones at the Pierre Menard home.

After our afternoon outing, we went home and I felt like working just a bit around the yard. I journaled, "I find such peace working in our yard. Kate took her iPod to the woods and took nature photos. Finn worked outside with me. Elise stayed inside and played. What started as a hard, hard day turned into a quiet afternoon and a peaceful night. The pain didn't go away. I still woke in the night and wanted to relive the time line, speculating what the boys would have been doing at that point last year, but God quieted my spirit and brought sleep back to me. The pain didn't go away. It was simply balanced with peace. God does not remove the pain, but He provides the means to get through it."

"January 13, 2014, journal: Their heavenly birthday. Having gotten through our wedding anniversary on January 11 and their journey on January 12, we have arrived at the one-year mark of their passing, January 13, the anniversary of them entering heaven, their heavenly birthday. The past few days have been a test of physical, mental, spiritual, and emotional endurance.

"I woke this morning planning to try to live the day as normally as possible. I walked my woods and sat at Dave's burn pile where he had cleared brush and chopped wood; his wood pile still sits there, and his clippers lie untouched. The place was cold, dreary, quiet, and dead. Dead trees, bushes. I started crying and asking God, 'What happened to the life of this place? There used to be sun, warmth, children laughing, boys climbing trees, dogs running, Dave working this little plot of land.'

"And after some time, the Father whispered to my spirit, There will be life here again, daughter.

"And I got a little glimpse of life on the other side: sun, warmth, a family laughing, running, and climbing at that spot—us together again one great day, life restored. It made me so hopeful, even if the reason for that hope will be fulfilled only on the other side of the veil.

"I took Kate to horse riding lessons and we went to counseling, but that all felt unnatural. My heart was drawn to one spot—Kate and I headed to the resting place. I wanted to be near my boys as best as I could be. I didn't even know what to say to them, but this was where my heart felt I belonged at that moment. Our wedding anniversary, January 11, marks the start of that weekend and our last nice meal as a family; January 12 marks their journey, and January 13, well, that marks the day they entered glory. But it also marks the start of my journey in dealing with that day.

"I recall lying with my boys one at a time in their beds. I held their baby-boy bodies as best I could, felt their hair, touched their faces, and told each of them, 'Go be with your daddy and your brother. Go be with Jesus. Mommy loves you, and I will see you soon. Rest well, my boy.'

"I said that to each. I wanted to tell them as best I could how much I loved them. But there were no words. It was a sacred moment, one I recall and write about only sparingly, because it is a sacred thing. To be the one to

bring your children into the world and then to tell them good-bye as they exit it - a sacred moment.

"Overall, I felt a calm to the day. I spent time out in my woods to start the day and then tried to keep the day normal with a horse riding lesson for Kate, counseling, visiting the resting place, and finally just home.

"Back home. I paid the sitter and there I sat.

"Here I sit journaling the day. The day is coming to a close. The weekend came and is almost over. I will lie down to sleep, so grateful that the past few days are behind us."

The next day, January 14, 2014, I awoke to a text from an aunt.

"Sarah, thinking of you and the babes today; it is a bright new day, a new start."

She was right, and I felt it in my spirit. I felt a brand-new start. The firsts were behind me, and by the grace of God, I had survived them.

Part III

Learning to Live Again

Chapter 19

A Precarious Calm at the New Year

God knew I needed to attend to earthly matters to keep walking the grief road and to bounce back to normalcy after having conquered the firsts. As January ended, I had to deal with several obstacles, and I was ready for the challenge.

Contractors were finishing work on my basement, and Dave's dad, David Sr., noticed problems with the workmanship when he and Dave's mom visited our home in December of 2013. The contractors balked at completing the work appropriately, and I ended up having to hire a lawyer to get the basement finished. The construction drama added a lot of stress in the last few weeks of January and all the way through February.

My lawyer gave the contractors a March 1 deadline for finishing the job. I was ready to have that part of my life behind me, since I had started hiring companies the previous summer to fulfill the dreams Dave and I had for our house. It had been several long months of tradesmen coming in and out of the house, and I was ready to reclaim my space.

Looking back, I see how God used that situation and the drama over the basement to keep a fire burning in me. To keep the life coming out in me. God allowed circumstances that required me to tap into His strength. I found it hard to feel hopeless when I had to be strong, to be a watchman, a protector, and a provider. What a wise God.

From Journal No. 4:

"Becky came to babysit today. I headed out to hash out deadline details for the contractors with my lawyer. Kate was concerned for me, wondering how the conversation that lay ahead would transpire. As I was walking out of the front door, I heard my dear friend assure my daughter, 'Don't worry, Kate; if anybody can hold her own, it's your mom.'"

I had finally scheduled my hysterectomy for February 2014. Having received my BRCA gene diagnosis several months before, I was ready to tackle the first of two major preemptive surgeries recommended for me to keep cancer from forming in my ovaries or breasts.

But when the situation started to go downhill with the contractors, I canceled my hysterectomy, reasoning, *I have to be strong to be able to fight these guys. I'm not going to be strong if I'm laid up post-surgery.*

I felt a surge of relief come over me as I canceled the surgery that February. I was not 100 percent on board with becoming barren, with having my fertility stripped from me, even though Dave was in heaven and I had no desire to have children with anyone else. The idea of yet another loss, the loss of my fertility, bothered me, and I was glad I canceled my surgery, though I did reschedule it for April.

February brought Valentine's Day and with it, my urge to have a Valentine's Day party for my nieces and nephews. It dawned on me that we had conquered all of the firsts and that we had already survived any holiday we would encounter without Dave and the boys. That realization left me with the desire to start new traditions, to make new memories.

As Valentine's Day 2014 approached, all the "couples only" events were being advertised. Romance was not an area of life I considered applicable to me any longer. It was no longer a part of my life, and I was okay with that. That time in my life was dead, and I was okay with that, too.

One evening at Finn's karate practice, I noticed signs hanging in the lobby advertising a "couples' night" karate class. My aunt Mary was there with my mom and me to watch Finn, and she asked if seeing things like that bothered me. I wholeheartedly assured her they did not. I explained to her that when I was single and in college, I had experienced many lonely nights when my friends had dates and I didn't, so I had trained myself to accept that some things were not applicable to me.

With Dave in heaven, romantic things no longer appealed to me or applied to me, and so I paid no mind to couples-related activities. I was almost emotionless, almost robotic. I had simply trained myself to block certain things from my consciousness.

I jovially prepared for my Valentine's Day party that year, packing goody bags and baking treats. As I did this, my mind drifted to Valentine's days past.

Dave and I were not huge on Valentine's Day. Neither of us felt a need to make a big deal of our love for one another on a certain day. That said, the romantic in me enjoyed at least acknowledging the day.

We had been married for only a month on our first Valentine's Day together and were at McGuire Air Force Base in New Jersey, completing the paperwork needed for me to move with Dave to the Azores. We lived on base for a few weeks. During that time, Dave drove me to the Jersey Shore, showing me around the area. We spent our first Valentine's Day together in nearby New York City. We walked the streets of Manhattan for hours, taking in all the touristy sights, strolling through Central Park, taking pictures, and otherwise enjoying our blissful day together.

Dave went to pay respects at the Dakota apartment building where John Lennon had made his entrance into eternity many years before.

We stopped for dinner at a delicious hole-in-the-wall Mediterranean restaurant. Dave and I were famished and ordered more than we could eat. Dave, however, surprised me and finished his meal. I could not finish and politely asked for a to-go container for my leftovers, much to the disdain of our waitress. Surprised at her dirty looks and sighs at my request, Dave and I realized that perhaps she was insulted that I did not finish my meal. Her questions—"You not like? Why you not eat?"—confirmed our suspicions.

Unwilling to insult the waitress or the cook any further, I again asked for a container so Dave and I could continue our Valentine's evening. When the waitress returned with the container, she brought with her two valentines—one for Dave that read, "Happy Valentine. Have good evening. Thank you," and one for me that read, "To you."

Convinced that I had offended the restaurant staff, a theory confirmed by the halfhearted valentine, I was anxious to be on our way and to redeem the rest of a blissful day. As we walked the streets of Manhattan the rest of that evening, Dave got a kick out of reminding me that the waitress "loved him" and not me. We laughed as Dave repeatedly looked at me and said, "To you."

Dave put a perfect period to the night, however. He bought me a single red rose from a street vendor as we made our way to the car for the drive back to the base that would end an unbelievable day spent together.

That beautiful Valentine's Day came on the heels of a much different Valentine's Day a year earlier while I was still living at college.

In 2000, I was near the end of my college career, almost having earned my degree in education. That February 14, I found myself alone in my dorm room. All my girlfriends had accepted dates and were off on Valentine's outings. A secret admirer had sent me a rose, and another guy had asked me out on a date for that evening, but I had no romantic feelings for this young man, so I had declined the offer and had elected to stay in my dorm room and watch a movie. But what I had thought would be a peaceful evening turned into a lonely one as I wondered why, at twenty-two years old, I hadn't had a boyfriend yet. I already knew the answer. I was extremely picky and brought that lonely evening on myself. But I felt sad nonetheless and decided to call home and talk to my parents.

My dad answered. He asked why I was in my room instead of out having fun, and I explained to him that I didn't have a date and why this was so. Though I didn't have a "deep conversation" kind of relationship with my dad, I found myself spilling my heart out to him and crying big tears as I explained my loneliness and my regret that I was so picky. My dad listened patiently, and when I was finished, he answered with words I will never forget.

"Sarah, I know one day you are going to meet a man, you are going to fall in love, and you are going to get married and have kids. Just hang in there."

I hung up feeling better about my situation. My dad was not an emotional person and not one for touchy-feely talk, so when he spoke those words, I took them as gospel. I knew deep within my spirit that if my dad felt led to say those words to me they would come true.

One year later to the day, I was in New York City with my brand-new husband, traversing the streets of Manhattan as newlyweds.

My mind returned to the present as I finished packing goody bags that Valentine's Day in 2014 and then drifted a little further down the time line to February 14, 2012.

Married eleven years, Dave and I were living in Germany. We had five small children and were staying very busy as Dave worked long hours and I homeschooled the big kids. Finn was a toddler and Elise a tiny baby. Our days were filled with diapers, tantrums, lots of hugs and snuggles, but also many tears, sibling fights, and crazy family meals.

I had done my best to muscle through that Valentine's Day, teaching the kids, making a Valentine craft, and baking some kind of goody while trying to throw together a family meal. After the family had eaten dinner and Dave and I had put the kids to bed, we sat on the couch and breathed a sigh of relief that the busy day was behind us. We intended to spend the rest of the evening relaxing. While Dave and I were in what we called the parenting trenches, we were quite content to celebrate Valentine's Day simply by enjoying the quiet after our wee ones had gone to bed for the evening. Before we opened up our laptops to dive into the evening's relaxation, however, Dave looked at me, eyed my outfit up and down, and without batting an eye, said, "Your shirt's on inside out."

I looked to see that indeed I had worn my shirt inside out all day and hadn't had a clue, since I was knee deep in teaching, cooking, cleaning, and otherwise mommying.

"Awesome," I exhaustedly responded. And making a feeble attempt to be festive, I added, "At least it's a red shirt. Happy Valentine's Day."

As my mind returned to the present and I set out the treats and put up the decorations for the party the next day, I was grateful for sweet family memories—whether it was my mom putting valentines on our pillows in my childhood or Dave and I going on a rare date to celebrate Valentine's Day. I found peace in the realization that Valentine's Day applied to more than just couples. It was a day to show love, and I was looking forward to giving my family and friends a fun party.

March came, and the contractors had finished the basement; my brother had started painting it. My hysterectomy was rescheduled for early April, so he was anxious to finish the painting before my surgery.

I felt as if I had turned a corner on my grief journey that early spring. I felt lighter and more content. I was starting to accept my new life with the assurance that I knew where Dave, Dom, and Grant were and that I merely had to press on until a reunion. I no longer felt like I was crawling through each day as I did the first year; some days, I felt joy. The kids and I spent our early spring days "doing school" and continuing with our extracurricular commitments: karate, horse riding, church activities, and gymnastics. Kate and I continued to see the Christian counselor we had started seeing a month after the accident.

I continued listening to video sermons in the evenings as my wind down-routine before bed, and we continued to get together with friends and family. We walked our woods and worked in our yard. Life was falling into a welcome routine.

Little did I know the peace in my spirit would be a brief reprieve. I was content as long as I avoided certain situations, certain triggers, and certain memories. I would soon learn that God was not content to let me stay stagnant. He was about to require me to peel back the protective layers, and while that would be painful, I needed to continue walking my grief journey. There is no progress in stagnant.

With my spirit, at least for that season, in a peaceful place, I decided I would have a spring party, a basement unveiling, after my surgery. Knowing my surgery was right around the corner in early April, I decided to have the party around Easter time and excitedly started planning for it.

Spring came, bringing the calm and the new beginnings it had brought the year before. The kids and I spent many days outside, planting, weeding, and planning what vegetables we would grow in our gardens in the upcoming weeks. I took pride in getting the house and the yard in order for my party.

I spent many evenings having dinner and conversation with my mom. She was a pillar for me, a rock, and a sounding board. I looked forward to Finn's karate nights and to the kids' church club night, knowing that meant dinner with Mom and that I could share my latest insights and struggles with her.

I was not whole, but I was content. I was willing to take what I could get and was grateful for the peace I had found since the new year had started. I was in precarious waters, but as long as no one rocked the boat, I reasoned I could survive that way for the rest of my life. But grief is not a calm ocean; it is a rolling sea, and the waters were about to get stormy.

One April afternoon, Kate and I were playing hooky from doing schoolwork. I got a babysitter for Finn and Elise, and Kate and I went to see a film at the local theater. It was the first time after our tragedy that I had allowed myself the joy of going to a movie. I had not allowed myself several past joys since Dave, Dom, and Grant had gone to heaven. Looking back, I see that I felt I needed to be punished. I thought I wasn't allowed happiness, wasn't allowed to experience the things that used to bring our family joy.

I had stopped taking photos as voraciously as I had done before our accident. I had virtually stopped reading despite having been an avid reader. I had stopped going to movies, intending to shut out the outside world and to focus on (or to wallow in?) the reality of my new life. Early on my grief journey, I had denied myself some of the basic joys of life. For instance, I no longer cooked the way I had. I cooked basic meals for the children and to entertain company, but I did not enjoy the cooking process, exploring new recipes, or experimenting with new dishes as Dave and I had done. The thought of having to do it alone sucked the joy out of me.

My cooking had vastly improved from my burnt bacon days, and Dave and I enjoyed being in the kitchen together. Dave was an accomplished cook and enjoyed the process—from shopping for the ingredients, to researching the perfect recipe, to preparing and cooking the meal. He liked treating the kids and me to homemade New Orleans-style beignets, "from scratch" jambalaya, and pastas—often making the noodles from scratch. He also tried out his mom's pot roast recipe and served his signature cold pasta salad. (In our Italy days, it was a staple at any function to which we were invited.) He and Dominic loved seafood, which they enjoyed several times a month. Dave would come home with a bag of shrimp, breading it and frying it up as a special treat for them to share with homemade fresh-cut french fries.

Almost every weekend during our time in Germany, Dave would wake us up in the morning with eggs, bacon, and biscuits, a breakfast we would enjoy around the table as a family. Actually, it was labeled brunch, since another thing Dave liked to do was sleep. (As did I; we were quite compatible that way.) On weekends, when Dave did not have to work ten- to twelve-hour days and fight Stuttgart traffic for an hour each way as he did during the week, he slept in. Sometimes he would make omelets, and still other times, a stack of pancakes. But at least one morning of each weekend we lived in Germany, we were almost guaranteed to awake to the sounds and smells of Daddy busily making us all brunch.

I treasured that tradition, not only because Dave treated his family so well but because I grew up having my dad make my family eggs and bacon many Sunday mornings. Besides the fact that Dave was making beautiful memories for our kids, this was a reminder of the times my own family spent around the table when I was a kid. Dave had many memories of his dad doing the same thing—cooking an eggs-and-bacon breakfast—many weekends in his childhood, so it was a welcome tradition all around.

Family time around the table was important to Dave and me. When the kids were little, Dave and I would generally feed them, put them to bed, and then enjoy a nice meal at the coffee table together. But we started eating as a family in England, did it more often in Italy, and by the time we were in Germany, we were having family meals at the dining room table nearly every night. This gave us a chance to catch up after a busy day of work and homeschooling and helped the family bond. Dave and I had grown up eating family meals around the kitchen table, and this was a tradition we wanted to impart to our children. And many times in Germany, when Kate, Dom, and Grant were older, Dave and I relaxed after a well-made meal as the kids, even at ten, nine, and seven years old, shared the responsibility of clearing the table and washing the dishes. Dave and I would then tend to babies Finn and Elise and get them ready for bed.

I had signature dishes myself, had belonged to a cooking group in England, and even started one in Germany. I also enjoyed the cooking process. While in Italy, Dave and I took an Italian cooking class together the summer I was pregnant with Finn. On many nights in our Germany days, we'd put the kids to bed and sit down to one of our TV shows with my bacon-and-blue-cheese potato treats and a bottle of wine. Bacon seemed to be a theme throughout our culinary adventures, and it certainly was a family favorite. As they say, the fastest way to a man's heart is through his stomach.

One evening, Dave and I were arguing about something. (I can't recall what, but as with many of our silly fights, this one was completely forgettable). I was usually the one to hold a grudge, but this time Dave was not budging. He eventually went into shutdown mode and stopped talking to me, ignoring my pleas to continue to hash it out. I tried talking anyway, I tried making him laugh, and I tried pouting, and nothing was working. But I had one more trick up my sleeve. After waiting a few hours to let the dust settle, I walked into the kitchen and quietly began making my bacon-and-blue-cheese potato treats. I said nothing to Dave, who sat just beyond the kitchen on the couch in the living room. After slicing the potatoes, I began frying the bacon, filling the house with the sounds and the smells of something delicious being made. Sure enough, I sensed a presence behind me. I turned to see Dave, scowl still on his face, drawn to the kitchen.

"So what's going on in here?" he asked.

And almost before he finished the question, both of us broke into huge grins and eventually giggles as we realized that the power of a snack enjoyed together far outweighed whatever score we felt we had to settle with each other. That evening, Dave and I enjoyed our treat and some wine, snuggling up on the couch, the argument far behind us.

Our love of cooking was rubbing off on our children, and for our tenth anniversary in 2011, Kate treated Dave and me to a spaghetti meal, complete with garlic bread and salad. She was nine years old. I had bought the ingredients for a spaghetti-and-meat-sauce meal to celebrate our anniversary that night, but Kate asked if she could make it and quickly got to work. I have the most adorable photos of her boiling the noodles, browning the ground meat, and tossing the salad. She also made place settings with "Happy Anniversary" written in her little-girl style and put them on the table. Then we sat down as a family to a meal prepared by our first baby girl to celebrate ten years of marriage.

Food was a big part of our lives and a part of many dear Decareaux family memories.

After our tragedy, I found it difficult to cook a nice meal when there were so few of us to enjoy it. Besides, Kate was (and is) a picky eater, and the babies ate toddler-size and preschool portions. I felt like I would be the only one eating a well-prepared meal. So, to avoid the sadness I knew that would bring, I didn't cook elaborate meals.

I felt much the same about movie theaters. Our family used to enjoy going to the movies together. It was hard for me to imagine going alone or with only a child or two when Dave and I often used to pile the whole brood into the van to go see a movie. So allowing myself an outing to go see a film with Kate was another step on my journey, another victory, and a welcome afternoon.

As Kate and I ate lunch before the movie, I got a phone call from the hospital where I was supposed to have surgery in a week's time. The representative told me that when the hospital called to verify that I was insured, the insurance company said that my coverage was terminated. I was not covered for surgery, nor were the children and I insured. I was confused and a little panicked, but I decided not to allow the potential bad news to destroy the small victory I had won by taking Kate to a movie that afternoon. I decided to enjoy the movie and to tackle the issue the next day.

I made several phone calls the next day and learned that paperwork was not properly filed a year before after Dave's passing. In fact, the insurance company did not know that Dave had passed. The company had been covering the children and me for more than a year, assuming Dave was still a federal employee. Knowing Dave's benefit package allowed the children and me continued coverage under his insurance, I was oblivious to any problems. Dave's HR department promised to get the matter straightened out right away. I was indeed still covered, and filing the proper paperwork would fix the glitch. I was calmed and assured all would be okay, but I canceled my surgery again, since I feared the glitch would not be fixed in time.

The children and I were uninsured for five weeks until the glitch was fixed, and while everything turned out fine, the hiccup in coverage, coupled with the fact that I had also canceled the surgery in February due to the house construction mess, made me wonder whether I was supposed to have the hysterectomy. I did not reschedule the surgery.

With no surgery on my calendar, I was even more excited at the prospect of what I had dubbed my "basement unveiling" party. I had always loved entertaining and opening my home, and I enjoyed it even more now, since it made my home feel less lonely. The absence of Dave,

Dominic, and Grant left a huge hole in our home, and I welcomed any opportunity to make our house come alive with company, noise, laughter, joy, family, friends, and celebration.

One afternoon, as my brother Richard was in my basement painting, I went downstairs to join him for his lunch break. In the several weeks he had spent at my house, we had many chats. I found myself talking to him on many mornings while Kate did independent schoolwork upstairs and while Finn and Elise were playing. I welcomed the company and was always eager to talk. We discussed many things: my family, his family, my kids, and his girls; we talked about history, events in the news, and each other's plans for the future.

That afternoon as we were talking about Dave, I shared humorous stories from our marriage and recalled our silly arguments and our adventures together. I finished one story by saying, "Dave was an unexpected extra just because God loves me."

"What do you mean?" my brother asked.

I explained to my brother how I had always felt called to singleness. Even as a teenager and a young adult, I felt quite content not dating. I was a bookworm, a studious teen, and was satisfied with my small circle of friends. Sure, I had crushes like most young ladies did, but I felt in my spirit that God was calling me to a single lifestyle.

I sometimes felt lonely as a younger woman, but I was extremely picky about what I was looking for in a man. I reasoned that since I couldn't find exactly what I wanted, I would stop looking and would stay single. While being a wife and a mother were among my life goals, the process of dating and of finding a mate seemed too daunting and seemed like too much work. I was fine going to the movies alone or with a group of friends; I had no problem sitting at a restaurant alone. I made the most of what I thought would be a solitary lifestyle. I made plans for my life. I would finish my education degree, teach for several years, and become a college professor by the time I was thirty.

But then I met Dave that cold December night, and everything changed. At twenty-three years old, I had my first boyfriend, and he became my husband.

After Dave had gone to heaven, I decided that I was indeed called to the single lifestyle but that God had gifted me with Dave because He is a good God and knew the brief joy we would bring each other. I reasoned that the children Dave and I made were meant to be made and to have a piece of me and a piece of him.

I consoled myself on my early grief journey by telling myself that I was always meant to be single but that God allowed Dave and our children to enter my life because He loved me. Now here I was, back to the singleness meant for me. But in addition to the life I pictured for myself as a young woman, I got to raise the three beautiful children left on earth with me.

I tried to tell myself that I was meant to be single, that I was good at being single, and that I would be able to do life without a man. But Dave was a good one. We had a beautiful, authentic marriage; we had a blessed relationship, a precious bond. I had had a taste of a good man, and it made being without one much harder to swallow. It made my "gift of singleness" more difficult to accept when I knew the beauty of togetherness.

My brother went back to painting and our talk had ended, but the conversation stuck with me long after I had walked back upstairs and joined Kate at the dining room table to continue her schoolwork. In the back of my head, I couldn't shake the realization that Dave had opened something in me. He had showed me the beauty of togetherness, of companionship, of true partnership, and I wasn't quite sure how to turn that off now that I thought I had been called back to singleness.

Chapter 20

Apprehensively Acknowledging the Void

I awoke on a spring morning in early 2014 to a blessed memory.

While living in a farmhouse on the grounds of a church in Illinois in 2007 after our move from England, Dave and I could not afford a washer or a dryer. So, before Dave headed for the night shift at work, we spent many an afternoon doing laundry at the local Laundromat. While our three small kids played with toys or colored in coloring books, Dave and I passed the hours playing a game. We had made it up one day while sitting, bored to tears, waiting for our laundry to finish.

It was a memory game. Since we missed our globe-trotting life so much during those months we lived in the farmhouse, we relished any opportunity to recall our past adventures. Travel was so much a part of our identity as a family.

One afternoon, while folding clothes at the Laundromat, Dave looked at me and said, "We had a baby here, we drove all over on day trips here, and we got a dog here. What place is it?"

"What?" I asked, confused yet intrigued by his challenge.

"I gave you three clues. It's a place we have lived in or visited. Try to figure out which one I am talking about," he answered with a grin on his face.

"Hm," I said as I folded laundry. "England is out of contention because we had no babies there. It could be the Azores because we had Kate there, drove all over exploring there, and got Bo and Cleo there, or it could be Idaho because we had Grant there, drove all over that state, and got Rex there." (I was referring to a Lab we had bought after moving to Idaho when Dom was a baby. We had Rex for the two years we lived there, and upon our move to England, gave him to a dear family that still had him in 2012, the last time we checked. Dave had pined for a Lab ever since and was overjoyed to get Bear years later when we returned to the States.)

"So which is it?" Dave asked.

"I need an additional clue," I said.

We decided that the rules of our new game allowed us to ask three yes/no follow-up questions or to ask for three additional clues before we had to guess the answer. We were allowed to make only one guess, so we needed to get as much information as possible through additional questions or clues.

"We swam there."

I told Dave that clue was no good, since we had swum at both the ocean coast swimming holes of our island home and in the lakes of the Idaho wilderness.

"Okay, we had company visit us there."

I told Dave that this clue was also no good, since his friend Mike came to see us in the Azores while on assignment with the air force for a few days, and my parents visited us in Idaho.

I decided to ask a yes/no question: "Did you try a new food here?"

"Yes," Dave responded, and I instantly knew the answer: "Azores!"

Since Dave had tried octopus while living in our island home, I knew the answer could not be Idaho, where we stuck to much more American fare and had many traditional barbecues.

"Yes! You got it!" he said with a laugh.

We chuckled at our newfound entertainment and played many rounds of our game as we folded laundry that afternoon. That game became a staple at the Laundromat.

As my mind drifted back to the present, I was reminded of how Dave and I so often turned situations around to our benefit and of how we transformed afternoons at the Laundromat into family fun as we recalled sweet family memories.

At the end of April, I had my spring party, my "basement unveiling." I had invited my parents, all of my siblings and their significant others, my cousins, a few good friends and their husbands, my aunt Mary, and my uncle Tim. I had a house full of family, friends, nieces, nephews, and kids, and the gathering was just what I needed to celebrate the new space in my house. I enjoyed preparing for the party, cleaning, cooking, and decorating.

As with Valentine's Day, I figured that I would ward off any waves of grief that might be lurking around the corner by making memories, by creating opportunities to be surrounded by family and friends, and by starting new traditions. I went on the offensive against my grief.

We visited for several hours that afternoon and evening in late April, and the party spilled out onto my new patio. We had a wonderful time, but I felt something rising in my spirit - I felt a hint of sadness. Looking at all the people surrounding me, I couldn't help but wish that Dave were hosting the party with me and that my boys were running around with their cousins. I hoped my offensive against grief did not backfire and produce more sorrow.

By the end of the evening, I couldn't have felt more alone. I saw all the joy around me but knew it wasn't mine to touch. I saw my good friends and their husbands in blissfully routine exchanges—handing children to each other with a quick kiss on the cheek, displaying the familiarity of couples who sit so close together you almost can't tell where one person stops and the other starts.

Remembering when that joy and familiarity were mine, I broke inside.

After everyone had gone home, I prayed and journaled, "God, why did I do that to myself? Why did I have couples over here? Why did I throw it in my own face that I do not have that partnership anymore?"

At my counselor's office a few days later, I recounted the events of that night and my sadness and journaling afterward.

"I can't understand why God throws it in my face that He took that away from me, that partnership, that companionship," I told her, recalling the simple exchanges between husband and wife that broke my heart.

And she said this - "Don't you think, instead of God throwing it in your face to hurt you, He is reminding you how beautiful that is? How beautiful that can be—that partnership, that relationship, that togetherness?"

"That is not for me anymore," I replied angrily. "I have a husband and I don't need another one!"

I had made great strides that new year and was not going to let one setback undo my progress. But I knew that something was shifting inside of my spirit; the layers were starting to peel. My path was getting rocky. Still, I was unwilling to accept the shift myself, much less to allow someone else to suggest a solution.

Whether I was ready to face it or not, I was starting to feel intense loneliness with my husband gone. This was not grief but the everyday emptiness of living alone. Up to that point, I had told myself that this was okay, that this was my lot in life, that I had been called back to singleness. However, something was shifting in me.

I had spent the first year after the tragedy trying to function again. I was worried about basic survival and the care of my children. Entering the second year, I had resigned myself to my new situation and had resolved to live alone. I did many projects, had family parties, had company over, went on trips, and shopped, all in an attempt to fill the void created by the absence of Dave, Dominic, and Grant. While I was glad to have my basement finished and to have honored Dave, I faced a problem with the projects completed. Now what?

One night after the basement was finished, I went downstairs, sat on the couch, turned on the fireplace, and enjoyed the scene around me. My eyes drifted to a framed picture on a shelf next to the fireplace. The crayon drawing was a layout of the basement that Dave and I had drawn the fall we moved into the house. That first week in the house, we sat down one afternoon and used a purple crayon to plot out on a piece of scrap paper our dreams for finishing the basement.

I used that design as my guide when I finally had the basement finished. When the job was completed, I framed our crayon blueprint and set it on the shelf next to the fireplace as a way of honoring Dave and his wishes for our home.

But as I sat in the warmth of the fireplace and the glow of satisfaction vanished, I had an overwhelming thought. *Now what?*

I was overcome with an anticlimactic sensation as I sat alone in the basement that evening. I thought, *Sure, the projects on the house are finally completed, but who do I share them with? Who do I sit in front of this fireplace with? Now what am I going to do to keep myself busy, to keep myself distracted? Now what?*

My spirit acknowledged the void in my life, even if my head and my heart were unwilling to face it. At only thirty-six years old, I found myself looking in the mirror, thinking, *I am still young, and I still feel young. I have the burdens of an old lady, but I am not an old lady! I have energy. I have fire. What do I do with it?*

I reflected on what I had discovered about holidays so far in the new year—Valentine's Day, St. Patrick's Day, and Easter. I felt secure and fulfilled in being able to celebrate with the kids I still had with me. I was still exercising my maternal instinct. But I thought about the other void in me. Not only did I lose children in the accident, but I lost a husband, my mate, my partner, my friend, my companion. I started to acknowledge, if only slightly in my spirit, that I had no partner whom I could give love and who would give me love in return.

I missed the simple things: having a partner in my house, someone to talk to, someone to discuss decisions with, someone to laugh with, to plan with—someone to live life with. I started to entertain the possibility that perhaps I had not been called back to singleness for the rest of my life, after all. But as quickly as the thought entered my mind, I banished it.

As I sat by the fireplace that evening, I realized sometimes I didn't know whom to mourn and when. Some days I was a mourning mother, and other days I was a lonely widow. On the toughest days, I was both. Some days the grief at losing my boys was so great that I couldn't breathe, while on other days, my missing my mate threatened to undo me. Sometimes the grief was stilled as I attended to earthly struggles.

I found much solace in retreating to sermons in the evenings. Part of my bedtime routine was to curl up on my couch to a sermon by JD Farag or Perry Stone. I consumed anything I could find about biblical prophecy, end times, and the second coming when Christ would gather and redeem His people and the fallen earth. I found great consolation in awaiting that blessed day when I got to heaven by my passing or by Jesus' return to earth to rapture His people. I hung every hope on that eventual reunion with my family and discounted the possibility of feeling alive on earth again. I had found a comfortable middle ground on my grief journey. I was functioning. It was too much to ask to also feel alive.

My confusion over the shift in my spirit, coupled with the loneliness my party brought as I watched the couples in blissful exchange, sent me into a tailspin that spring.

Chapter 21
An Answer

Despite the progress I had made, the darkness constantly threatened to overtake me, and that April it did. The gloom was brought on by my confused feelings as I watched the couples at my spring party, and it got worse from there.

The school year was nearing a close, and we started to receive invitations for high school and college graduations and parties to follow. One invitation brought tears to my eyes. It included a poem the student had written about her life dreams when she was in junior high and about how she was now fulfilling those dreams as a graduate. It was a precious sentiment, but reading that poem sent me into darkness as I sat on my back porch steps one spring afternoon sorting through my mail.

"God, my boys had dreams!" I said aloud. "My boys were going to be many things! Dominic was so intelligent, Father. He was extremely bright; he was more observant than most adults I know and could carry on a conversation better than any children I know. Grant was the most knowledgeable child about dinosaurs and animals I had ever met. He taught me things, God. He taught me how to pronounce names of extinct creatures; he was so gifted, unusually gifted, in all things animals. Why, God? Why would You bother gifting my boys beyond a normal child's intelligence just to take them back home so early? Why didn't You leave them here to lead a full life with those gifts You had given them in abundance?"

Already despondent and speaking to God through tears, I started to get angry.

"You have promised us abundant life, God. Where is my boys' abundant life? Where is Dave's abundant life? Where is my abundant life living with this grief now? Where is Kate, Finn, and Elise's abundant life living here now without a father? You promised us abundant life, God, and I don't see it! No, what I see, God, is that You let two very promising little boys die out on a trail when they were just trying to spend time with their daddy; I see that You let a man full of love, life, and generosity crawl to his death on the ground in a forest. Where is their abundant life, God?"

I was so angry. I ran down my porch stairs, not knowing where I was going or what I was doing, just knowing I needed to move. I could not sit still on my stairs, yelling at God. I needed to run. I was boiling over with anger and despair. I was desperate, and my spirit demanded answers. I reached my driveway, not knowing where to turn.

I got in my car and turned on the Christian station. The praise songs blaring through the speakers were usually comforting, offering me a lifeline and providing prayers from my heart to the Father. Now I felt as if those praises were jeering at me; those prayers the artists offered to God were just wishful thinking. "What is the point, God? What is the point of praising You?" I demanded. "You let things like this happen. You snuffed out bright young lives that could have been something for You here on earth, could have done great things."

I was losing my grip on reality and coming undone. My only foundation, the only sure footing I had felt since Dave, Dom, and Grant entered heaven, was slipping out from under me, and I started to doubt my beliefs and to question God about what I saw as His contradictions.

"It says in John 10:10, 'The thief comes only to steal and kill and destroy; I came that they may have life and have it abundantly.'"

I quoted His own words back to Him from Scripture and demanded, "You said You came so we could have abundant life. Where are my boys' abundant lives?"

I was at the end of my rope. I pounded my hands on the steering wheel and screamed and cried until I exhausted myself. Then I laid my head on the steering wheel and whimpered softly with my eyes closed, my energy spent. My will was broken.

As I sat with my spirit crushed under the weight of my anger and my weakness, I sensed something off to the left through my closed eyes. I could detect a light becoming ever brighter. I slowly lifted my head and immersed myself in the glow that was overtaking the darkness under my closed eyelids. I turned my head to the left, to the source of the light, and opened my eyes. Before me was the most glorious sky I had ever seen.

To the west, the sun peered out from behind billowing white clouds, glowing ever more brilliantly as it emerged. As I watched the sky, something happened in my spirit. I felt that light was an answer to me. I felt a communication and an assurance from that sky. God was speaking to my spirit.

I did promise you abundant life, My daughter. I promised all My children abundant life. I promised your Dave, your Dominic, and your Grant abundant life. I promised you abundant life; I promised your Kate, Finn, and Elise abundant life. Daughter, abundant life is not limited to what you can see with your eyes. Abundant life goes beyond your earthly realm and continues on to eternity. I never promised life on earth would be painless. What I did promise you is that you would have abundant life. Your life encompasses more than just the time you are on earth. Trust Me, My daughter, your boys are reveling in abundant life even now. They are living life to the fullest right here in My care. I did promise Dave, Dominic, and Grant abundant life, and they have received it. That life started on earth under your care and now continues here under Mine. Those gifts I gave them are at their fullest capacity here. Those gifts weren't wasted. They continue to grow in them, to hone them, and to use them here. Don't limit yourself to thinking that abundant life can only happen there; it is at its fullest here.

Just as surely as I felt that light was a communication from God and heard that word from Him in my spirit, I was certain at that moment that God does indeed keep His promises. The fulfillment of those promises may look a lot different than what we expected, but He keeps them in His way and in His time.

As I got out of my car, dried my tears, and headed for the house, I was assured of something else. My God hears me when I call to Him. My God hears me in my despondency. My God is always with me in my pain. Like a father watching as his child throws a fit and demands answers, He let me vent my frustrations, my doubts, and my anger, waiting for the moment when I was ready to fall back into His arms. And when I could not hold up any longer under my own will, He got my attention with the light. He answered my spirit and soothed my soul.

That night, in my emotional exhaustion, I fell asleep on the couch as Elise snuggled up next to me. When we awoke the next morning, Elise said, "Mommy, I had a dream with Daddy last night."

I immediately turned all my attention toward her, having found much comfort in her dreams of her dad and her brothers since our tragedy.

"What happened in the dream, Elise?' I asked anxiously.

"Daddy was on a boat, and he waved at me," she said, "and then he got off the boat and came to our house. We held hands and I showed him all around our house. Then he came to the couch to say hi to you, but you were sleeping and didn't hear him, so he lay down next to you and hugged you."

I immediately started crying. As the tears welled in my eyes and slowly ran down my cheeks, I thanked my girl for telling me her dream and grabbed her up in a hug. Then she was on her way, ready to start her day, seemingly without a care in the world.

I sat a moment on the couch, recalling everything Elise had told me about her dream. I was overwhelmed with love, with gratitude, and with the realization that my God and my family were far closer than I could ever imagine. As I got up from the couch to start my morning, I wondered how much of that encounter was a dream and how much of it was a glimpse our Father had given my baby girl of her daddy in bliss usually unseen. But spotted that morning by my pure, precious daughter.

Chapter 22
Another Summer

As spring came to a close and summer began, the kids and I stayed busy. We went on day trips to the surrounding area, had many play dates, brought our school year to a close, and planned possible vacations. But the intense loneliness that I had started to feel in April remained beneath the surface. This new sensation was still stirring in me. I was increasingly dissatisfied with the place where I found myself and knew it was time to go to the next level of healing. I didn't know how to do that. I didn't even know what that next level looked like, but I knew something was changing in me.

I put these thoughts on hold, however, as the kids and I prepared to spend time with Dave's family, and to welcome them to our home. His parents and his aunt and uncle came to see us that summer in back-to-back visits. Later in the summer, the kids were also able to travel with Dave's family to Oklahoma to meet up with extended Decareaux family, and to meet their new baby cousin.

Living in Louisiana, Dave's mom and dad—Nana and Popsie to the kids—were able to see the children and me a few times a year since Dave, Dom and Grant had gone to heaven. We kept in touch with notes, cards, photos, phone calls, and text messages. The kids were always willing to pose for adorable photos, to make homemade cards and crafts, or to send a quick text to Nana and Popsie. We looked forward to Nana's seasonal goody boxes and to shopping for and packing gifts in return. These exchanges with all our family and friends across the miles, were among the many pockets of joy we found on our journey.

The kids and I would think of creative ways to keep in touch with our family and friends living far away. Receiving a package, a card or a note in the mail added a bright spot to any day. Relatives and friends never left us disappointed. We were blessed beyond measure by family and friends.

After our tragedy, I was not feeling strong enough to take the kids to Louisiana. I was afraid the sights, the sounds, and the memories of the area where Dave grew up, and where we had taken our kids to soak up some of Daddy's culture, might undo me.

Our last visit there as a family of seven, at the beginning of January 2013, was precious, and I was afraid of what seeing familiar sights might do to me if I returned without our family intact. Dom loved fishing off of the dock in Nana and Popsie's backyard. Grant enjoyed "hunting" for alligators in the canals near their home. I could not face going down there without my sons—not yet, anyway.

So I welcomed the chance for the children and me to visit with Dave's family in my haven, my safe place, my home. Upon Dave's family's visits to our home they were able to attend a couple of Finn's karate practices and Kate's gymnastics practices. One karate practice a month, was parent participation night. Upon David Sr.'s visits, he participated a couple of times with Finn during those special practices. As I watched Dave's dad stand side by side with Finn, I was overcome with emotion. I had to fight tears as I watched both of their faces so filled with joy as they seemingly each forgot about anything but that moment; grandfather and grandson filling a void for one another. And while Dave was not there to have that moment with his son, the replacement of pain and loss, with joy, was evident as we watched Finn and Popsie battle it out through smiles and laughter.

His parents came up again in the early summer of 2014, and has since become something of a tradition when they visit, we sought out a fun kid activity in the St. Louis area.

During their visits, we went to the St. Louis Science Center and Planetarium, the City Museum; and that particular visit, we explored the Magic House Children's Museum. As we walked the halls of that high-energy, kid-friendly place, I was overcome with gratitude. In the science wing, Dave's dad showed Finn how a machine worked, and Dave's mom played with Kate and Elise in the museum's make-believe wing. At one point, we were among many people randomly selected to appear in the background of the filming of a local news channel story on the volunteers at the museum. Further, the reporter interviewed Finn as he painted in the art section of the museum. We have precious video of Finn making his "television debut" on *Show Me St. Louis*, showing off his purple and yellow castle art creation.

As I walked the halls of that children's museum, I recalled the memory of Dave telling me about his parents when we first met and when we talked in my apartment, the following night.

"My parents are really hard workers," he said.

He told me about his parents' careers. Dave's father was a firefighter and his mother worked as a nurse, but each held additional jobs.

My mind going a bit further down the timeline, I pictured Dave and me snuggling in bed with several children between us hogging the covers. Dave never minded when the kids wanted to snuggle or even when, as babies, they occasionally slept with us. He recalled snuggling with his mom in her bed when he was a child and how safe it made him feel to be held by her in those early years. He wanted our children to have that same sense of security as we shared our bed with them.

I recalled one of our visits to New Orleans when Kate, Dom, and Grant were tiny. Dave couldn't wait to go fishing. He talked about some of his favorite fishing expeditions with his dad along the waterways of Louisiana many years before and told funny stories about how he had fallen out of the boat when it hit waves on lakes and rivers. He also spoke about the bonding between father and son that those fishing trips enabled. He wanted to instill that same sense of togetherness in his boys and hoped to create that bond between his father and his sons.

As with many family relationships, Dave and my dynamic with his family was filled with its ups and downs, lots of lessons learned and priceless memories made. I heard Dave's voice as his dad spoke, and I saw him in his mother's face and mannerisms. I was grateful for their visits because it helped us to heal and to stay connected after the tragedy and because each time they came to our home, they brought a piece of Dave and my boys with them. Dave's childhood and his heritage came alive for my children and me as we visited with "Daddy's mommy and daddy."

Dave's parents' presence also reminded me of all of the times we shared with Dominic and Grant. These were sweet memories. I recalled Dom's love of fishing, and Dave's pride that Popsie's love of the sport had passed down to his grandson. I remembered Nana's update on her pets each time she spoke to the kids on the phone, as she knew Grant's great love of all living creatures. Once, she even sent him a photo of a soaking wet bunny she had corralled to safety during a storm turned flood.

I could see Dave's parents in all our children. Kate had been passed Nana's creative flair for all things crafty. Nana made homemade and hand sewn scarves, pillowcases, and even clothes for the kids through the years, and Kate picked up on that creativity. Even as a little girl in Germany, she was finger knitting, sewing and creating crafts that impressed all of us. Finn got his chocolate brown eye color from Nana and his athletic ability from Popsie. Even as a toddler Finn showed such an agility far beyond his age that Dave and I knew he had the makings of a born athlete. As Elise has grown, traits of her grandparents have become apparent in her as well. She is very neat and organized, just like Nana. She likes everything in just the right place in her bedroom.

Even living overseas, we were able to have Dave's family visit us many times. They met Kate when she was three-and-a-half months old. Dave and I were living in the Azores and took a short flight from there to Norfolk, Virginia, one March weekend in 2002. My parents;

Dave's parents; my brother David (then fifteen); Dave's sister Brittany (then thirteen); Dave's grandmother, Maw Maw; my cousins Colleen and Hilary, and my dear friend Becky converged on Norfolk to meet Kate and to visit with one another.

Dave's parents and sister visited us in Idaho in 2003, England in 2006, and Germany in 2010 and 2011, and we traveled together to Belgium, Wales, and Italy upon their visits. We saw them in New Orleans many times on our stateside visits. In 2007, we traveled to Disney World with Dave's parents, his sister Brittany, and her boyfriend Joel, now her husband. In Germany, we traveled all over the Stuttgart area with Dave's mom and dad, Brittany, and Joel. On our most recent overseas adventure, Dave's parents flew to Germany and traveled to Venice, Italy, with Dave and me and our children the night before Finn's third birthday in October 2011.

When they came to see us in England, Dave, his sister, and I traveled together to Belgium for the day while Nana watched Kate, Dom, and Grant. Dave's mom was with us in Germany when Elise was born, just as my mom had been with us in Idaho and Italy when Grant and Finn were born.

The kids knew that a visit from Nana and Popsie meant lots of presents, lots of laughs, lots of love, and lots of fun. And I was grateful.

As we headed from the museum to my house for a barbecue on the patio, I was reminded that Dave had left us a heritage of precious family memories, a legacy of love, and principles of peace. He lived on in his parents, his family, our children, and in the bond he and I shared.

Dominic and Grant lived on in the laughs and the smiles of my children as we enjoyed Dave's parents that day. They lived on in the many memories of their sweet faces and of their hilarious antics.

Driving back home after a day well spent, I decided it was time, sooner rather than later, to take that trip down to Louisiana.

We were also blessed to welcome Dave's aunt Chris and his uncle Bob to our home that summer.

I had grown close with Aunt Chris, a sister of Dave's dad, since the tragedy. Our texts and phone calls, some lasting an hour or more, were filled with encouragement, hope, tears, and laughs.

I was so grateful for their company. Their smiles as they played with the kids calmed my spirit. I was comforted by the proof that family bonds transcend titles. While Dave lived in heaven and I was no longer his wife on earth, we were still family and our cord remained unbroken. And the dear man and the gracious woman sitting at my patio table still welcomed the kids and me as part of a larger family.

As I watched Finn and Uncle Bob play and saw the smiles on their faces, I was reminded of several dear photos Dave's godfather, Uncle Ted, had given me the year before. They showed a three- or four-year-old Dave ("Davey" as he was known then) and a younger Uncle Bob playing on a beach, piling up and dumping sand with a toy dump truck.

I was comforted by the notion that my children could build a bridge from here to there. I prayed that as my children grew, they would be a comforting reminder to Dave's parents, his sister, his aunts and uncles, and his cousins of the Davey they remembered, the Dave they loved. I prayed they would see that Dave and our boys lived on in a legacy of strength, of love between a father and his sons, and of endurance. I believed that Dave, Dom, and Grant would live on in the faces of Kate, Finn, and Elise.

In turn, I was grateful that the kids and I could get to know a side of Dave that we never knew—the little boy Davey—in the stories told, the memories recalled, and the photos shared. We would see the whole person—not just the husband, the father, the friend, the leader, the aspiring chef, the musician, the artist, the outdoorsman, the football lover, the avid photographer, the intellect, the computer genius, the hopeful hobby farmer, and the man of God we knew and loved, but also the boy, the Hollywood child (as his mom called him), the teen, the student, the son, the brother, the nephew, and the cousin.

I was comforted and thankful that my kids could learn their daddy's heritage through his parents, his aunts, and his uncles.

During that visit in the summer of 2014, Aunt Chris, Uncle Bob, and I recalled the last trip Dave and I had made to their home in Louisiana, in January of 2013, days before our family's tragedy. We visited with them and Maw Maw over spaghetti and king cake. Dave always looked up to Aunt Chris and Uncle Bob, a retired military couple who had friends all over the country after having been stationed in many places. Dave wanted to emulate them and was proud that we also had friends at military bases all over the world.

During our visit with Aunt Chris and Uncle Bob, we had fun at the playground, enjoyed dinners out and a trip to the St. Louis Zoo, spent time in my "Mom Cave", as Aunt Chris dubbed my basement, and had a barbecue on the patio.

Our time together culminated in a visit to the resting place of Dave, Dom, and Grant. My sister Deanna joined us. As we stood holding one another in our individual, yet shared pain, I imagined Dave looking down on us, our boys and the Father by his side, pleased that his legacy of love, peace, and family lived on.

Chapter 23

Coming Up for Air

As summer continued, my birthday arrived. I had learned that to get through each birthday, holiday, and special day without Dave and our boys, we would have to come up with new traditions, to be open to new ways of doing things while remaining grateful for memories of the way Dave and I had done things in the past. For my birthday, I took the kids out to lunch and came home for a celebration put on by Kate and the babies, much like the one Kate had given me the year before. My mom took me out to dinner. My dad was quickly succumbing to cancer and was not feeling well enough to join us, so I stopped by my parents' house after dinner to visit with him for a few minutes.

My dad and I did not always agree some big things. We were strikingly alike in personality but differed some on religion, and greatly on politics. After arguments in the past, we learned to no longer broach those subjects with each other, but my dad respected the fact that I held the religious beliefs I did.

My parents gave me a precious gift for my birthday, one I treasure, since they signed the inside cover "Happy Birthday, Sarah; Love, Dad; Happy

Birthday, Sarah; We love you! Love, Mom." The gift was a book on prayer with Scripture passages and devotional stories on the power of prayer. I treasure that book because they had given me the gift of encouragement, a true act of love. My dad, willing to put aside our differences in beliefs and knowing how comforting I found Scripture, gave me something he wouldn't have chosen for himself but knew I would enjoy, a gift in the purest form. And I couldn't have asked for anything more as I visited with my parents that evening of my thirty-seventh birthday.

A year and a half into my grief journey, I was tired of feeling dead. I was tired of seeing life go on all around me and feeling like I was on the outside looking in at something I could no longer touch. I missed living. I longed to lay my burden down.

This change in attitude was not a conscious decision; it was something that happened deep in my spirit, and only God could have produced it. This was a natural progression, the next step on my grief journey. I felt God whisper to my spirit, *Daughter, it's time to come back to life.*

I fought the sensation a bit. It was easier to feel dead inside. I didn't know what "coming alive" meant. I didn't know how to reconcile my deep yearning for Jesus' return and my focus on heaven with living here on earth again.

How do I do both? I wondered.

God directed my thoughts to the Scripture verse about "occupying until He comes" (Luke 19:13). We are always to live with the expectancy of our Lord's imminent return, but we are to *live* until He does return! We are to be about the Lord's work, which in turn causes us to live. We must fulfill our earthly mission and experience the ups, downs, joys, sorrows, and disappointments of this life—all while anticipating eternal life, the best yet to come.

During the first year and a half of my grief journey, I had lived yearning only for eternal life. I had written off this earthly life. While we must always live with hope and joy and expectancy of the life to come, it was all I wanted; I no longer wanted life here.

I was one step above suicidal. I still wanted out of earthly life desperately but no longer wanted to cause my exit by my own hand, to get sick, or to fall victim to a tragedy. I just wanted out. And the best compromise seemed to be awaiting our Lord's return and the rapture of the church (His people, Christians). This was the best of both worlds for my aching spirit. I would be reunited with my family and didn't have to die. Perfect.

With my awakening in the summer of 2014, I knew God appreciated my eagerness for His return, but I felt Him say to my spirit, *Yes, daughter, I do want you to anxiously await that glorious day I have promised My children when I will come and make all things new. But daughter, I need you to live there first. I need you to do your mission there. You still have a mission, or I would have brought you home when I brought Dave, Dominic, and Grant home. But I didn't. I'll see you when it's time, whether that be My return in your lifetime or your eventual passing to heaven. Either way, I'll see you. You'll be reunited with your family when it's time. But for now, there's work to do. Wake up!*

And I awakened.

I came up for air.

I felt like I had been drowning for a year and a half, and I came up for a huge gulp of air. It was a strange but welcome feeling, though it was scary to come back to life when my spirit had been dead and broken inside. The ebb and flow of the brutal grieving became less frequent and intense. The grief remained, but the hardest grief, the times that took my breath away, now came in waves instead of tossing me about constantly in a sea of despair.

My stamina to recover after each wave, increased. The time between each wave that knocked me to my knees became longer in between. The sea calmed just a bit. I was able to live a little more in between each wave. And my reserve of endurance increased, helping me to bear the brunt of the inevitable next wave.

No longer drowning in the waves of grief, I came up for air, grabbed the hand that was reaching out to save me, and climbed into His boat of reprieve from the storm. I reined in my grief and braced myself for each wave instead of allowing myself to be tossed about by those waves. With God's grace, I started to exert control over my grief instead of letting it control me.

I stood the summer of 2014, feeling a little lighter. I had regained some control over my life. I was ready to make life happen instead of letting life happen to me. I added new dimensions to my life. I began to see life in color again instead of in the dark grays my world had become. I started to work out again. I exercised every day on my elliptical, and I continued to walk on the country lane outside my house. I started going out with my girlfriends more—a dinner here, a glass of wine there. I allowed myself to sit down at the end of a day to a movie or to a book. I poured over photos I had taken, current and past, and compiled them into albums.

I felt cautiously optimistic about my new path. As I was about to learn, however, everything—including my newfound light and awakening—had to happen in God's time for optimal results. And just as there was an ebb and flow to grief and I had to learn to control it, I needed to learn how to control my new aliveness.

On a warm late May afternoon, my friend Rachelle and I took our kids to the Science Center in St. Louis. While there, I ran in to a friend from college whom I had last seen fifteen years before. She and caught up for few minutes, since she knew nothing about my life's events. I found it hard to sum them up in a few minutes. ("Well, after college I met and married a guy in the air force. We had five beautiful kids and traveled and lived all over Europe. But last year, my husband and two of our sons passed to heaven in a hiking accident.") She offered her heartfelt condolences and then said something that left me stunned and speechless and wondering, *Father, what are You trying to say to me with that?*

As we said our good-byes and parted, she yelled to me from across the way, "Hey, Sarah! When God closes one door, He opens another one!"

Instantly, I felt a surge of hope run through me, and I had no idea why or what it meant.

My friend continued on her way down the hall of the Science Center with no idea what her words had just done to my spirit. I stood in the hall, thinking, *Okay, Father, what on earth do You have in store for me?*

In the summer of 2014, I contacted a friend whom I hadn't seen in years. We went to college together and had talked a little over the years. I remembered him as a sympathetic ear, a kind face with a big smile, in college. Knowing he had received some spiritual training and religious education, I hoped to get insight on my theories about living life here while awaiting life in heaven. I wanted answers on how to do both. I reasoned he would offer a welcome new set of ears to hear my latest questions, revelations, concerns, and observations.

He and I started having dinner and conversation together early that summer. Each carrying our own burdens, we certainly weren't the carefree college kids of years ago, but our dinners were a breath of fresh air nonetheless. We got together much of the summer for dinner and drinks, to talk and to spend time with each other. It was nice to talk to someone outside of my usual circle of support. He had not heard about my family's tragedy, so I got a fresh perspective on some points that I ran past him and I could vent in a different way. And I reciprocated, listening as he told me of challenges he was facing. We went on that way through the summer.

As the summer continued, on the evenings I was getting ready to see him, I sensed a familiar feeling returning—anticipation. I hadn't felt anticipation in quite a while, and I cautiously welcomed this old sensation back into my spirit. As I readied myself those evenings—putting on my makeup, fixing my hair, finding just the right outfit—I felt an excitement. I was starting to care again about how I presented myself to the world. I took more notice of my appearance, much the way I had many years earlier. I looked forward to our evenings together, and it did not escape me that I had not looked forward to anything in a long time, since I was always looking back.

As our rekindled friendship continued, I started to question myself on my theory of reacquired singleness. I also started to ponder my redemption. I felt God would call me to redemption, but I had no idea what that meant. When I awakened in May, I felt God say to my spirit that He was going to restore my life; He was my Redeemer, and I would see restoration and redemption. I had always believed that was so in spiritual terms. God would give me the strength for my spirit to endure and would allow my eventual reunion with my family in heaven.

But that summer, I started to wonder if my redemption could also come in the earthly realm. I was prepared simply to endure the rest of my life. Now I started to wonder if God was telling me that joy would be returned to my life as well.

I was grateful for what my friendship with my friend represented. It reminded me that I was more than the pain I carried every day, and I was glad for the brief reprieve from darkness that my evenings out with him allowed me.

I often acknowledged to God in prayer His message to my spirit that I would see restoration. But what did that mean? Ideas about restoration flooded my mind. Would restoration happen by becoming a missionary, by taking a new career path, by gaining a volunteer position, or maybe even by becoming a foster mom? Coming back to life, I found, was exciting yet terrifying.

As the summer wore on, a transition slowly but surely started deep within my spirit.

For a year and a half I would snap at anyone who even mentioned "moving on" with another man. Though I wasn't seeking a new relationship or even ready for one, I was now open to the possibility. I admitted that perhaps I was not called back to singleness for the rest of my life. My life with Dave had made me aware of how beautiful togetherness was, and I decided not to limit God. He would restore me in some way, though I didn't know what that might be.

My journal reflected the many changes my spirit was undergoing that summer.

From Journal No. 6:

"What if this life truly is easier to shoulder with an earthly partner, Lord? Dave will always be my love, but what if my heart can expand? What

if it can have room for eternal admiration and respectful love while still loving in the earthly sense? Partnership can be beautiful. I don't know, God. Lead me …

"Father, I am not designed to impress anyone. That should not have to be in my life goal right now. But as a single mother, a single woman, it is my present reality. I resent that. Dave loved me as I was. We were growing old together. We giggled at each other's faults, remembering each other as our best selves in the past. We had such a comfortable love for one another. My workouts are for me. My time on the elliptical, my sweat, it's for me. It makes me feel strong, back in control a bit."

As the summer continued, despite my newfound aliveness, I had real life to attend to. My father started to succumb to his terminal illness during those summer months. He stopped the chemo treatments that had been done to prolong his life for the past year and a half, and he was put in hospice care.

When I heard the news of my dad's terminal status that summer, I was waist deep in mourning Dave and our sons and trying to find my footing in my reawakened aliveness. I had no strength left in me to deal with my father's crisis.

In my confusion, I didn't know how to handle the new place where I found myself. I recognized that when I was walking my grief journey with God, He kept calling me out of comfortable (albeit stagnant) places and telling me to continue peeling back layers so I could take steps forward. While I was grateful for my aliveness, I had no idea how to handle it. And with all the stress and the changes of that summer, I decided to take a detour on my grief journey and try to go it alone.

I wanted an easy, scenic path instead of the rocky but authentic path God was trying to walk me through. I took my newfound aliveness, mixed with confusion, and ran down a detour. I stopped listening to the sermons that had brought me so much peace. I virtually stopped journaling. I nearly closed the avenues from which I could hear my Father speaking to my spirit. I stopped walking closely with my Father, the hand that had led me along the rocky path, had stilled the waters, and had carried me over stretches when I had no more strength. I did not turn my back on God. But instead of walking alongside, I said, "Okay, God. I've got this from here. Thanks."

I tried to step out into my newfound aliveness my way. I thought perhaps my way would be easier than the authentic path God was leading me down. He kept asking too much of me, I reasoned. I didn't want to peel back layers. I wanted to stay right where I was for a while. I was no longer willing to face the reality of what lay ahead and of all the growth that would be required of me to continue to heal. Healing was too painful; I wanted to stay stagnant. I wanted to be distracted from the reality of my life. Instead of continuing to grow, I stayed blissfully distracted and stagnant that summer.

But as the summer drew to a close, God closed off a portion of that detour. As one day, my friend and I stopped writing; we stopped talking. Just as suddenly as we had started talking again after all those years, it was over just as suddenly. Each of us had pressing matters, real life, to attend to, and our friendship seemed to fade just as quickly as it had started months before.

I felt God say to me, *Daughter, I brought you back to life. I did it so you could live for My purposes, to fulfill your mission for My coming kingdom. I need you to be alive, to feel alive, to be willing to live, to fulfill those things. But you do not want to do the growing that comes with returning to life. You tried to find an easy path, a path that allowed you to stay stagnant when you wished. So I am pulling the reins back in.*

I used that man in your life to make you aware that you are still capable of feeling emotion for another man again in time. Do not put Me in a box. Do not limit the ways in which I may restore you in the future. Daughter, I do want you alive. You are on the right track, but don't limit Me. Let Me do this and all things on all points along your journey in My way and in My time. Do not be afraid to continue with Me. Yes, I will ask things of you. Yes, I will require you to move, to grow, to keep moving forward. But

I am asking you to trust Me. Restoration is glorious, but sometimes the path to it is hard. I will be with you the entire way, My child.

I had heard my Father clearly whisper to me. I knew the friendship with my friend had run its course and had served its purpose for that season of life. I decided to focus on what our friendship had taught me and had reawakened in me. I further realized that my Father allowed certain people into my life at certain periods for a purpose. He opened and closed doors to people and circumstances to bring out what He needed in me, and what He needed me to learn, as I progressed along my healing road. He continued to mold me into the person He wanted me to be.

Once again, I was forced to face the reality of my life in all its rawness, in all its ugliness, and in all its beauty. I was placed back on my path.

Hesitantly, I again placed my life in the hands that had led me thus far. I was ready to face my dad's illness, ready to face my confusion over coming alive, and willing again to endure the pain it took to grow and to heal properly. I was willing to live.

From Journal No. 7:

"I have been strong. I have been focused. I have been firm and sure and protected. I have put up the barrier to human emotions. I have focused above and beyond. I have focused on the unseen and have given up on the seen. I have planned for my life in the next existence and have put a big red X through my life here beyond raising my kids. I have counted myself chosen to have a focus beyond romance, beyond earthly love. I have dreamed of a family restored. I have pictured being loved from beyond. But something is awakened."

The rocky path to which God had called me was better for me than the easy, scenic detour. Each time I stumbled on the rocky path, God took the opportunity to steady me, to lift me, and to guide me. Every time I was bruised or broken on the treacherous path, God took the opportunity to mend me and to put His healing balm on my wounds.

I would bypass a lot of hurt by taking the easy detour of denial and distraction from my life, but I would miss all the ways God wanted to help me, to guide me, and to heal me along His tougher, rockier way. God awakened me to the possibility of redemption. He pulled me back to His side. He asked me to trust Him. He told me that healing and growth would be painful but that I should not limit Him in what my redemption might look like.

In the summer of 2014, I also had to face a truth that God had been trying to speak to my spirit. When Dave went to heaven, he no longer needed me. We are told in Scripture that marriage between a man and a woman on earth is a picture of Christ's love for us in heaven, and He refers to Himself as our bridegroom and to us as His bride (Ephesians 5:27; Revelation 19:7, 21:2, 21:9; 2 Corinthians 11:2; John 3:29; Isaiah 54:5; Matthew 25:1–46; Isaiah 62:5).

When Dave went to heaven, he became completely fulfilled, perfect, and whole. He had reached Christ, whose love marriage merely reflects. He didn't need me anymore. At the beginning of my grief journey, that thought broke my spirit. Now I started to release him to God a little bit more, to release him to that fulfillment.

As God whispered those truths to my spirit, I decided it was time to remove my wedding rings from my finger.

I removed my wedding ring and Dave's ring, which I had started wearing with mine on the same finger after the accident. I did this as an outward sign of an inward transition. I allowed myself the possibility of a life here on earth in whatever form God saw fit. Whether that meant a job, adopting a baby, or eventually having another man, so be it. Removing my rings was my way of commemorating that shift in my spirit, the next step on my journey, my coming alive.

I knew at the moment I took Dave's wedding ring off of my finger that the bond we shared would transcend titles and would never end, that he was my best friend and that nothing would ever break that cord.

I still believe our family will have a heavenly reunion one fine day. But I have come to accept if God chooses to allow me to have the love, the bond, the friendship, and the support I shared with Dave again with another man, I will not fight it. If God orchestrates a brother in Christ to come alongside me in providing for our children a godly heritage and a solid foundation in Christ, bringing his unique gifts and his passions to our family's table, I will not fight it. I will not dictate to God the ways in which I will be restored; I will let Him make those decisions.

No matter how much I love Dave, there is more to give. Just as a mother's heart expands with each child she births, I have the capacity to love more and to love again. What a rare gift it would be indeed to get that kind of love twice in one lifetime.

When the summer, with its confusion and awakening, was done, I had been brought back to life. I was again walking alongside God and was allowing Him to show me what to do at this new point, accepting that growth might bring pain.

I started journaling consistently again, and a peace returned to my spirit. I started walking closely with my Father again, studying His Word, listening to sermons, attending to what He wanted to teach me so I could continue my mission on earth, whatever that might be. I was reminded that no matter how God might restore me, He considered me His beloved, like all of His children, and that "I am my beloved's and my beloved is mine" (Song of Solomon 6:3). He would see me through my coming alive. I had finally found a good balance between longing for life in heaven and being willing to live a life on earth, all the while continuing to let God lead.

I have had a friend call my life a "crazy, beautiful life." I couldn't agree more.

Chapter 24

Dad—No Hill Too Steep

My journey continued that fall with the many ups and downs I had come to expect. I was newly awakened, newly alive, facing life head-on again, and was open to redemption. But I had to stop theorizing about redemption while I attended to the life right in front of me.

My dad was succumbing to pancreatic cancer and entered hospice care. My mom found out in August that her cancer was back. She had fought cancer on and off for years. In 1997, she was diagnosed with renal cancer. After surgery, chemo, and radiation, she went into remission for several years, completed her bachelor's and master's degrees in education, and fulfilled her life's dream of becoming a special education teacher, all while in her forties.

From 2009 onward, however, my mom battled breast and ovarian cancers. Mom had surgery upon surgery and chemo treatments on and off for years. She'd go into remission and then have cancer pop up in another part of in her body. All the while, however, she taught and lived as normally as possible. In between battles, Mom was her old self.

In August of 2014, right before the doctors decided to end my dad's treatments and put him in hospice care, my mom found out her cancer had returned. Our family was devastated, and so was my mom. She had taken on a caregiver role as my dad fought his battle, and now she would be down, too. Our family braced for the challenge ahead with two very sick parents.

In mid-August, my mom had major surgery to remove the cancer from her colon, intestines, and stomach lining. My dad, always self-sufficient, asserted his independence by driving himself to the hospital to be there for Mom. We sat in the waiting room all day, awaiting word on her progress.

It was hard to watch my dad sitting in that waiting room. He was frail, weak, and almost skeletal. Before his illness and even during his chemo treatments, he had been a fit, active man. An avid cyclist for forty years, my dad could ride twenty miles after work in the evenings, and in my childhood, he would ride forty to sixty miles on a weekend like it was nothing. So to see the way he looked now was difficult.

We set up a vigil at the hospital. My dad, my sisters, my brothers, several aunts and uncles, a few nieces, and I visited and waited for hours.

Finally, the doctor came out and said that all visible cancer had been removed and that Mom was in recovery. My dad asked to be notified as soon as he could see her. He wanted to be the first face Mom saw as she awoke and to tell her they "got it all."

I captured that time in a letter to a dear Christian sister in the fall of 2014.

> Ami: I have had a trying day. God and I had quite the conversations to and from the hospital. The day started out well enough. I worked out and mowed the lawn. But then I went to see my mom. She is having a setback. She has been back in the hospital since Monday, and they want to keep her until at least next Monday. In the meantime, Dad is at home alone. After visiting Mom, I grocery shopped, went to visit Dave and the boys, and cried to Dave. He would be so supportive of me right

> now. He'd help where he could, help me shoulder the burden, hug me, support me. I miss him so very much. Then went to see Dad. He's alone; he's worn. His house was a mess. I straightened up and talked with him. He needs Mom's companionship.
>
> It's pathetic to see him this way—sick, dying, and alone. There are five of us kids. My siblings and I have all been helping around the house, as have many family friends, aunts/uncles, and Mom's church family. I guess I stopped by on a night when he was alone. It's hard to see my dad that way. This is natural to lose a parent. If I can survive the unnatural (burying a husband and children), I can survive this by God's strength. But I'm tired.

The Wednesday after my mom's surgery, my dad was due for a procedure. He was having a drain put in his abdomen. As his body started to shut down due to the advanced cancer, his abdomen filled with fluid, leaving him in excruciating pain. The drain was not a life-saving measure but simply a way of making my dad's last days on earth more comfortable.

Driving to the hospital with my dad the day of the outpatient procedure, I was struck with the realization that while my mom was in the hospital after having surgery to save her life, my dad was headed to another hospital for a procedure that would only make him more comfortable. There were no more life-saving measures my dad could undergo. Even chemo had been called off.

We drove in virtual silence that afternoon. The Christian radio station played softly in the background, and my dad and I had only light conversation. He slept most of the way. As we arrived and slowly navigated our way through the parking lot and into the waiting room, I was overcome with sorrow. My dad—my capable, independent, take-charge father—was so helpless, weak, and frail. I felt like I wasn't with my dad—not the dad I knew and loved, the avid cyclist, the artist, the painter, the witty comic, and the opinionated commentator on current events. That was not the man sitting next to me in the waiting room.

My heart broke for him. And as I watched the nurses try to get an IV into my dad while he was being wheeled away for his procedure, I was overcome with the injustices of sickness and death. I wrote to a dear friend while I sat in the waiting room.

> Christy: He is getting a drain inserted in his abdomen right now. They debated whether he was well enough for this procedure, but thankfully they took him back. They just started. It's really hard to see him this way—very frail, weak, ill, throwing up—especially knowing this is no kind of healing. This drain is simply to make his "transition" go more smoothly. Please pray he has peace. Sickness is a disgusting injustice. There's no dignity in it at all. I'm just praying over him. It's so strange to have parent and child reverse roles, making him comfortable. It's just horrible. I'm just praying he is at peace and feels some control over his situation with this drain.

As my dad was having his procedure done, my mind traveled to memories of him, of my boys, and of my family.

I thought of all the traveling my parents did with my family. My mom and dad visited Dave and me and our children in Virginia, Idaho, England, and Germany. My mom also came to see us in Italy. We had many adventures together during these visits.

Our castle hunting trip to Wales during my parents' visit with us in England, summer 2006.

Still living in the Azores, Dave and I flew to Virginia to introduce a brand-new Kate to our families in March of 2002. My family and Dave's got to know one another as we visited in the hotel that weekend. We were joined by several members of our families as we converged on Norfolk. We toured the Jamestown Settlement, enjoyed Colonial Williamsburg, and climbed aboard the USS Wisconsin, all together.

Over crawfish, my dad and Dave's dad talked, and my mom and Dave's visited. Dave and I reveled in our parents getting acquainted while meeting our new baby girl, their shared granddaughter.

When my parents visited us in Idaho in 2004, we took many day trips together, though I was pregnant with Grant and couldn't go on the more adventurous outings. Dave and my dad mountain-biked, summited the Bruneau Sand Dunes, and went whitewater rafting together, while my mom and I stayed back with toddlers Kate and Dominic. Together we visited the ghost town of Silver City, admired the Sawtooth Mountains, drove through the Danskin Mountains and stopped for a picnic in the forest. We took pictures at Trinity Lakes and let toddlers Kate and Dom wade in Redfish Lake. I remembered, with a smile, my dad holding Kate and Dom on his lap as he colored with them in their coloring books, while visiting at my home that trip.

On my parents' visit to England in 2006, we went castle hunting in Wales, visiting about eleven castles in a weekend. Further, Dad, an avid history buff, soaked up the history all around him, posing proudly in front of Captain Nelson's *HMS Victory* in Portsmouth. Mom, a Henry the VIII aficionado, posed humorously with a statue of the infamous king. We traipsed through London, showing Mom and Dad all of the typical British sights, and ate lunch at the Sherlock Holmes restaurant. My parents stayed with us at our home that trip, and we enjoyed family meals around our dining room table, together. My mom and dad woke many mornings to Grant climbing into bed with them for a snuggle and Dom showing off his latest dance moves. After each day's adventures, we gathered in our living room to watch a slideshow of the photos from that day.

In 2008, my mom came to be with us in Italy for Finn's birth. Days before his due date, Dave and I, along with Kate, Dom and Grant, showed my mom around some of the local area. We drove the Amalfi Coast, stopped in Positano, ate traditional Margarita pizza, and took photos of Mount Vesuvius from a distance. While I was recovering after giving birth to Finn, my mom even "substitute taught" Kate, Dom and Grant their homeschool lessons, as I was on "maternity leave".

When my mom and dad came to see us in Germany in 2009, we took a weekend trip across the border to Paris, ringing in Finn's first birthday together. My dad held him for a photo in front of the Eiffel Tower. An avid photographer, my dad relished the opportunity to take in all the sights—castles, mountains, and nature scenes of Europe. While on a day trip to Rothenberg, Germany, my dad and Dave went off on side streets throughout the day, hunting down the perfect shot. Mom and I, kids in tow, had to hunt them down when they vanished on their photographic endeavors.

We had many laughs and many adventures (sometimes misadventures) as we traversed Europe together. As I sat in the waiting room, I remembered my dad insisting I take a photo of him in front of a castle in England over and over again to get "more turret." I recalled my mom in Wales asking for her burger to come with "no burger, just the bun and lettuce, please" to looks of utter confusion from the dear

Welsh behind the restaurant counter. Then I thought of the bond my parents shared with my boys, and I was almost brought to my knees.

My dad and Dom were very much alike. Dom looked like my dad had as a little boy, and I was often astounded at how Dominic shared my father's mannerisms. Upon my parents' visit to us in Germany in 2009, we took a trip to Bavaria. We arrived at the base of the Zugspitze, the tallest point in the German Alps, on an October day, and snow had started to fall. Most of us opted to wait in the van, but my dad and Dominic braved the snow to walk to Lake Eibsee, which sat at the base of the mountain. They finished their trek to the lake, and as I watched them walk back to the van, I got out, camera in hand. I moved a bit closer to them and took what has become one of my most treasured photos: my dad and Dom, walking side by side, snow falling all around them, bundled in their coats, with the mountain behind them in the distance and snow-covered pines surrounding them on every side.

While Dom and Dad were close, Grant and my mother shared a special bond. My mom was with us in Idaho when Grant was born. Dave and I were grateful for the help she provided. My mom took care of Kate and Dom at home, while Dave stayed with Grant and me in the hospital. I have the most precious photo of my mom in the hospital room. She had brought Kate and Dom to meet their baby brother, and they flanked her as she sat in a chair holding Grant. The look on her face as she gazed at her grandchildren was nothing short of magnificent. The love she had for her grandchildren radiated from her eyes, and I was blessed to capture the moment on film.

Home from the hospital with baby Grant, I watched, succumbing to tears, as my mom held him in her arms and sang to him, read to him, and cuddled him.

Returning to the present, I thought about my dad and the lessons he had taught me, and the one that stuck out most for me was that there was no hill too steep. There was no obstacle too hard to overcome. When life brought challenges, there was no option but to fight and to stand.

As the nurses wheeled my dad out of the treatment room and readied him to return home, I looked back to a long-ago afternoon when I was a little girl. My dad, an avid cyclist, was driving my siblings and me on the back roads near our house after a hike. He pointed out of the window and said, "You see that hill—that one, the big hill over there, the steep one? I ride that hill. I ride up that hill. I do not get off my bike and walk it. I ride up it."

And as I looked at my dad, steadied and ready to walk to my car, I was reminded that there is no hill too steep.

With the drain inserted, my dad and I were on our way back to his house. He slept the entire ride home, absolutely spent from his session at the hospital. Back at his house, he assured me that he was going to rest and that it was okay for me to go. I had no idea that within a few days my father would be under the constant care of my brothers. Dad was so good at masking his true condition that we were not aware that he should have been monitored at all times well before then.

A few days after I dropped off my dad, my sisters and I got calls from my brothers telling us to get to our parents' house, since they thought Dad would pass away that night. I found out that a day after Dad's procedure, he had fallen. My brother was at the house. It finally became apparent to all of us that Dad could not be left alone at any time. In an email, I relayed the events leading up to this decision to a dear friend.

> My siblings and I have had two scares, called in Sunday and yesterday, both times thinking this was it and he was going home. But then he stabilized. My two brothers are his primary caregivers, since Mom is in the hospital. They both took off from work and are there with Dad 24/7. We are on watch this entire week. Our big concern has been getting Mom home to him first! She is still recovering from her own cancer surgery. Finally, they feel she may get to come home tonight. We think this may be why he is hanging on. My prayers are for Dad's smooth transition to heaven (my mom says he accepted Jesus a few weeks ago), that Mom is home tonight so they can say good-bye to one another, for

her emotional health, and for my brothers' endurance as Dad's primary caretakers.

We held a vigil the entire week leading up to Dad's passing to heaven. Visitors included Aunt Judy and Aunt Mary, two of my dad's sisters; Uncle Greg and his wife, Aunt Leslie; Uncle Darrin and his girlfriend Stephanie; many cousins, and dear family friends, including Jim, Doug, and Brian, who had known Dad's since early childhood. Uncle Greg and Dad were especially close, since the two brothers were born only eleven months apart and were bicycling buddies for decades. We often had multiple visitors a day.

First Baptist of Waterloo, the home church for my mom and me, brought meals every day. My dear friend and babysitter Faye watched my kids for hours each day as I spent time with my dad and my family.

Doug, my dad's best friend from childhood, who had built the shelves in my basement and had helped me with yard work after my tragedy, came to my parents' house to play guitar and sing for my father. Dad closed his eyes and listened, resting to the soft melodies. I was overwhelmed at this example of love in action. I was blown away as that man displayed the hands and feet of Christ. Their friendship of more than sixty years culminated in that moment— Doug doing what he could to make my dad more peaceful and comfortable during his transition to heaven. I am forever grateful to Doug and to his wife Julie for being such outstanding friends to my parents.

As we held our vigil, spending time together with my dad that week, it dawned on me that while people gather to welcome and to celebrate the beginning of life with the birth of a baby, we had gathered to celebrate a life on earth coming to a close. We were ushering Dad into the next life. I sat amazed at the beauty of that week as we poured over photos and laughed at memories recalled, and I watched my brothers tenderly care for my dad in much the way he cared for them when they were small children. I was overwhelmed, and I was grateful for a God who allowed such moments of beauty.

With my dad's condition worsening, we were on almost an hourly watch, knowing that his passing was imminent. Our major concern was getting Mom home from the hospital in time to say her good-byes to Dad before he passed. When she entered the hospital a week and a half before, she had no idea that while she was recovering from surgery my dad would take such a drastic turn for the worse.

Almost unaware of the dire situation at home, my mom had also taken a turn for the worse. Her recovery was not going as planned. She was under heavy medication, since she was in great pain. Visiting or calling her at the hospital, several of us tried to alert her to the gravity of Dad's condition, but we were not sure if she fully grasped the news.

Fortunately, Mom's doctor allowed her to come home briefly, telling her she would have to return to the hospital to continue her healing after my dad had made his transition to heaven. Two days before my dad's passing, my mom came home. She got to see my dad, her husband of thirty-seven years, and to help us all usher him into the next life. Our prayers were answered.

From Journal No. 7:

"Mom got to come home today! They had a great reunion, albeit a low-key one, considering their weakened states. We all visited as a family—we five kids, our families, and our parents. Precious moments. I'm very grateful Mom got home. My brothers are amazing at providing them both with 24/7 care. Church, friends, aunts, uncles—everyone is playing a part, from meals to prayers to transportation to babysitting. This is God in action! Dad is still precarious and will be going home soon, but at least now we are all together."

"Today was also Elise's fourth birthday—spent eating lunch out, just me and the kids, then a small celebration at Grandma and Grandpa's. There is no other place we'd rather be today!"

Two days later, on August 22, my dad went home to heaven. He was surrounded by his five kids, his legacy. And while I knew I would miss him, I was happy for him. I was happy that he was free of pain, in bliss and glory, had met Jesus, and was with my boys, off on another adventure. I captured much of what transpired surrounding my dad's entrance into heaven in a letter to a friend.

> Ami: Thank you for everything. When Dad passed, we siblings went into overdrive—planning everything for his services. Mom was and is still incapacitated and drugged up from surgery. You know what? God did something amazing. He enabled me to walk boldly through Dad's services. I walked with the confidence of having been there. God is so good to offer such calm and grace. This is going to be a different kind of closure. And to think of my boys welcoming Grandpa. It actually makes me swell with pride! My Dad's passing has set me on a new course. Strangely enough, while there is grief, a confidence is back: I was finally able to use some of what I've endured to help someone else through a similar experience.
>
> We had beautiful services for him on Monday and Tuesday—celebrating his gifts as an artist, a painter, an avid cyclist, an outdoorsman, and a father/son/grandpa/uncle/husband/brother/friend. I am honored for him! My sister and I spoke of him in eulogies. I read a paper I wrote on him in college as someone I admired. My two brothers continue the same level of care for Mom in her healing that they gave to Dad in his last days. Beauty. Absolute beauty. I would have given anything to see what he saw at the moment of his last breath! Glory! Jesus, our Father, celebrating angels, my babies. I just kept praying as he was breathing his last, "Jesus, wrap him in love and light right now!" I wanted Dad to see the glory just ahead as he was transitioning to what awaited him moments away. It was beautiful.
>
> I really feel we honored him, and I am so happy for him.

God absolutely covered me—and not just covered me but rejuvenated me with a sense of mission. I feel on mission to walk Mom through this widow road.

She could use your prayers: she was taken back to the hospital tonight. They released her too soon last week so she could be by Dad's side. Please pray. Thank you for everything, dear sister. I should add that Dad made a profession of faith to my mom before his passing. And when he and I were talking the week before he passed, I flat out asked him if he was ready, and he said, "Yes, I am ready. I am going to see Jesus and the boys."

That has been my mom's saving grace as she mourns him; she knows she will see him again! Praise God!

Chapter 25

Laying Former Things Down

That fall as I mourned my dad and I watched my mom spiral downhill, I continued to trudge the new path of aliveness on which God had placed me. I was angry and depressed. My sense that I had a mission to walk my mom along the widow road had given way to sorrow and to depression, manifesting itself as severe loneliness. I was still trying to figure out what to do with my newfound desire to live even as death and loss continued all around me. I asked God, "What is redemption for me? What does it look like?"

I felt God say to me, *Daughter, when are you going to see I am enough for you? You keep striving and seeking on this new leg of your journey. When will you see I am enough for you? Daughter, I have so many blessings in store for you that you won't be able to contain them all. But first, My daughter, I need you to see I am all you need. I will supply all your needs. I will continue to walk with you and to heal you. I will walk you through pain that you know is inevitable, and I will guide you through the new sense of aliveness I have given you. I never promised this life would be easy. Following Me is the more difficult road. I have promised abundant life to My children, but as I revealed to you earlier this year, only I know if that abundant life will fill to overflowing while you are on earth or come to its fullness when you arrive here with Me. Either way, you will have abundant life, and I am asking you to trust Me to bring you to it wherever the road may lead.*

God gave me a peek at my redemption and at my purpose through His Word while I was reading Scripture and journaling one fall afternoon.

"Those who were rebuilding the wall and those who carried burdens took their load with one hand doing the work and the other holding a weapon" (Nehemiah 4:17 NASB).

From Journal No. 8:

"Father that is me. I build these walls. I rebuild this life. I try to help my babies rebuild their lives while carrying this burden with one hand and a weapon with the other. I am now protector, gatekeeper, provider, comforter, mother, and father to my children."

With all the losses surrounding my children and me, I decided I needed a change. I could no longer shoulder all the mourning, all the pain, all the grief, all the confusion, while in the same environment. I wrote a friend that I "could not take another ounce of bad news just staring at my walls." A change of scenery would be good for my spirit. In spite of all my losses, I needed a gain.

I was still searching for a place to hang my hope with my newfound sense of life. Joy was nowhere to be found, so I decided it was time to go out and make it; create my own joy. I would take another step forward and add a gain despite my many losses and the losses still to come. I prayed for direction, and with boldness in my spirit I decided to put the kids in school.

A seven-year homeschooling veteran, I realized I had nothing more to give my kids in terms of education. I had too much on my plate. Further, Kate was at the age where she needed her peers. Her brothers were her classmates, her friends, her peers, and her companions.

Grant was Kate's best friend; they shared (and share) a special bond. Kate, only three years older, took to Grant from the moment he was born.

In one particularly scary instance, Grant, just a few weeks old, was crying one morning when we were in Idaho, and before I could get to him Kate tried to carry him to me.

When Kate was five and Grant was two, we were at a friend's home in England. The children were all playing downstairs as my friend gave us ladies a tour of the upstairs. As I was coming down the stairs, I saw Kate carrying Grant as best she could, her arms firmly around his waist with his legs dragging on the floor. She told another child, "You will not hurt my brudder!"

Grant returned her affection. Just days before our tragedy, we were visiting Dave's family in New Orleans and spent the day on the water in his father's boat. We docked at a sandy beach on a lake in the afternoon to let the children play. Grant used his time on the beach to draw in the sand with a stick, and we all went to see his masterpiece. He had drawn a girl and under the picture had written, "Kate."

Grant and Kate usually sat next to one another in family pictures. They were each other's preferred playmate. They were best friends. That was one blessing of homeschooling. My children had lots of time together and with me. We had time as a family. Kate and Grant shared a special bond, and I can't wait to see that beautiful friendship restored one fine day!

Without Dom and Grant with us at the dining room table doing school, Kate spent many days working alone on her lessons at her computer as I worked with Finn, a kindergartner.

God whispered to me gently that Kate needed more than that. She needed routine, structure, discipline, excitement, and adventure. She needed to be out of the house, to be a kid, and to make friends. She needed to lay down the burdens our family had shouldered for almost two years and to start on her journey.

God was asking me to release Kate to her full potential. He whispered to me that I was smothering the spirit, of my strong, beautiful, courageous young lady.

I was grateful to God for showing me that I was trying so hard to cling to my old life and to the way we did things before. I released Kate to her great unknown, trusting God to take her by the hand and to lead her down her path just as He had so faithfully led me down mine.

In addition to putting the kids in school, I reactivated my state teaching license and signed up to substitute teach at Kate and Finn's schools.

Staring at the teaching certificate in my hand that fall afternoon as I left the regional office of education, I fought tears. The paper reminded me of the education I had received, of the degree that I had earned. I was gently reminded of who I was before Dave, before marriage, before kids. I was a teacher; I was Sarah.

I realized that if I could be Sarah before my marriage to Dave, before my children were born, then I could be Sarah after my marriage and after my kids were in the hands of their heavenly Father, released on their brave new journeys in the public school system, or under the watchful eye of a babysitter while I began my new adventure in the classroom.

As I drove home that day, a hope took over my spirit. I was more than the grief that had defined me for almost two years, and I was excited to see where this new hope took me.

With the decisions I had made about school in the fall, I had resolved to let one more piece of my former life go. No longer was I a wife. No longer were we a military family. Now we would no longer be a homeschooling family.

I had been torn apart a year and a half before as the gates of Scott Air Force Base receded from view and I watched another piece of my life vanish, but I relinquished my role as a homeschool mom with a calmer heart. With all that God had walked me through in the twenty months since my grief journey began, I knew that if He was asking me to lay former things down, He had new paths and new adventures planned.

I stepped out boldly in faith, anticipating what God had in store with the new chapter He was writing in my story.

Chapter 26

On Finishing Well

As the fall progressed, my mom's health worsened.

Her surgery in August did not get all the cancer as was originally thought, and we found out that while my mom was burying my dad, the remaining cancer had taken over her body. My brothers and one of my sisters took turns giving my mom full-time care. My other sister and I filled in and helped where we could. My aunt Lee, my mom's sister, an RN and a nursing instructor at a university, was a constant caretaker for Mom as well.

My mom—usually a quirky and goofy but energetic and intelligent woman—was quickly succumbing to the struggles with her sickness and to the grief that had overtaken her at losing my dad. Someone had to tend to the incisions from her surgery and to change the dressing every day; she wore a waste drainage bag, since the surgery had required that her body's plumbing be rerouted.

I thank God for my brothers and my sister Elizabeth, who took such good care of Mom during those months when she fought her last earthly battle. Watching her waste away was hard to endure. I had watched Dad waste away and had written about the injustices of sickness and death, and my mother's condition produced the same feelings.

My mom was fighting daily to keep her spirits above water. After an examination, my mom was told her condition was terminal, barring a miracle. She wisely decided she would refuse to endure any further surgeries but cautiously chose to give chemo a shot until it made her too sick. She decided to finish well, to finish her way. She chose quality of life over length of life, and we all had to swallow the news that months after burying our father, we would likely be burying our mother in a few months as well.

From Journal No. 8:

"God is stripping me to need and to lean only on Him. It's very painful, but I am used to pressing on through pain, sadness, and confusion. Been there. I don't want pain and endurance to define my life, but so be it. I've got to look at the joys that surround me every day. I'm trying …

"God will never introduce something into my life simply to hurt me. No, there's always a lesson to glean! Shaping, molding, refining, stripping—I have to understand that God is walking with me. Dave's support is with me. I have to believe; I have to walk on. I don't have a choice. And it is not about me. It is about how God can use me through it. I told Him to use me, and I am getting what I asked for. Earthly, this hurts. Heavenly, it's glorious."

That late fall brought plenty of ups and downs in my spirit. I recorded many in a letter to a friend.

> Dear Kim: We are in the honeymoon period of the kids being in school. They love it; I love it. I do miss them here, but I feel we need this in this season of our lives. I have subbed three times—twice at Finn's school, once

> at Kate's—and go again tomorrow. I'm looking for just a few days a week.
>
> Mom is doing okay for now. I am so glad to be able to go see her during the day. We spent Tuesday together, just Elise, Mom, and I, and she was in such great spirits. She is back at home after having lived with my aunt for a bit. The cancer is in her colon. They did not end up getting it all with her August surgery, and she has resigned herself to her mortality. Her body is perhaps not prepared for another fight. We will see. She is peaceful and mentally back to her old self. We take one day at a time.
>
> We are all hanging in there. After awakening back to life this summer but experiencing some choppy waters after Dad's passing, I feel my spirit leveling out a bit again. I spend my days getting my house in order. I enjoy organizing and tossing out things around the house. This helps me feel more in control of my circumstances. I'm still working out on my elliptical. The kids are thriving in school, just seeing where God leads. I'm trying to be patient with all these losses and to prepare myself for His rain of restoration. I'm hanging in there, trying to live in the moment, one day at a time. Love you.

There were moments of clarity, of resolve, yet still moments of sorrow throughout those fall days.

From Journal No. 8:

"Once again, I feel empty. I have visitors, but everyone leaves, and again I'm alone. No plans today. No plans tonight."

That fall, Finn started asking me tough questions about being the "only boy" in our family. I recorded much of the fall of 2014 in my journal.

From Journal No. 8:

"I took the kids to the drive-in tonight; while waiting in line for our snacks, Finn looked all around him, then looked up at me and asked, 'Mom, why are we the only ones here without a dad?'

"My heart broke all over again for my boy as it does every time he asks me that question. He went on to ask, 'Why am I the only boy in our house?'

"I wanted to tell him, 'Buddy, if you only knew the ladies used to be outnumbered in our family.' But instead I pulled him close to me, covered him in a hug, and told him how much his daddy and I loved him. Sometimes I don't know what to say."

I continued to journal a great deal in those late fall days leading into November:

From Journal No. 8:

"I'm trying to find the blessings and the light in this day. I find when the world is held at bay, I see them more clearly. A rough, rough day. But I found peace doing laundry and listening to sermons as the storms rolled all around me. I had a calm, quiet night of baking and making a good dinner and sitting with my kids at the table—the world blocked out, just us. At peace. Grateful. I have had a productive, calm day but a yin and yang day, as it was also very rough.

"I try to stay in my ark. Journal like crazy. Pray. Stay still. Try not to sin in my grief and anger. I don't expect too much from myself right now. I don't try to figure out how to save the world. Just exist. Just be and listen. Stay still . . .

"I have retreated all weekend back into my home, my family, and my memories. Cleaning, organizing. I feel calm in the mundane. Friday I spent a peaceful evening with Mom, Saturday night I had a short, quiet visit with Heather, but all weekend, and especially today, I have just stayed on my ark. Cleaned, organized, and had minimal contact today, and it feels good. I'm almost living in my memories: sorting old notes and drawings from our England days with itty-bitty Kate, Dominic, and Grant …

"Becky said I would crawl. These are the days I am crawling. Remember: endurance. I feel the pain, yet I feel protected from it. I do feel the weight, the burden, the heaviness of grief and loneliness, of having to live in the past, in memories, while other people live and love in the present. But it is what it is. I persevere. I endure. Perhaps it is my lot. I daydream and fantasize about the past but also about the future, and I scold myself for the latter. False hope. Ridiculous. I live my mundane yet peaceful days. I have my memories and my present. My future is a question mark. Hope is waning; the only hope I feel right now is heavenly hope, nothing earthly. I don't know why I go on. I just do. As long as I am in my ark, my sanctuary, my home, I can retreat to solace, retreat to memories."

I recalled in my journal a blessed visit I had with my mom one late November day.

From Journal No. 8:

"I'm feeling so many different things: sadness, loneliness, quiet, resolve, confidence, peace, confusion, wondering.

"It was an honor and a blessing to sit with Mom yesterday from 3:00 to 8:00 p.m. We had a wonderful time. Uncle Beas was there until about 3:30 p.m. She rested and I made the house cozy and comfy. It was just Mom, Elise, and I. After I cleaned her up a bit and David and I changed her bedding and her clothes, it was just us. (David left at 4:00 p.m.) I gave Mom her meds, and she lay down in her bed. I did laundry and a few dishes; it was

quiet, peaceful, and cozy. Elise played quietly and rested. I found a cute Thanksgiving movie on, and that played softly in the background. Then I rested and held Elise, and she slept on me. Mom wanted up about 6:30 p.m. She and I drained her bag, then got her sitting up in Dad's chair. We talked a lot about God, about endurance, about finishing well, about fighting bitterness. We talked about my crazy life. We talked about Dad, his dad, Dave, and the boys.

"Mom said something neat. She had a really rough night last night and a painful day. It was not what she had planned. She had planned a different day—Uncle Beas's visit and the nurse to change her dressings—and she was disappointed at the additions (extra pain, bag leaking), but she pointed out that she did everything she wanted to do that day, just not in the way or in the order she had planned. That really hit me. She is so wise."

Chapter 27

Medicine for My Soul

Relaxing on the couch one fall afternoon, my mind drifted to a memory.

I was standing in the living room of our Germany home with seven-year-old Grant. He was suiting up for our upcoming walk. The kids and I liked to spend our summer days and our afternoons after school walking the paths near the creek across the street from our house. Grant was putting on his zookeeper vest. Grant used the fishing vest Dave had bought him a few Christmases before to help play the part of a zookeeper, a zoologist, or a paleontologist, whichever he chose to be that day. On our walks, Grant recorded every animal he saw, real or imaginary, in his memo pad. In his younger days, he used inventive spelling, but as he got older, he became pretty good at jotting down what he saw on our safaris.

His vest securely zipped, Grant stuck his memo pad in one pocket and a pencil in the other. As we got ready to leave, Grant and I were discussing his aspiration to be a zookeeper when he grew up, but Grant stopped speaking and got contemplative for a moment. Concerned, I turned to him. "Are you okay, Buddy? What's wrong?" I asked.

"Mom, I just don't know one thing about being a zookeeper, though," he answered.

"Okay," I responded, "what's the problem?"

"I just don't know how I am going to trap the lions and get them to the zoo," he lamented.

Stiffing a giggle but with a smile showing in my eyes, I assured my boy that I was certain there were ways he could get lions for his zoo without having to trap them in the wilds of Africa. As I watched Grant gear up that day, I was amazed at the little boy in front of me—so innocent, so pure, small in stature but with big dreams. I was reminded not to underestimate my Grant David. Sure, he was small, but in his mind and in his spirit, he was ready to conquer lions.

Chapter 28

Grant's Birthday

I would like to say that leading up to the Decareaux birthday season I was busy preparing myself to withstand the inevitable pain as I had done the previous year. But with Dad passing to heaven, Mom quickly fading, and everyday struggles confronting me, I was treading water. I was barely making it day to day and didn't have enough strength to prepare myself for the upcoming onslaught of birthdays and holidays.

My mind and my spirit seemed capable of taking only so much pain, and when I reached my quota, I would close down. The sensation was different from what I felt in my early days of grief. In those days, the pain was all-encompassing. There was nothing but the pain. I had lost my boys; I had no desire to live and wished for death. But as I faced the onslaught of upcoming milestones, I was in a different place on my grief journey.

In that sense, I was stronger. I saw a clear distinction again between joy and despair. I could recognize the days when I was able to feel joy and the days that brought me nothing but despair. This was in contrast with the early days when all was dark and painful.

In the days leading up to Grant's birthday, I was in pain. But more than pain, I felt confusion, a restlessness in my spirit. I was mourning Dad, mourning my husband and my sons, and mourning Mom even though she was still with us, since I knew her passing was inevitable. And watching my mom suffer, I knew that my hysterectomy had to happen sooner rather than later if I was to avoid her fate. That knowledge added sadness to my spirit as I started to mourn my upcoming barrenness following the surgery.

The pain was not the hopeless pain of a year prior, but it was pain nonetheless. As I faced trial after trial, I wondered if suffering was my lot in life. I did not want my life to be defined merely by endurance. At that point on my journey, I wanted some kind of life back, though I was still searching for what that meant.

With that mind-set, I arrived at Grant's tenth birthday—eight years on earth and two so far in heaven. School was in session, so the day started like any other. I got the kids on the school bus, walked back from the bus stop, and crawled back into bed with Elise. I thought, *All I have to do is hunker down and survive this day.*

I had no plans for the day, as I had the year before. I was dry, I was spent, and I needed God to guide the day.

Adding to the challenge of my son's birthday, my uncle Tony, my mom's big brother, was being buried that day, having passed days before. Not only was he being buried on Grant's birthday, but he was being buried at Jefferson Barracks National Cemetery, where my boy was laid to rest. And while I felt proud that my uncle was getting buried with the full military honors he deserved, there was no way I could make myself attend those services. My family understood. I couldn't be there on my boy's birthday, not in the same place where he lay, unable to celebrate his big day with us.

The pain that day was different from the pain a year before. On Grant's birthday the year prior, the pain was all internal. The grief lived in me. On his second birthday while in heaven, however, the pain was caused by outside sources—the loss of Dad, Mom's illness, pending surgery, daily struggles. In a sense, the pain was easier to handle. If the pain was coming from outside of me, I could control it. There was a start and a finish to the pain. I decided when to put it on and when to take it off, when to allow it and when to banish it, whereas the pain of the previous year had been continual.

God is a good God, and with all the added burdens He knew I would face that year as the birthday season approached, He had brought me further along on my grief journey so I could have a firmer footing as I continued the battle.

After snuggling Elise a bit, I got up and decided to go through the motions of the day and see what happened. I knew that when the children came home from school, we would celebrate Grant at his resting place (long after my uncle's funeral was finished) with apples and cupcakes, as had become our tradition. Other than that, I decided the best way to honor my boy was simply to hold on and to get through the day. I cleaned, I organized, and I played with Elise. I took breaks here and there to contemplate and to journal. As I entered Kate's room to collect laundry that afternoon, I couldn't help but notice her calendar on the wall. I saw "Happy Birthday, Grant" written on the space for November 3. I quickly flipped through the calendar and found that she had noted no other birthdays, just her friend Grant's.

My mind drifted to memories of my boy.

Grant was a quiet, unassuming, gentle soul. He was small for his age, had a smile that could light up several feet in front of him, and looked just like his daddy. He was the only one of my kids who would always give me a "good morning" after he got up. Grant was the consummate middle child. He had a big sister and a big brother, a little sister and a little brother. He could hum any melody in tune, and I had dreams of him becoming a musician like his daddy. Grant was the mediator of our family, and while he and Kate shared a special bond and spent most of their time together, he was happy to play with any of the other children.

There were things only he and Dom shared (hiking and Scouts) and things only he and Finn shared (a love of dinosaurs), and since he and Elise looked so much alike, I could see a special bond developing between them. He liked to make his baby sister laugh, and she willingly obliged every time Grant made funny faces, tickled her, and spent time with her.

But Grant was more than gentle and sweet; he had a fire in him that was often overlooked. Even I had to be reminded of that, since the fire lay under the surface. Grant had a strength in him. He had the dreams of a grown man housed in his tiny body, hidden behind his unassuming, pleasant demeanor. Sometimes that fire would show itself. He and Dom liked to dress up and play make-believe. They would put on a scene from *Lord of the Rings*, playing music from the movie in the background as they acted out scenes from the movie in costumes made from what they could create with clothes we had around the house.

As I watched my boys act out a scene for me one day, I noticed that Grant David was holding his own against his big brother. Grant reminded me so much of David in the Bible, small and unassuming but not to be underestimated. And just as David became a mighty warrior and eventually a king, I knew big things were in store for my boy.

Grant was so easy to please, so easy to get along with, an absolute joy. When he was born, Kate was not even three years old, and Dominic was months from being two. We moved from Idaho to England when Grant was only five months old, and I had my hands full. One night I held him in my arms as he lay asleep, while Kate and Dom slept in their beds. Dave was doing work toward his master's degree in the other room, and it was just baby Grant and I on our couch. My mom called and asked me how we were adjusting to all of the recent changes.

"How are you doing with the three little ones being so close together, Sarah? How is Grant? What kind of baby is he?" she asked.

"Mom," I answered as I stared at the precious life I held in my arms, "he is a joy, just a joy."

And I meant it. Grant was easy and pleasant from the moment he was born. What a rare gift indeed.

Grant had a silly streak in him, something largely unknown to many family friends, since he saved many of his shenanigans for family-only entertainment. One day, while we were living in Italy, Grant thought it would be fun to make his version of stone soup, which we had read about in the famous children's tale earlier that afternoon. As he gathered ingredients from our yard—grass, rocks, sticks—he took bits of cactus that he had somehow broken off and added them to his mixture. We had small cactus plants, lemon trees, and a few palm trees dotting our yard. Kate and Dom joined him in his endeavor and eagerly gathered items for the soup.

I was inside, very pregnant with Finn, and suddenly heard Grant run into the house, trying to tell me something through whimpers and tears. He was followed quickly by Kate and Dom, who were translating for him. Looking at Grant, I noticed small, hairy-looking protrusions coming from his lips. As I got closer, I could see he had many needle-thin prickles from a small cactus plant sticking out of his lips. Alarmed and almost speechless, I quickly sat him down on the kitchen table and removed the needles one by one. As I was working, he stuck out his tongue to reveal even more prickles there as well.

Once Grant had calmed down a bit, I tried to get an explanation without coming right out and asking, "How does something like this even happen?" As Kate and Dom surrounded Grant and me, trying to stifle their laughter, Grant explained that he wanted to make his brother and sister laugh, so he licked a heaping tongue-full of the yard mixture—turned stone soup—and received a quick reminder of why that was not a great idea.

Turning my head, I stifled a giggle as best I could before turning back to my boy to continue freeing his lips and his tongue from the prickles. As I worked, I laughed inwardly at how committed Grant was to a part. When he played make-believe, he was all in.

But above all, Grant was sweet. He was blessed with a calm, gentle, inquisitive soul. One afternoon in January of 2013, just days before our lodge trip, I was running around the house doing everything that needed to be done to sustain a household of seven people. I was cooking something, cleaning something, and correcting someone or some pet; I was busy. Grant came over to me as I took a short break on the couch to write something down. He was carrying several boxes. I could see he held the five puzzles he had received as gifts on recent occasions, including one from my parents for his birthday and one from Dave's parents for Christmas.

"Mom," he asked, "can you help me write on the boxes who gave me what puzzle?"

Sighing inwardly, since I had so much more I needed to complete that day, I wondered at the seemingly unusual request, but my spirit quickly corrected me and reminded me that this request was indicative of Grant's precious nature. As he put together each puzzle, he wanted to know who had given it to him. This was a sweet gesture by a sweet boy.

"Yeah, Bud. Come over here," I said with a smile, patting the couch beside me.

I put aside the list I was making, and he and I worked together to write "From Nana and Popsie, Christmas 2012," "From Grandma and Grandpa, Your 8th Birthday, Nov. 3, 2012" on the backs of the puzzles. It was a precious moment, a rare moment. He and I talked, smiling at each other and recalling pleasant memories as we figured out who had given him each gift. We finished our project and Grant walked off, but I remained grateful for that moment—that brief reprieve from my busy day spent with my precious little boy.

Looking back, I see that was not a random request at all. God orchestrated this moment so I could have just such a memory of time spent with my treasured Grant David.

My mind drifted back to the present. During one particularly peaceful point on the afternoon of Grant's birthday, I sat on the couch as Elise played make-believe with her dolls. I watched her facial expressions and listened to her voice inflections. I smiled as I watched her live out that blissfully innocent, carefree childhood moment. I watched her play and imagine and dream with no cares in the world, and I was happy for her. I wanted her to revel in that moment and stay in it as long as she could. That moment encompassed all that was beautiful about life, about childhood, and about motherhood. Parents can ask for nothing greater than to be able to provide that joy and that innocence for their children.

And I was comforted in my spirit as I pictured Grant David playing in a similar way as his sister, setting up his dinosaurs, lining up his animal figurines, blissfully living his innocent childhood moments. I knew that Dave and I had enabled Grant to have those moments while he was under our care on this earth.

In his short time with me, he was immensely loved; he knew nothing but love. I felt I had fulfilled my mission for my boy while he was on this earth with me, and I was grateful.

As I got up from the couch to press on with my day, I could almost hear Grant David still playing, still running, still laughing, still blissful. And I was happy for him. Knowing oh how thin the veil that separates us. If only I could see what my spirit heard that day, I would see joy, activity, and a life that continues. Except now not under my care, but in the mighty, capable hands of our Father.

Chapter 29

Sometimes He Says Yes

From Journal No. 9:

"A gorgeous, productive day. Dropped Kate off in the morning at church to go on an outing with the youth group, then ran errands with the babies. Back home, we did much: played with the cats, took care of the pets, fed the chickens; I sipped my pumpkin spice coffee while sitting at the patio table. Then I headed through our woods to the creek with my babies and Bear, our loyal companion. We played out at the creek a while. What a covered and calm day spent with my family. Thank you, God."

I found much peace, especially in those fall evenings, walking up and down the country lane near our house just as the sun was getting ready to set. With a cornfield to one side and woods to the other, the hilly lane leads to wide-open skies; to the west, there are views of breathtaking colors and of unobstructed sunsets.

On just such an evening, I was taking a walk up and down the lane, over and over, slowly taking in the sights before me, the smells around me, the sounds just beyond me. I have always felt close to God out in His creation, and that evening, I felt peace and calm in the cool, crisp fall air.

In a calm place in my spirit, I told God, "I just don't understand why You always tell me no. Why, Father, are some things just beyond my reach? Why are some things not allowed for me? Why wasn't I allowed to keep my guys here? Why did You tell me no? I feel like You tell me no a lot."

As if by way of an answer, my mind drifted to a memory.

I was fourteen weeks pregnant with Finn and was on a plane flying from St. Louis to Rome with Kate, Dominic, and Grant beside me; Cleo was riding along in the cargo hold. We were moving from Illinois to our new home near the US naval base in Naples, Italy. Dave had flown over to begin work in February of 2008. The kids and I were following seven weeks later, in April.

I had stayed behind to sort our belongings, to box up items we were leaving in Illinois, and to ship items that we would need to set up house in Italy.

I had to drive to Chicago to secure visas for the children and me to live in Italy, and I had to make all the necessary arrangements for Cleo to fly with us. I had to do all of this while in my first sick trimester pregnant with Finn.

When Dave accepted the job in Italy, we had no idea I was pregnant. We stopped at a restaurant for lunch before taking Dave to the airport, and I started to feel awful. I thought, *Wow! I am taking Dave having to go on before us kind of hard. I actually feel sick about it.*

Two days after the kids and I saw him off at the airport, I took a pregnancy test, and sure enough, we were pregnant. I called Dave in Italy. "So guess what?" I said. "You know how I didn't feel well when we dropped you off at the airport? Well, it wasn't nerves. We're having another baby!"

Dave was always excited each time we found out we were pregnant. If it were up to him, we would have had ten kids. He loved children and wanted a huge family. He had dreamed of big family dinners around the kitchen table, surrounded by his brood, since he was a boy. We were well on our way there, since we found ourselves pregnant with our fourth child.

So there I was, finally on the plane headed for Rome with all of the logistics necessary for our move behind us, knowing Dave would be waiting at the airport to pick us up on the other side. After landing, gathering my kids and our carry-on luggage, deplaning, and finding our way to Cleo and then through the airport, I couldn't wait to be reunited with Dave.

I was walking up one section of the unfamiliar foreign airport and then another, all the while dragging our luggage, urging the kids to "just keep walking," and pushing Cleo in her kennel, which had been placed on a cart. And finally, there he was; I saw him walking toward us, a smile on his face, and I started crying. I was so grateful to be back with him and so ready to share some of the burdens I had been carrying. (I'm sure the pregnancy hormones had something to do with my tears as well.)

We had been a military family and had been separated while Dave finished up his time in the Azores and took work-related trips, so we were used to the airport reunion scenario, but this one was among the best.

I collapsed into his arms, crying as he pulled me near and reassured me while trying to greet the children, who were anxiously pulling on his jacket, grabbing at his pants leg, and calling for Daddy. But Mommy was hogging him.

Reunited, we found our way to the car Dave had borrowed to pick us up, and off we were to start our Italian adventure.

Our home for one month before securing a rental house was a beautiful hotel near Dave's workplace. We had a suite with a bedroom, kitchenette, and balcony—the perfect place to call home until our Italian rental was ready for us.

I slept so well that first night reunited with Dave. I felt a great sense of relief at being able to share parenting with him again, anticipating what lay ahead on our Italian adventure and excited at knowing we had a new baby on the way. But my peace and relief quickly turned to worry and dread as I awoke the next morning.

I felt a strange sensation and ran to the bathroom to find that I was bleeding heavily. I called Dave in, and through tears said I had better get on the phone to the US naval hospital on base to see what I should do.

After I explained to a nurse what was happening, she said, "Ma'am, if you think you are miscarrying, you need to get here right away."

Driving the twenty minutes to the base hospital, Dave and I had no words for each other; we didn't even hold hands. We each sat in silent grief, certain that we were about to experience a miscarriage. I was devastated and scared. I don't remember praying. My thoughts came more in snippets, such as *God, please,* the implication being, *God, please don't let me lose this baby. Please heal whatever is happening in me right now. Please let us have a strong, healthy child.*

When we walked into the ER, I was rushed to an examination room, continuing to bleed and vomiting and crying as well. The doctor checked for several things, I was given something for my nausea, and I rested. The doctor decided the best course would be to do an ultrasound to see if there was any movement or a heartbeat from the tiny baby inside of me.

I was terrified as I was wheeled to the ultrasound room. *God, please prepare me for whatever this ultrasound might reveal.*

As I lay on the ultrasound table and a tech applied gel and a wand to my stomach, my breath caught in my throat. I waited. I watched the face of the ultrasound technician, trying to decipher any news from her expressions. She looked very serious. She applied the wand to my stomach, lifted it, and then applied it again. Finally, I asked, "Is everything okay?"

Continuing to apply the wand to my stomach while watching the screen in front of her, she replied, "Well, I'm trying to get accurate measurements here, but your baby won't stay still."

I burst into tears and laughter at the same time. My baby wouldn't stay still. My baby was so active that the tech couldn't get him to remain still long enough to take a reading on his measurements. My baby was just fine.

I was wheeled out of the ultrasound room and told Dave the good news. The doctors had me rest in the ER for a while. When I was cleared to go home, I was given my discharge paperwork. There was no explanation for my bleeding, but the paperwork read "threatened miscarriage," and I knew I was blessed to still have that precious life inside of me as we drove away from the ER that afternoon.

Our healthy Finn Nathaniel was born six months later, and he has remained just as active as he was in my belly that day in Italy.

My mind returned to the present. As I continued to walk up and down the country lane, the thought hit me: Sometimes God says yes. Sometimes God says, "I will."

Sometimes God says no. His answer depends on His purposes and His plan. I prayed that morning in the barn almost two years earlier for God to warm my boys and to let them come home to me. And He told me, "No, daughter; they are already home with Me."

But on that long-ago morning in Italy, I prayed—not with words but with my spirit—for my baby to be safe and protected, and God said, "Yes, I will."

As I walked into my house that night, the sun having set, I saw Finn Nathaniel playing with his Legos on the living floor, and I heard a reminder whispered to my spirit: *Sometimes I say yes.*

Chapter 30

Late-Fall Transitions and Big Decisions

From Journal No. 9:

"There are days I am done, and right now feels like one of them. Father, I feel I have no strength left, none to fight. Too is much going on—Dad died, Mom dying, my health scare or upcoming surgery, single parenting, trying to live again but not knowing what that means. Makes me realize there cannot be a man who could deal with the intense pain I will always carry. Who would voluntarily take that on? That 'giving up' is a freeing feeling in a way; it makes me ever more dependent on God, too. I have had a beautiful life! I have been blessed beyond measure and have had unbearable pain. I have known both. I have had a beautiful, full life; perhaps it's ungrateful for me to want more, to want that joy back. I had it with Dave and our family—blissful joy beyond measure. Now I settle in to the remaining pieces and do the best I can to give these kids joyful memories, even if

they are not as full as they'd be with all of us here. I pray some of these burdens are lifted, but I do not reach too far. I stay content in the middle ground, because hoping for joy restored here is tiring. I will be content in the middle ground, the pieces, living off of the abundant joy I knew until I have fullness of joy again in heaven. Endurance. Pockets of joy. Realistic hope, not false hope or ungratefulness, just being grateful. And living in these ashes, I will not see life or live life as others do. I will always live deeper, live with more pain. I will not be normal, but I have to accept that and live in the ashes as best I can."

The late fall of 2014 became rougher as the weeks wore on. I was bombarded with single-parent struggles on every side. Kate was learning and growing, but that growing was accompanied by growing pains. We were trying to get accustomed to our new routine. Kate was adjusting to the public school setting. Finn was bucking me as I took over the role of disciplinarian, a role Dave used to occupy. The fall was defined by many frustrations and challenges.

From Journal No. 9:

"Sometimes I wish I were still dead inside. In so many ways, it was easier to feel dead. The first year and a half of my journey, I was dead. There was no life in me. But then God brought me back to life, and while my head understands He brought me back to life for His purposes, my spirit grows weary trying to live again. I don't know what that means—to live again. It was easier when I didn't care, didn't want to thrive, and didn't want to feel. I couldn't feel. I was numb. I couldn't go lower, so nothing hurt me anymore. I had no expectations, so there was no such thing as disappointment anymore.

"But I am alive; God the Father breathed air back into my lungs, life back into my spirit, joy back into my being, feeling back into my heart, light back into my eyes, fight back into my soul. He has pulled me out of the muck and the mire. He has set me on dry ground. But where do I go from here? I

don't know how to do this. I feel, I hope, and I dream. But of what? Like a baby, I am learning all over again how to walk, how to move, how to be. It is painful. I am vulnerable and open."

As I mourned my dad and watched my mom succumbing to her illness, something else plagued me that fall: I knew that I needed to make decisions about my surgeries. I was not at peace. God had laid it on my heart in the late fall that it was time to decide about my hysterectomy. I had watched my mother suffer through many surgeries for her breast and ovarian cancers and undergo many treatments for many years, and now ovarian cancer was killing her. I knew that it was within my power to avoid that fate. I had to do all I could to avoid ovarian cancer.

Having received the BRCA gene test result a year and a half earlier, I knew the recommended course of action was a full hysterectomy, a removal of my ovaries. But while I was all set for immediate surgery after learning that I had the mutated gene, I had begun to change my mind since then. I felt relief at having to cancel my hysterectomy in February and April of 2014 due to outside circumstances, and I had not rescheduled my surgery.

In fact, after coming alive in the summer of 2014, I started to wonder if my redemption meant having another baby. I wondered if my life restoration meant that I would be gifted with another family. I was only thirty-seven years old, after all, and another baby was not outside the realm of possibility. I often speculated about this in conversations.

"After having to lay two boys to rest, what a beautiful gift it would be to give birth to another one."

And I meant it.

I researched ways in which I could have the best of both worlds—how I could have my surgery in a timely manner but still have another child, even on my own. I looked into freezing my eggs so I could use them in the future to create a child in the event I was ready to have another family. I even briefly considered using a donor from a sperm bank and getting pregnant so I could have another baby before I had to have "all my parts taken out," my description of a hysterectomy.

God quickly used hard facts to disabuse me of those ideas. The cost of harvesting and freezing eggs and using a surrogate to nurture them and to give birth to a child was more than I wanted to invest in. And the thought of using a surrogate to carry my child left me feeling unfulfilled. The notion of being artificially inseminated, getting pregnant, and carrying and birthing a child alone lost its luster after my sister encouraged me to think about "what that really looked like."

Did I really want to go through pregnancy and childbirth without a partner? Did I really want to knowingly bring a child into the world without a father? Did I really want to raise such a child alone when I was already struggling to raise the ones God had left with me?

After several weeks of researching my options and of trying desperately to hang on to something that was not mine anymore—my childbearing years—I slowly released the idea of ever birthing another baby to God.

And God used mighty women to cement the idea that it was time to say good-bye to my fertility and to schedule my hysterectomy.

I awoke one morning to the dread of knowing something heavy was lying on my spirit. I did not want to face it. I knew it was time to schedule my hysterectomy. I grabbed my phone off of my nightstand to check my morning messages and to read my daily devotional. I had received a text from a mighty sister in Christ, Jen, a friend from our England days.

She had written me a beautifully worded text.

"Not sure where you are today or what you are doing, but just know right now this morning, the God of Israel is keeping you in His mind and heart. He has me thinking and praying for you right now. You are so deeply loved and blessed. Just know God sees, knows, and has already provided the stick to sweeten the bitter waters He leads us to. May He show you that stick today" (Exodus 15:22–26 KJV).

I sat up in my bed, completely amazed. Jen had no idea of the struggles I was facing, since our last conversation had taken place when my dad passed to heaven. She knew nothing of my other challenges: my terminally ill mother or my internal conflict over whether to have my surgery. I grabbed my Bible off of the nightstand.

> So Moses brought Israel from the Red Sea; then they went out into the Wilderness of Shur. And they went three days in the wilderness and found no water. Now when they came to Marah, they could not drink the waters of Marah, for they were bitter. Therefore the name of it was called Marah. And the people complained against Moses, saying, "What shall we drink?" So he cried out to the Lord, and the Lord showed him a tree. When he cast it into the waters, the waters were made sweet.
>
> There He made a statute and an ordinance for them, and there He tested them, and said, "If you diligently heed the voice of the Lord YOUR God and do what is right in His sight, give ear to His commandments and keep all His statutes, I will put none of the diseases on you which I have brought on the Egyptians. For I am the Lord who heals you" (Exodus 15:22–26).

Overcome with astonishment, I said aloud to God, "Okay, I'm listening."

As I sat there, the conversation continued in my head.

I am in the desert, God. I have been led to bitter water after bitter water. You want me to know You are sweetening the waters I have been led to, and if I heed Your words, You will not allow this sickness to touch me. I hear you, Father. I hear You. Now I need to step out in faith and to let You show me the stick You will use to sweeten these many waters I am led to. I am listening, Father.

I got out of bed and started my day sure about the decision I had to make. Seeking confirmation, I had one phone call I wanted to make first.

That afternoon I called my doctor. I had come to look at her as a confidante and an encourager. She had given me the BRCA gene results a year and half before, and I felt I could trust her. She was always honest with me, realistic but compassionate. I dialed Doctor Mahon. We exchanged pleasantries, and I briefly filled her in on my internal struggles over scheduling a hysterectomy and saying good-bye to my fertility. "Just tell me what I need to hear to be able to make this decision," I said.

"Sarah, from what we can tell now with all the imaging we do on you, you look healthy. From what we can tell, you are healthy—for now," she said.

The doctor was referring to the many screenings I underwent twice a year—pelvic ultrasounds, internal exams, and cancer-screening blood tests for my ovaries; mammograms and MRIs for my breasts. But what she said next made my breath catch in my throat.

"But I am afraid we are going to lose our window with you."

Ovarian cancer is known as a silent killer. Usually, by the time it presents noticeable symptoms, it is already too far gone for remission. Some research I had seen suggested BRCA patients get their hysterectomies at as early as thirty-five years old. There is a window of time in which it is recommended that a woman with the BRCA gene mutation get her ovaries removed. Having the double mastectomy to avoid breast cancer, urgent and important as it was, took a back seat to getting my ovaries removed. Imaging for the breasts is very effective, and so I had a bit more leeway on when to have them removed. However, with my ovaries, there was no truly effective screening to assure finding cancer at a curable phase.

I hung up with Doctor Mahon, called my surgeon's scheduling office, and asked to be put on the calendar for the first available appointment for a hysterectomy. My surgery was scheduled for December 16. I called back and said that if there were any cancellations between now and then, I'd like to go in earlier.

I knew I should have the surgery done before I changed my mind again.

Later that evening, I went to see my mom. I walked into my parents' house, so quiet without my dad, and found my mom there in her room; my siblings, who had been taking care of her, were occupied for the evening in the other room. I sat at the foot of my mom's bed as she lay resting, and for a while, I just watched her. When she awoke, we chatted quietly. The room was lit only by the small glow of a lamp on her nightstand.

I started sobbing. I cried for my mother, lying there so helpless and weak. I cried for all she had to endure, all of her physical sufferings while having to mourn my father, her mate, her partner, her friend. I cried for Dave and my boys and for the loss that continued to plague my soul. And I cried for me, for the upcoming loss of my fertility, for having to say good-bye to one more thing.

I felt so terrible, as she lay dying, to be the one crying. I quickly apologized to her and tried my best to dry my tears.

"What's wrong, Sarah?" she asked gently.

Despite her dire condition, she was still my mom, and I allowed myself to vent to her as I had during our many dinners together shortly after Dave, Dom, and Grant had entered heaven.

"I scheduled my surgery," I said.

"Oh, Sarah," she responded quietly as she grabbed my hand, knowing full well the struggle I had faced in the weeks leading up to my decision.

"I don't want to do it, Mom. I don't want to have to say good-bye to one more thing," I said, sobbing again. "What if I was meant to have one more baby? What if God wanted to restore me in that way? I thought that God was going to restore all He had allowed to be taken from me."

My mom let me get everything out of my system. And then she quietly but ever so wisely answered me with a question: "Sarah, have you prayed on this?"

"Yes," I said, assuring her I had prayed about whether I should do the surgery and if so, when I was meant to do it—if I should wait a short while, wait a year, wait a few years.

"Okay, let me tell you some things," my mom said. "First, you have to think of the kids you still have here, honey, and what would happen to them if something happened to you. And don't ever forget when you are ready, you can always adopt, with or without a man in your life."

She was repeating what I had told her in earlier conversations as I was debating the pros and cons of surgery.

"I know," I said, letting her know that I remembered our talks.

"I know you want back some of what has been taken from you," my mom said. "But Sarah, you have to look at what you still have left here, what God has allowed you to keep here. Your children need you. They need you healthy. And Sarah, look at me. Look at how they have to take me apart piece by piece because this thing has taken over my body. Do you want to have to go through what I am going through? Do you want this to have to be your life in the future because you put off surgery too long?"

I assured her I did not want that fate, and she finished with one poignant piece of advice.

"Put the date you have scheduled surgery on a card and stick it in your Bible. Pray over that date every time you see that card. And if the date is meant to change, it will. And if it is not meant to change, you can go into surgery that day knowing you were meant to go on that date."

As I left my mom's house that evening and drove home, many thoughts swirled through my head. I knew that God was asking me to lay another thing down. Just as He had asked me to lay aside the things of my former life, my titles of wife and of homeschooling mom, He was asking me to lay my fertility at His feet.

And just as He had asked me to release my daughter to the public school system, He was asking me to release my desire to bear another child to Him.

I also realized I was trying to custom-make my restoration by trying to plot out how I could parent another child in the future. God, however, wanted full control of how He would restore me.

As I drove that evening, I was assured of two things. First, if God was asking me to release my childbearing years to Him, it was because He had treasures in store for me, and He would reveal those treasures to me as I stepped out in faith. He had plans for me that I could not imagine, and He would restore me in His ways. He would sweeten the bitter waters to which He had led me.

And second, He would ask me to release many more things to Him in the months to come.

Chapter 31

Mom, Mighty Woman of God

From Journal No. 10:

"I believe in Jesus' name, He can heal Mom miraculously if He chooses! If He chooses not to heal her, I believe in the name of Jesus Christ, that her journey will be used to bring many to Christ! Amen!"

On a Wednesday in early December 2014, I spent the evening talking with my mom while the kids were in church club.

In the past, I dropped off the kids at church on these nights and then picked up my mom for dinner out. But in the several months since her health had worsened and we had lost Dad, I went over to Mom's house simply to visit with her. Weakened by cancer and weighed down by grief, she sat in my dad's chair as we talked. I treasured those visits. We shared our struggles, our common widowhood, and our fight against bitterness and despair. My mom, ever wise, offered encouragement and words of wisdom. But we also laughed as I recounted Finn and Elise's latest exploits, and we reveled in Kate's increasing maturity as a blossoming teenager.

That Wednesday night, I sat by her chair and we talked about Dad, Dave, Dom, Grant, and heaven. I did not know, could not know that would be the last night we would get together to talk and that she would transition to heaven the very next day.

On Thursday, December 4, Elise and I drove over to Mom's at 9:00 a.m. to spend the day with her. I wanted to visit with her, but I also wanted to relieve my brother David from his shift. He and Richard and my sister Elizabeth had shared the responsibility of caring for Mom 24/7, much as my brothers had cared for Dad in his last earthly days.

Walking in the front door, I could immediately see my brother was concerned. He told me that Mom was breathing oddly and had been suffering flu-like symptoms since five in the morning. In her weakened condition, even a minor problem could be life-threatening, and he was watching her very closely. He had contacted Aunt Lee, the RN, for advice on what to do about Mom's changed condition. He had also called her doctor to report what was happening. He did all that was needed to make sure Mom was closely monitored.

But when I walked into the living room, I found my mom was calm and resting, and the situation did not seem alarming.

David decided to get Mom cleaned up, medicated, and comfortable before heading to his apartment to freshen up. I watched as he tended to her, carefully changing her dressings and cleaning and redressing her incision, and then draining her waste bag. I was in awe of that young man, my parents' youngest son, who had risen to the challenge of caring for our aging and sick parents for several months.

I was grateful beyond words for him and for my brother Richard. These two men had walked me through many days of my grief journey. Days after our family tragedy, they had hiked the trail that took my boys to heaven, gathering information, formulating a time line of events, and piecing together my boys' last earthly moments. My brothers had accompanied me on the trail, had hiked with me, and had allowed me to sit on the ground and to cry at the place my boys met Jesus. My brothers had obliged when I asked for help at my house, in my yard, or with my dog, in those early grief days. They had walked my dad through his last week on earth, tenderly caring for him the same way they were caring for our mom.

I was exceedingly grateful for the two young men I got to call my brothers. I was thankful for a God who allowed such beauty, such Christlike love, to be shown through two tough but compassionate young men.

"Have you ever considered doing this as a profession?" I asked David as he tended to our mom's incision.

"No," he said. "I can do this kind of thing only for my own parents."

Before leaving to take a brief break, David showed me how to take Mom's blood pressure, instructing me to check it and her temperature often, and wrote down the medicines she needed for the day. I assured him I had everything under control, and he was off.

My mom was awake after having rested, and I asked if she were hungry.

"I don't want to eat," she said softly.

"Mom, you're not gonna put that one over on me. You're gonna eat. What sounds good?" I asked with a smile.

We decided I would make her some boiled potatoes. As I cooked, washed a few dishes, and got Elise occupied with crayons and paper, I thought about my mom and all she had overcome. I thought on what an awesome woman she was, a woman of strength and wisdom, endurance and resolve. Like Grant, my mom was made up of so much more under the surface than she showed. She was a woman of strength and ambition; and she masked both beautifully with her humble and gentle nature.

I handed Mom her potatoes, and as she took a few small bites, I got Aunt Lee on the phone. I described Mom's symptoms, and my aunt suggested we call Mom's doctor and then call an ambulance to take her to the hospital for a routine checkup. The medics would provide better transportation for Mom in her precarious condition than any of us could do in our vehicles.

My mom agreed that was the best plan. After talking to the nurses at her doctor's office, we agreed that getting some antibiotics and fluids in her might rejuvenate her and that she could perhaps come home the next day.

David soon returned, and we were joined by Richard, who had come by on his lunch break. We called an ambulance, but as we waited for it, Mom started to breathe strangely. She panicked a bit. My brothers and I assured her that this was probably a routine situation and that she needed to stay calm.

When the ambulance arrived, my mom was in full panic mode. She looked me square in the eyes and said, "I can't breathe. I can't breathe."

Figuring her difficulty was probably due to nerves, I assured her, "Mom, as soon as they get that oxygen on you, you will feel like a new person. Let them do what they need to do for you."

As the paramedics got Mom on a gurney and put her into the ambulance, I thought she was in good hands. David would follow behind the ambulance to be with Mom at the hospital, Richard would return to work, and I would finish straightening up at our mom's house and head home to await further news. I told my brothers I would contact our two sisters at work and keep them abreast of the situation.

I washed a few dishes and texted my sisters, informing them of our mom's situation and of what hospital she was being taken to. When my sister Deanna responded, "I will be right there," I knew things were worse than I was allowing myself to admit.

Moments later, David called.

"Where is everybody? They are taking her to a different hospital; they want to stick a tube down her throat. Tell everybody to get up here *now*!"

David said Mom had started to crash in the ambulance; her blood pressure had gotten dangerously low, and the ambulance had to divert to a closer hospital. I grabbed up Elise, left every light in the house on and dirty dishes in the kitchen sink, and took off for the hospital.

On the twenty-minute drive to the hospital, my mind started swirling. I prayed in snippets, my mind too foggy to compose a comprehensive prayer. Nonetheless, I was sure that God could feel the urgency of my message through my spirit.

About five minutes before I reached the hospital, Aunt Lee called. She had arrived at the hospital with David moments before.

"Sarah, is everyone on their way?" she asked.

"Yes," I assured her. "Why? Is there a change in her condition?"

"She's not good. She's not good, honey," Aunt Lee said.

"What does that mean?" I wanted to know.

"It means she could die, Sarah. She could die today."

Hanging up the phone, I heard it. I heard a familiar song coming faintly from my car speakers. It was the song I had played at the funeral for Dave and the boys. And I knew instantly that my mom was going to heaven that day.

I entered the ER to see that most of my siblings and many of my aunts and uncles and cousins had arrived. I walked into the room where my mom was being observed.

She was alert, awake, and calm. She was hooked up to many machines, and I was told that doctors had done tests on her and were awaiting results.

I called my dear friend Heather, whom I had known since kindergarten. She had become a rock for me during my grief journey. She and I had quite a history. We had graduated from high school together, and she was one of my nurses when Dominic was born. When our family returned to the States, her daughter and Kate had become fast friends.

I asked Heather to pick up my kids from school and to come get Elise. Always willing to help, she offered to take all three back to her house so I could have time alone at the hospital with my family.

As I hung up with my friend, I saw a doctor leaving my mom's room. I pulled him aside and said, "I want to you to tell me exactly what we are looking at here. Tell me what is going on."

"Your mom is very sick. She has pneumonia, and I do not think she is going to survive the night." He told me matter of factly, just the way I needed to hear it.

With a sympathetic look on his face, he walked away. I stood there a moment, knowing I would soon have to say good-bye to my mother.

Deanna came out of the room. She had heard the news moments before. She came over to me and we held each other in a firm hug. Deanna softly whimpered and we released one another. There were no words, but the look between us said everything we needed to say: *How are we going to do this again? How are we going to say good-bye to yet another person?*

As we were about to return to our mom's room, my other sister, Elizabeth, arrived. As she walked down the hall, I could see her facial expression change from confused concern to fear and despair as she saw the crowd of people that had gathered at our mom's room. I explained what was going on, and she started to panic.

"Is she dying? Is she dying right now?" Elizabeth demanded.

Aunt Lee came at that point to calm Elizabeth and to fill her in. My aunt Lee was a pillar for our family. She took care of my mom, acted as her advocate, and was always there when anyone needed anything. My uncle Darrin, one of my dad's brothers, had once referred to Aunt Lee as my mom's guardian angel. I couldn't agree more.

As my aunt walked away with my sister, I stood tearless in the hallway. There were no tears, no emotions. I had again put up that wall. That same wall that had gotten me through the early days after Dave, Dom, and Grant had gone to heaven. The same wall I had put up as I watched my dad transition to heaven.

Or was it a shield that God had allowed? A protection? Whatever it was, I knew that it would see me through ushering my mother into her new life.

Heather arrived to pick up Elise, having retrieved Finn and Kate from school. I was surprised to see Kate behind Heather as she entered the hospital. She told me that Kate had asked to stay with me.

"Mom, I want to be here," Kate said, begging me with her eyes.

I looked at my strong, beautiful young lady. She had the same strength and determination as her daddy, and I knew she was not going to take no for an answer. I decided that my girl had earned that moment and should join the vigil we would hold for her grandma to usher her into heaven. I knew Kate had been through more than any young lady her age should ever have to endure. She had shouldered far too great a burden, missing her dad, her brothers, and her grandpa. She needed that moment for her closure. She needed this time to say good-bye to her grandma.

"Okay. Okay, Kate, you can stay," I calmly told her.

As I watched my dear friend leave with my babies in tow, I knew they were in good hands, and I turned with Kate to walk the other way down the hall to my mom's room and to what lay ahead of us.

As I held my mom's hand, she said something, but through the oxygen mask, it was hard to hear her.

"What did you say about Uncle John, Mom?" It sounded like she had said something about her brother.

"She said…that she's dying," my brother told me.

I looked to my mom and she gave a slight nod. She knew that she was about to transition from earth. She again spoke, asking if all her children were there, and we assured her we were all with her.

The doctor came in to brief us further on her condition. He looked at my mom and asked, "Mary, do you want to know exactly what we are looking at here?"

My mom, never afraid to face the truth about her situation, nodded her head.

The doctor braced himself and said, "Mary, you are very sick, and I don't think you are going to make it through the night."

My mom sat very still for just a moment. Then, lifting the oxygen mask ever so slightly from her face, she said, "You mean I don't get to die at home?"

That was the last full sentence my mom ever spoke aloud. She was transferred to intensive care, and we all followed her.

A huge group of us gathered in the waiting area outside her room. Besides Aunt Lee, my aunts Bonnie, Nancy, and Mary were there. Aunt Mary was my dad's sister but had become a sister to my mother over the decades. Uncle John and Uncle Beas (my mom's living brothers) and Uncle Darrin (my dad's brother) and his girlfriend Stephanie also joined us along with many cousins, family friends, and our pastor. We took turns going into Mom's room to have our good-byes with her.

While I awaited my turn, I looked at my sisters. They both wore looks of despair on their faces but allowed smiles to shine through as they spoke with relatives. I was overcome with love and admiration for these two women. Their personalities were far different, but they were so alike in the character that our parents had instilled in them.

Deanna had been a rock to me since Dave, Dom, and Grant had entered heaven. In the early days of my grief journey, she was at my house daily, doing everything she could to help me. She once told me through tears that she had prayed that God would allow her to carry some of my burden. Deanna's love and devotion were unshakable and undeniable. She was there every time I came up with a spiritual truth I wanted to share with someone. She was always willing to listen and to offer her own revelations from our Father.

My sister Elizabeth, a firecracker, was never afraid to say exactly how she felt. I found that honesty refreshing during my grief journey. So many people tried to sugarcoat my experiences, but Elizabeth never did. She would listen as I cried and vented, and then with a sympathetic look, she would give me a realistic assessment of what my next steps should be. Elizabeth was a realist. She helped me shoulder my burdens by babysitting and by comforting me and making me laugh, and she would always offer practical advice.

I looked at those two women and was thankful that my God had made them exactly the sisters I needed. The three of us, while wildly different, complemented each other beautifully, each balancing out the extremes of the other. I was so grateful that I got to travel through life with them by my side.

My turn with Mom had come. I sat by her bedside and took her hands in mine. She was lucid but barely responsive. She looked at me as best she could to indicate she was listening. I talked about God and about the glory that awaited her. I quoted Scripture to comfort her in her transition. As I said good-bye to my mom during those precious moments, I knew she was headed for something glorious. I knew she would be with the same Jesus she had taught us about and had worshiped her entire life, and I was happy for her.

I was overcome with joy that my mom was embarking on the last leg of her journey toward the goal she had pursued her whole life. She was about to lay her burdens down, and I was exceedingly grateful to the loving, merciful God who offers us such joy.

Not long after I said my good-bye to my mom, she became completely unresponsive. Soon after that, Aunt Lee, who had her medical power of attorney, approached us siblings and asked us to make a decision. She told us Mom was on artificial life support, with a machine keeping her blood pressure at a life-sustaining level.

Knowing my mom had asked not to be artificially supported in any way, we knew our only choice was to have her disconnected from the machine.

We knew it was time to say good-bye.

Once the machine was removed, the nurses applied the oxygen mask to my mother, since my aunt had promised her as smooth a physical transition as possible to the other side.

With her five children, her granddaughter Kate, her brothers, and her sister surrounding her bedside and with aunts, uncles, cousins, and family friends lining the walls of her hospital room, my mom took her last earthly breaths and entered into glory.

As she was making her transition, I kept saying with my spirit, *Thank you, Mom. Thank you.*

I wanted her to know how grateful I was for the woman she was and for the faith she instilled in her children. I was happy for my mom and wondered what she saw as she entered bliss. I pictured her running to her Father, to our Jesus, and never wanting to leave His arms. I pictured my boys running to Grandma as she stooped down to grab them up into hugs, with Dave standing right behind them. I saw her welcomed by her mother, my grandmother, and by her brother.

But then I saw her stand to see my dad, a little off to the side, waiting for her to notice him. I saw her look at him and smile a grateful, confident smile, knowing they would never be apart again.

And when the nurses removed the oxygen mask from my mom's face after she had passed to heaven, there was a hint of a grin upon her beautiful, peaceful face.

The morning after my mom passed, I woke early and recorded this journal entry.

"Slept, grateful for my home, my shower, and my bed. Wrestled a bit, tossing and turning, then slept at midnight. Woke at 5:00 a.m. to that familiar pit in my stomach. Saw Dori's text to me about Mom and what Mom loved about me—a well-placed text. I felt peace. I have many thoughts. I feel much sadness and fear but also thankfulness and a wonder at what her homecoming was like. There is also loneliness. I told God she was and is one of my greatest comforters, and now I don't have her. I contemplated how I am called to do this alone. I long for strong arms to be holding me tonight, but am reminded that there are strong arms holding me. 'Yet I am not alone, for my Father is with me' (John 16:32). I was awake until 7:00 a.m. Two hours of tossing and turning, yet peace. I slept again and had a dream I can't remember. I slept an hour until eight. I woke to plans for the day, getting the kids home from Heather's, answering messages, getting to the funeral home to help plan Mom's services. My stomach feels sick, though not literally. I feel that sick feeling of grief, sorrow, and loneliness in the pit of my stomach, in my throat. Remember, sorrow has a taste. Yet I have joy for her, an overall peace that surpasses my understanding, deep in the core of my being. My spirit is comforted."

I described my mom's funeral services to a friend in a letter.

Mom's services were beautiful. What an honor to be a part of it. We lined the halls of the funeral home with photos, as we did for Dad. The same pastor who spoke for Dave, the boys, and Dad spoke, but before that, we had open mic for anyone who wanted to speak. The testimonials lasted forty minutes! She was and is an amazing woman. One of her students came to the wake, and his mother said, "I just thought you should hear from a parent how much of a difference she made in my son's life."

Other students wrote letters, and one of these special-needs kids said, "Thank you, Mrs. Hartrum, for making me feel important."

Oh, I will miss that woman! She was and is a mighty woman of God.

Our church had a banner made for us that says, "Thank you, Mrs. Mary, for teaching us about Jesus." And it is signed by generations of kids, some now adults, whom she taught in Sunday school. What a legacy. If I am an ounce of that woman, I'd be happy. But she's back with my dad, with Dom, Grant, and Dave, with her mother (my grandma Dorothy), and most important, with the Jesus she learned about, taught about, and followed her entire life. I'm happy for her. We joked that the Pepsi vs. Coke debate continues in heaven now that she and Dave are there together. When she would come see my family for visits, Dave (a Coke lover) would say, "Hey, go get a six pack of Coke in the fridge just to see what your mom says when she gets here." He liked to tease her.

I love that woman and know she is in bliss. That fact alone comforts my soul like nothing else could.

I realized in the days after my mom's passing to heaven that I did not properly mourn my dad. I couldn't mourn my dad.

When he passed to heaven, I was so overcome with everything happening in my life—his passing, my mom's illness, my pending surgery, my grief journey—that I had nothing left to give. I had nothing left to mourn him with. And I feared that if I allowed myself the emotion to mourn him, I would destroy the defenses I had built to withstand my mom's illness, to come to terms with my impending surgery and the barrenness it would bring, and to deal with all the stress in my life. I had also resolved to help walk my mom through her grief journey as a new widow, and I didn't think I could do that if I was falling apart myself.

But after Mom had made her transition to heaven, I felt free to mourn Dad. I felt free to let my mind wonder to memories of him suited up to ride his bike and of our many adventures when he and my mom visited my family and we traveled throughout England, Wales, Germany, and France.

My parents came to see Dave and me and our kids in Germany, fall 2009.

My mind wandered to memories of Dad from my childhood. I allowed myself to mourn and to cry. I was grateful for the father I was given, for the man who taught me that life is not easy. He believed in overcoming obstacles.

My dad knew grief, having lost his own father when he was just eight year olds, and he was an overcomer. As a teen, he was in a severe motorcycle accident that almost claimed his life and then almost claimed his leg. But my dad fought, and his leg was restored. He suffered a limp for the rest of his life, but he overcame that by becoming a bicyclist, riding sixty miles in a weekend, twenty miles after work, like it was no big deal.

My parents, Keith and Mary Hartrum, taking a punt ride down the River Cam in England while visiting my family in 2006.

My brothers and sisters and I used to ask Dad why he didn't go to church with the rest of our family when my mom took us each Sunday. Dad responded that he felt closer to God out on his bike, in all that God had created.

I have since come across the log my dad kept in 1986, recording memorable rides and his mileage for the year as a New Year's resolution. My dad rode more than 2,500 miles annually, even up to the year he started to succumb to pancreatic cancer. In fact, he remained a strong rider even during his chemo treatments, feeling weakness brought on by his illness only toward the very end of his journey.

I recalled a conversation my dad had with me not long after my marriage to Dave.

Because Dave and I married so soon after meeting, we had our doubts in the weeks after our wedding, wondering if we had made the right decision. As we prepared to move overseas, we faced the reality of what married life would look like.

I was struggling with saying good-bye to my family, and despite my excitement at being with Dave, I feared leaving my old life.

One afternoon, we set out for New Orleans to say our good-byes to Dave's family. From there, we would catch a flight to New Jersey, ultimately heading to the Azores to begin our overseas adventure. We had not gotten far out of my hometown when Dave and I were in an argument. Only about twenty miles out of town, Dave pulled into a gas station, turned around, and started going the opposite way on the highway. I asked him what he was doing, and he said, "I'm taking you back to your father. I can't handle you."

"Good," I responded, adding that I couldn't handle him, either.

Embarrassed, yet determined to air my grievances as we pulled back into my parents' driveway after having left only thirty minutes before, I stormed into the house. My mom was out running errands, but my dad was still there.

I was crying and my dad asked what was going on. Dave and I recapped our argument and said we felt we had made a bad choice and were reconsidering our decision to set out on this adventure together.

My dad, in his quiet, practical wisdom, sat us both down. He let us vent our frustrations with each other and then said, "You two are both adults and have made a very adult decision. It is time you own up to your choices and stick to the decisions you have made."

My dad coached us on the topics we presented to him and about our frustrations with each other.

After about an hour of talking with my dad, Dave and I were okay. We had a better understanding of each other. My dad had calmed the storm.

And as we got up to leave and to resume our journey, my dad called after us, "Dave, she's got a German stubbornness and an Irish temper. Good luck!" he said with a smile on his face.

Righted again, Dave and I were ready to face our great unknown together.

Looking through cards, letters, scrapbooks, and photos after Mom and Dad had passed, I came across a thank-you note I had written to my dad months after that episode. From the postmark, I could tell I had written it in March of 2001 and had mailed it from our home in the Azores. I thanked my dad for the dinner he and my mom had hosted when Dave and I got married, but I finished it with this: "Thank you, Dad, for putting me in my place that day Dave I talked with you."

As I folded the letter and put it back in the scrapbook, I was filled with gratitude for the man who first modeled for me how to live a good life. My dad taught me how to stand, how to fight, how to persevere, and how to make life happen instead of allowing it to happen to me.

I was grateful as I pictured my dad, welcomed home by the Father, amazed at all he saw before him. I saw him being greeted by my boys, each running up to him. I saw my dad bend down to grab and hold each of my boys in his arms. I saw Dave, standing behind my boys, share a knowing smile with my dad. I saw my dad's mother, my grandma, overjoyed to see her boy, surrounded by my aunt and uncle, Dad's sister and brother that had gone on before.

And then I saw him stand to see off in the distance a familiar face, a face from long ago. I saw his father, whom my dad had pined for since he was eight years old, standing there, smiling, walking over to welcome his son home.

I have often been comforted by the picture of my father playing with my boys, hiking with Dave, continuing his adventures in our true home, and taking long, long walks getting to know his dad.

Chapter 32

Another Good-bye, yet a Relief

From Journal No. 10:

"God spoke to my spirit today: He told me my mission right now is my children. In time, it may be another family, it may be becoming a missionary, or many other things, but for now, it's to be a mom to the children I have with me. I should not underestimate that role. He brought to mind the fact that I am now mother and father to my kids. I am still molding lives. I am still raising children. He reminded me of the preciousness and importance of that role. I am Mom. Perhaps there is more in the future, but for now, I am Mom."

"My ears had heard of you but now my eyes have seen you" (Job 42:5).

We laid my mom to rest December 7 and 8, her funeral taking place on my meeting anniversary with Dave.

As I poured over notes and cards I had received after my mother's passing, I was comforted by the love coming through each message I read, each story of my mom and the difference she made.

Looking around my living room, I was comforted by the flowers, the plants, the cards and the gifts sent by family and friends. My eyes fell on the beautiful stepping-stone Aunt Chris and Uncle Bob had sent from Louisiana. I had put it next to the fleur de lis decorated vase they had sent with flowers for my dad's passing just months before, and I was so grateful for those dear people. I was grateful for all the people who had showered our family with love over the last few months. And I was grateful for the people who continued to walk beside me on my grief journey. Besides missing Dave, Dom, and Grant, my family now had to deal with the loss of my mom and dad.

Mom had been laid to rest, and that part of mourning her was mercifully over. However, I couldn't let my guard down. One big challenge still loomed. I knew that in a week I was due for my hysterectomy—the surgery I had put off for months, the surgery that meant a good-bye to my fertility, but the surgery that could save my life.

I recognized that God was asking me to trust Him yet again. He was asking me to make a leap into another unknown, into uncharted territory for me—into barrenness.

Grateful for the five beautiful lives that Dave and I had brought into the world, I had decided it was finally time to have my surgery. I would release the idea of conceiving or carrying another baby. No longer experiencing the fear and anxiety of wondering whether I would succumb to my mother's fate and get ovarian cancer, far outweighed never having another child by natural means.

I decided to trust my God yet again. If He was asking me to lay down my fertility at His feet, to say good-bye to that part of me, just as I had surrendered so many other areas of my life, then He surely had greater treasures in store for me. He wanted me to take a step of faith to receive them.

With that bold faith I prepared my spirit for the surgery that was only a week away. But first, knowing I would be laid up for a while after the operation, I decided to cram the Christmas season into one week. The children were going to get a Christmas.

We laid Mom to rest on December 8, and my surgery was scheduled for December 16. In the time in between, we visited Santa twice, had photos taken with a reindeer, drove through a lighted nativity display, baked, made treats in the kitchen, wrapped gifts, and snuggled up to Christmas movies with hot cocoa in hand. Thankfully, by late November, we had already bought, put up, and decorated our Christmas tree, and I had done all my shopping and even had most of the gifts wrapped.

The night before my surgery, all arrangements were secured: my friend Karen (another dear sister in Christ) was set to bring me meals during my recovery, and Sue, my Sunday school teacher from childhood (now Elise's church club leader), would also visit and bring meals.

Aunt Lee planned to stay over at my house the night before surgery, since we had to leave at 4:45 a.m. for a 5:30 a.m. show time at the hospital. The kids were spending the night at my friend Heather's house, and she would take them to school the next day. Everything was squared away logistically in preparation for my surgery. But first we had Finn's kindergarten Christmas program that evening at school.

Aunt Lee came with the kids and me to watch Finn sing Christmas carols with his kindergarten classmates. His daddy wasn't there to see his first concert, and Grandma wasn't there to cheer him on as she had done at all of his other endeavors, so having my mom's sister next to me as I watched my boy sing his heart out meant so much to me.

As Finn and the other children sang, I couldn't help but look at all the families around me, at fathers and mothers, at grandmas and grandpas, and for a moment, the thought of my immense losses threatened to undo me.

But God reminded me of my aunt sitting next to me—the love she showed, the way she displayed the hands and feet of Christ by taking time out of her busy life to support my son and to care for me as I faced surgery—and I was grateful.

I was overwhelmed with the realization that where God takes away, He will always refill in His way (Joel 2:25). I was further comforted by what I heard said to my spirit that night: *You are in deep darkness now, but I will be bringing you out into the glorious light.*

I was reminded that God is my Redeemer and that He would restore my life in His time. But for now, there was this concert—and there was that surgery.

Awakening bright and early to head out for my surgery, I felt calm and peaceful. *I will do this surgery in honor of my mother, who fought the good fight*, I resolved.

My mother found the information about the gene she carried too late for her, but she gave my sister and me the knowledge to do something to avoid her fate. My mother gave me a gift that could save my life. I headed into the hospital that morning with my mom and Aunt Lee walking right beside me.

With registration papers filled out, my IV in, and the surgeon scrubbing up, it was time for surgery. Having had five C-sections, entering surgery was no big deal for me. I joked with Aunt Lee that it was the first time I would ever undergo major surgery without leaving with a baby. She very wisely replied, "Nope, you'll be giving them something instead!"

My spirits and resolve were lifted even further when I was about to be wheeled into the operating room and a nurse looked at me and said, "You should be just fine; you are a very healthy young lady."

That was the sendoff I needed and one of the last things I remember before my world went black. I didn't dream. I had hoped I would dream while under anesthesia during the hysterectomy. After surgery, I awoke in a fog but with a blessed sense of relief. Even moments after surgery as I was still waking up, I had the conscious thought, *I am so glad that is over.*

Back in my room and out of the anesthesia, I heard the two things I needed to hear: there was no visible cancer, and everything was removed laparoscopically. That meant a much shorter recovery time when I got back home. I thanked my God for a successful surgery and resolved to recover as quickly as I could. I had just gotten through Grant's birthday, buried my mother and my father and had major surgery, but I knew that Dave's birthday, Christmas, Dom's birthday, and the anniversary dates of my family going to heaven were coming up, and I wanted to heal and to be on my feet so I could withstand the emotional waves ahead.

I was an easy patient, doing all I was told to hasten my healing. I was visited by my brother and his family, by my sister, and by my friend Heather, who brought my kids to see me.

"Mom, now you're not going to have to go to heaven like Grandma, because the doctors gave you shots in your belly?" Elise asked me.

"Sure, Elise—kind of," I said.

But I assured her it seemed as if Mommy was here to stay for a while.

With my company for the evening gone, Aunt Lee having left to take a break, I found myself alone in the hospital room. I was encouraged at the success of the surgery and was peaceful in my spirit at having done it.

I gingerly got out of bed to take a walk up and down the hall as the doctors recommended. As I hobbled along, I laughed to myself at feeling like a little old lady walking ever so slowly through the hospital wing.

Returning to my room, I had just gotten myself back into bed and was about to settle in for a good night's rest when my nurse, Tammy, came in to check on me and to administer medicine. After she had done all that was needed for the night, she turned to leave but stopped for a moment at the doorway and looked at me.

"You are determined," she said quietly.

"What?" I asked, not having heard what she said.

"You are determined. You have courage. I can tell," she repeated.

She smiled at me and left, closing the door softly behind her.

As I sat in my hospital bed that evening before falling into a peaceful sleep, I was in awe of my God and I was grateful. *You have angels everywhere. Don't You, Father?*

God knew I needed reassurance at just that moment. He used my nurse to send me His message of love, His message of calm, His words of, "Well done, My child."

I fell asleep that night encouraged and sure in my spirit at the decision I had made.

Chapter 33

Dave's Birthday

Dave's birthday had arrived, and I was woefully unprepared. I was healing well from my surgery, but my defenses were weak. I awoke that morning with a pain in my heart and in my body. Determined to honor Dave on his special day, I got up off of the couch, six days after surgery, and prepared myself to go to his resting place. I captured the day in my journal.

"Dave's Birthday:

"Physically I am healing on schedule. I send that report out to anyone who asks. But inside, it's my Dave's birthday—only thirty-eight, thirty-six years on earth, two so far in heaven. And my heart is breaking. It is breaking. I miss him so badly I can't breathe at times. My partner, my friend. I try so hard to muster the strength I carry every day, but with surgery, with Christmas, with Mom and Dad, my defenses are weak. I wake this morning to journal him. I write down all birthdays of his we

shared together on earth. I laughed and cried as I wrote this morning. Precious memories—memories you can almost reach out and touch, feel, smell, and taste, memories I want to retreat to. I'm tempted to go backward, not wanting to go forward. What is forward? Unknown. I feel pain in my heart, and right now, pain in my body—pain he would be nursing me through so lovingly. I miss him. Sometimes there are no other words than just those three: I miss him.

"Probably not supposed to drive yet, I take a Motrin to take the edge off the pain, and I get my kids in the car to go visit Daddy's resting place. The kids sit in the car; I ask to have a moment alone. I shuffle to his stone; I stand in the drizzle with my hoodie tied tight around my head, thinking. It's the least I can do. I feel so alone, so very sad, so lost at that moment. Me, my pain, my physical pain, my husband's name in stone, and the rain. Crying, crying. The kids get out, we sing to Daddy, leave him and the boys cupcakes and apples, as has become our tradition. Then I ask for more time alone. I cry for him. I call out to him. I would crawl to him if I could.

"There is no saving grace in that moment, just inward pain, physical pain, absolute longing. There is only past joy and present pain. There is no future in that moment. I owe him more, but what more to do I do not know. I want to convey more to him, but the words won't come, only groans and moans mixed with tears. I would give anything to make him appear to me—to wrap his arms around me, to hold me, to lead me back to the car, to drive us home, to nurse me back to health, and to tell me as I lie at home that this has all been a dream, a nightmare.

"But reality beckons, and my eyes drift from his name in stone to my babies' names in stone, and I remember there is more to endure in the coming weeks. This isn't even the worst of it. Heaviness is on me, the heaviness of grief as I stand in the rain. I shuffle back to my car—the only pieces I have left of him, our babies, waiting for me—and I drive home. No emotion, just robotic movement.

"But there is a seed of something, a reminder of something. I dare not even outwardly call it hope. But it's a reminder of an unseen hand holding me, of someone who has held me and will continue to hold me, of someone who tells me that Dave, Dominic, Grant, Mom, and Dad are in a place unseen and are on mission. They see me struggle, see me in pain and suffering, and love me. I do feel loved.

"I praised my God to the music as we drove home, because there is a bigger picture, more to this story. They see the full picture.

"I determined that I will cry, sing, do whatever comes, and all that matters is this drive home. Will I still praise Him? I will. And I did. At home, I rested. I heard Dave remind my spirit, 'Give our kids the same sense of family we were giving them together. You will be okay.'

"I snuggle my babies. I look in their eyes and see Daddy looking back at me, and I feel for a moment as if I am hugging him. I am reminded Dave, Dom, and Grant will one day come up out of that place. And I press on. Kate wraps gifts for me, the babies play, and I rest. I feel content here with our tree twinkling, our plans upcoming, and memories of my visitors yesterday with warm meals brought from church. I am reminded to put one foot in front of the other—to see a bigger picture and to honor him by pressing on."

Chapter 34
Sweet Reprieve

I awoke to a memory. My mind drifted back to Germany and our home there. I was lying in my bed when Dom walked in the room.

"Good morning," I said.

"Good morning," he said with a sigh.

"What's wrong?" I asked, noticing his sigh and his defeated attitude as he sat down next to me on my bed. I could see a crusty white residue on his upper lip and the same residue, mixed with fur, on his fingers.

"What on earth is that?" I asked.

"You don't want to know," he answered.

Laughing, I asked him again to tell me what happened.

"Well, you know how I've been reading about the Civil War guys?"

"Yes," I answered. Dom's days had been filled with researching all things Civil War, reading histories of the war, playing make-believe in our backyard, setting up his army men in formations from Civil War battles.

"Well," he said, "I wanted to look like the men in the book, so I took some of Cleo's fur and Super-Glued it to my face. But then the Super-Glue smell started burning my eyes, and I tried to get it off with my fingers. And, well." He glanced at his fingers and then at me.

I was laughing so hard that I wasn't even making a sound, the scene playing out in my head as he spoke. I saw Dom pulling loose fur off of Cleo, our husky and Super-Gluing it to his face to try to create a beard and a mustache, only to have the fumes from the glue start to burn his eyes. As he tried to wipe it off, the glue made a hairy, sticky mess on his fingers as well.

At Cub Scouts that night and for the next couple of days, Dom had hairy hands and a thin, crusty white mustache above his upper lip.

As my mind returned to the present, with the smile from that memory still on my face, I got out of bed and started my day.

Chapter 35

Dominic's Birthday

I awoke to thoughts of my Dominic. The night before his birthday, I stayed up until midnight so I could commemorate the first moment of his birth date, much like he used to do while here on earth.

On his last earthly birthday, in early 2013, we were in Louisiana visiting Dave's family. Dom stayed up until midnight the night before his birthday, fishing off of the dock in his Nana and Popsie's backyard, so he could say his birthday had officially started. That birthday, his tenth and his last one on earth, was magical. We spent the day on Popsie's boat on a lake, docking at a lighthouse and later at a beach.

Back on dry land, we headed to Chuck E. Cheese to celebrate the birthday boy with Dave's parents, his uncle Larry, and his aunt Kathy. We rounded out the evening with Nana's homemade cake, gifts, and a celebration at their home. Dave and I gave Dominic a microscope for his birthday. That shows what kind of child Dom was on earth. He did not want a video game or a piece of sports equipment; he wanted a telescope and a microscope, and Dave and I gladly provided him both—the telescope for Christmas and the microscope for his birthday. Dom—having become a quiet, gentle soul in his older years after having been a rambunctious toddler and preschooler—excused himself from the party to fish off of the dock in the backyard. I have said several times that Dom was an old man in a little boy's body.

Much the same as Grant and Kate shared (and share) a special bond, as did (and do) Finn and Dave, and Finn and Elise do now, Dom and I did (and do) as well. A large family tends break off into groups, and family members can't help making connections to those closest to them. And Dom was mine. He is my kindred spirit.

From the start, Dom and I shared a special connection. He looked just like me and looked just like my dad as a little boy. As he grew into a young man at nine and ten years old, he was more than my son; he was my friend. We had the same sense of humor, and when someone made a joke that wasn't very funny, he would shoot me a look, and I would shoot one back. We knew what each was thinking.

We would spend many afternoons and early evenings in the kitchen talking as I cooked, washed dishes, planned a grocery list, and filled in the month's calendar. In fact, Dominic would do so much talking, I sometimes had to ask him to give me a break for a few moments so I could get the rest of my thoughts down on paper before he continued. He could do a spot-on imitation of Kip from the movie *Napoleon Dynamite* and loved making his momma laugh as he tirelessly acted out scenes from the movie. In the evening, I was almost guaranteed to hear him ask, "Mom, do you want pumpkin-spice or green-tea pomegranate?"

Dom made us hot tea almost every night, and he boiled water on the stove. No microwave for Dom. He was too much of an old man for that; he wanted to do it the right way, the old-fashioned way, on the stove. As we sipped our tea together, we'd sit down to a television program, usually a nature show or a documentary, or have a conversation. I am so grateful to God that although we lived in a bustling house with five kids, pets, and lots of commotion, the evenings he and I carved out for tea and conversation went virtually uninterrupted. My God knew I would need those memories to sustain me even now.

We'd talk about many things. Dom would tell me about his latest Lego creation or about his research on the most recent subject or person to catch his interest—historical figures, spiders, snakes, monkeys, the world's tallest buildings, ships. It could have been anything. And it wasn't enough for him simply to talk about these things. During school hours, he would research, document, and write about his latest interests.

Dom's lists of varieties of spiders and snakes remain taped to the wall of his bedroom. The door to his bedroom (now Elise's room) still has a picture of an orangutan he drew, colored, and taped up there. When I went on a cruise with my cousins in the fall of 2012, Dom became intrigued with all things concerning ships. He researched the *Titanic*, drew it, wrote about it, and even built it with his Legos. His drawing of the *Titanic* still hangs on his bedroom wall. Our talks in the evenings over tea were priceless moments spent with my boy.

Grateful for all the memories swirling in my head, I had arrived at Dominic's twelfth birthday—ten on earth and two so far in heaven. The year before, as I was going through all the firsts, I dreaded the onslaught of birthdays and holidays. But that year, each birthday seemed to sneak up on me, since I was so knee deep in all the other struggles plaguing me. I was woefully unprepared for Grant's birthday in November, but God turned it into a peaceful day. I was certainly unprepared for Dave's birthday. That was a rough day, but even then, I still felt I was being carried by unseen hands.

On Dominic's birthday, however, I felt a little stronger. Mom and Dad had made their transitions to heaven, and I had come to a place of peace in my spirit while mourning them. I had gained a closure with them that I didn't have with Dave and the boys. Further, the surgery I was dreading was behind me, and I felt relieved at having made the decision to do it.

I captured some of Dominic's day in my journal.

"Last night, after midnight, I talked with Kate about Dom's birth story.

"I slept peacefully that night; I woke to pleasant, peaceful thoughts and to church bells from the country church down the road . . .

"After journaling about his past birthdays and spending the morning sitting in my bed writing, praying, thinking, reflecting, and looking through pictures, it was time to get ready for the day and to go to his resting place. There were snow flurries outside, and the day was calm, peaceful, and beautiful.

"We got ready and headed out. I was grateful for the normalcy I felt. When we arrived at the resting place, that's when the emotion came. Dee, Meg, and Nick had left an apple, a cookie, and three coins for Dom—my boy, honored by his aunt and cousins. I was touched, and grateful for the card that was addressed to Dom, saying how much joy he brought to our lives and how there's a celebration in heaven.

"After reading the card aloud to Dom, the kids and I did the traditional things. We sang to Dom, and the kids ate the birthday cookies. (We did cookies this year instead of cupcakes.) Then each spoke about one thing they love about their brother. Then they waited in the car while I sang Dom his baby song and talked to him a bit. I closed my eyes as I talked, prayed, and cried; as I talked, I could see the light from the sun coming out from behind the clouds send a glow through my closed eyelids. I felt the crisp breeze blow against my face, and I felt for a few moments, in that place of light and of prayer with the wind on my face and in my hair, that God the Father and the Holy Spirit were standing right in front of me. I felt that Christ heard every word I said, heard every cry, heard every prayer through my tears, saw every single tear, saw my anguished face as I closed my eyes and lifted my face to heaven to feel closer to my boy.

"I felt so sure—no other word for it, sure—that my Dominic Christian was with Daddy, Grant, Grandpa, and Grandma, hearing Momma, and just fine.

"Finally, I remembered that a man buried near my family had the same birthday as Dom. Sure enough, the World War II vet, who lived into his eighties, was born on the same date as Dom, but in 1925, and lived until a few days after Dom. Thinking how very appropriate, with Dominic's love of all things concerning war and history, that a world war vet shared his birthday and was buried right next to him, I left him a cookie and wished him a happy birthday.

"Leaving there, we saw deer—bucks—and that brought us joy. I love that feeling of smiling with pure joy through a heavy heart; it's like laughing through tears. We stopped to feed a deer a couple cookies. I drove the children through some of the historical areas of Jefferson Barracks, and then home we went.

"I am so proud of my boy, of my guys, of my parents, and I have a strange comfort in knowing they are all there together. They are the alive ones. They are more alive than we are here. It is my intension to press on, to endure, but now to thrive until it is my turn to be with my Father.

"I love you, my family. I love you, birthday boy, and I am so proud of you. I cannot wait to see you again! We will laugh and talk and never say good-bye. Praise be to God for His indescribable gift!"

I had made it through Dominic's birthday another year. As I walked away from the resting place and headed for my car, I could almost hear it—giggling, a slight hint of a laugh. And I felt as if Dom was reassuring Momma that he still laughs, he still grins that knowing grin, and he still researches subjects and people of interest. But now he doesn't need books; he can ask the historical figures directly to tell him of their adventures. And I felt assured that when I got to heaven, when it was my time to go home, Dom would be waiting there to tell me all about it, hot tea in hand.

Part IV

Paving a New Path

Chapter 36

Two Years

From Journal No. 10:

"I was always a woman of conviction, but now my goal is to be a woman of God. I had loyalty to God, belief in God, conviction to live for God. But now I have a relationship with God. Amen!"

Approaching the second anniversary of my guys entering heaven, I prayed and asked God to show me how to commemorate the upcoming milestone. *How do get through it, Father?*

He directed my attention toward the piles and piles and boxes upon boxes of photos, scrapbooks, and memorabilia that I had brought home from my parents' house and had stacked in my bedroom.

During the first week of January, my siblings and I had started the arduous task of emptying our parents' home. In the week leading up to the anniversary of Dave and the boys entering heaven, I poured over our family legacy represented in the pages of my dad's old junior high school projects, black-and-white photos of my mom as a girl, newspaper clippings, and postcards from all over the world from my great-grandpa to his daughter, my grandma when she was a young woman and a young mother—family treasures.

I was very close to my grandmother. My dad's mom, my grandma Mary knew struggle; she knew grief, and she knew how to overcome and endure. She and my grandpa Dick married after a whirlwind courtship, much like Dave and I. In fact, as Dave and I were dating, we talked about my grandma and grandpa's love story, and how it was strikingly similar to ours. But unknown to us, the similarities would not stop there. Grandma was left a widow in her early thirties after only ten years of blissful marriage, with seven kids aged nine and under. I was left a young widow in my early thirties after twelve years of blissful marriage, with three kids left with me on earth. But Grandma was a survivor. She was a spitfire with a tenacity to live that I found admirable as a young woman looking up to her. My grandma remarried years after my grandfather's passing, and even had one more child. Only to be widowed for a second time, as my grandpa Bob passed months before I was born. But Grandma overcame. She rebuilt a life out of broken pieces.

I listened intently upon our visits, to her recount memories of her life, to my cousins and me, to my sisters and me. As I thought on Grandma and the lessons she taught me on strength through adversity, my mind drifted to memories of her from my childhood. Having huge Irish family gatherings on holidays, my grandma knew to get any quality time with her twenty-plus grandkids, she needed to make smaller dates to visit with a few of us at a time. I remembered homemade sundaes around her kitchen table, and sleepovers in sleeping bags on her living room floor. Grandma had a taste for style and class having been raised in a wealthy home as young girl, and treated her granddaughters to outings at local tearooms. She was a bold woman and never shied away from saying exactly what she wanted to say. As I got older, my grandma and I remained close. We stayed in touch by phone and letters during my years overseas, and Dave and I always went for visits with her, upon our trips stateside. She and I had many laughs and meaningful conversations, and I always felt understood by her. Grandma was a confidant, a friend. She and I have birthdays in July only two days apart, and she often opened her cards to me, "To my fellow moon child…" and signed them, "Your loving Grandma."

Grandma got to meet my first three babies, and formed a bond with Grant. While my family was living in the farmhouse in Illinois in 2007, preschoolers Dom and Grant and I would visit with my grandma while Kate was in kindergarten. One afternoon while having lunch at a local café, Grandma and I were having conversation. It was just she, Grant and I. Dom wasn't feeling well and my mom offered to babysit him at my home. Three-year-old Grant was playing with his toy cars on the table. As he acted out races with his cars, complete with sound effects, I was afraid Grant's playing was a distraction to my grandma as she and I talked. Newly pregnant with Finn, my emotions were all over the place and my patience wore thin. I kept shushing my boy and reprimanding him, when Grandma stepped in and said, "Sarah, I've had eight kids. Trust me, he's fine." She handed him an orange cracker and gave him a reassuring smile as they each took a bite of their snack. Little Grant took to my grandma from that moment on. And upon our move back to Europe he often referred to her as, "the grandma that gave me the yummy orange crackers".

My grandma passed to heaven in 2009 after a lifetime of ups and down, beauty and heartache. Dave and I were living in Germany, and I was not able to go home for her services. On the day of her funeral, at the same time I knew my family would be gathering across the ocean to celebrate Grandma's life, Dave held down the fort at home while I took Cleo and walked the trails in the woods behind our house. As I walked in the fresh air of that early April afternoon, I spoke aloud to my grandma and told her of all the ways I loved her, what she meant to me, and I recounted many precious memories. With only my companion Cleo by my side, I traversed the leaf strewn paths and thought on Grandma's strength, my admiration for her, and my gratefulness that she was now pain free and reunited with all those that had gone on before her.

As my mind came back to the present, I longed to talk to my grandma in that moment. I longed to talk with her about my grief road, about our shared widowhood. She would offer advice, she would listen as I cried, questioned, and wondered. But while I could not talk with her face to face, I knew my grandma was aware. I knew she was urging me on. I knew that I had her example of perseverance and strength to use, as I continued on my path. I knew I had her stories of proud family legacy to use as my foundation in my rebuilding. And I was grateful. I pictured she and Grant up there together, and the thought of the grand reunion of all those that had gone on before overwhelmed my spirit with pride. My heart felt full.

I had photos, cards, and letters spread out all over my bedroom. I immersed myself in reading through every single item. I felt like I was on a journey into the past, a beautiful journey.

On top of that, in a box in my closet, I had found photos of two trips to Yellowstone that Dave and I had taken in 2003 and 2004, and I started putting them in albums. I was surrounded by family history and beautiful memories.

From Journal No. 10:

"Surrounded by my life—my photos of our travels, my childhood photos, my journals, and letters written—I am overcome with a surge of gratefulness. I fall to my knees in thanks to my Savior, who has chosen to save me, to mold me, and I pray, to use me. I asked God to let me be used to bless and to touch others. I will sow these seeds of blessing I have received.

"Those praying for me for these next few days are crucial to my strength. I feel the power and grasp of my Savior's mighty arms upholding me even now! Praise be to God, my mighty Father from whom all blessings flow."

Staring at all the photos and the family treasures in front of me brought memories of my childhood.

We were a middle-class family, and my parents knew how to create adventure and make memories for us without a lot of money. Camping was a big part of my growing up. I have many memories of the Hartrum clan—all seven of us—piling into our family sedan, sharing seat belts in the back seat, with bags, tents, camping gear, and food piled up all around us—many times past the heads of the smallest in the back seat. Then we would be off on our latest camping adventure. An avid outdoorsman, my dad knew how to pack adventure into each camping trip we took. Whether we were swimming in a river, floating with the currents in a canoe, roasting marshmallows by a campfire, or sitting around the picnic table of our campsite to a meal of barbecued burgers and 'dogs, we always had a great time.

I recalled trips to the zoo, exploring caves, hiking trails in the woods, visiting Fort de Chartres, an old French fort in Illinois, and seeing the annual reenactments and rendezvous. I remembered with a smile the one time my parents took us to Six Flags. My dad was not one for crowds, and we were lucky beyond measure that they treated us to that amusement park outing when I was a small child. I remembered my dad driving our rented pontoon boat all over the lake during our family vacation to the Lake of the Ozarks when I was thirteen and fishing off of a dock for the first time on that trip. I also recalled the annual Hartrum family Thanksgiving hike. After my dad got "the bird" in the oven early Thanksgiving morning, he would take all five of us Hartrum kids hiking, allowing my mom to have the quiet and the concentration she needed to get all the side dishes and the pies made while we were gone for the afternoon. I remembered my parents, especially my dad, being as excited about Christmas morning as we children. I recalled our Christmas Eve tradition of my dad reading a Christmas story to us. My mom followed every year by reading the accounts of Jesus' birth from the Bible.

I also had sweet memories of my mom taking us children to the grounds of the local courthouse for picnics on summer afternoons. She would treat us to band concerts on the courthouse lawn on Tuesday nights throughout the summer. We would all get a snow cone from a stand and sit with our mom on a blanket, listening to the municipal band play.

My mom knew just how to make each one of her five children feel special. She invented "special days," as she dubbed them. She had a rotating schedule for which child to take with her each Saturday for grocery shopping and errands. After grocery shopping with Mom, we would head to the department store to pick out one special-day gift, priced at five dollars or less, then go to lunch at a place of our choosing. Special days were a staple of my childhood, and all five of us children looked forward to our day well into our teen years.

I also remembered all the preschool snuggles with my mom on weekday afternoons. She stayed home with all five of us children until we entered kindergarten. On the fourth Sunday of every month, we would go with a church group to sing to the old folks at the local nursing home. Mom instilled in her children love and respect for the elderly. I recalled sleepovers in the living room with our mom on the weekends my dad went camping with his brothers. Sleepovers came complete with a rented movie, popcorn, and snacks. I remembered joining my dad on the Moonlight Ramble—an organized bike ride of about twenty miles through the streets of downtown St. Louis in the middle of the night. He routinely took part.

I coupled all of those memories with the precious memories of Dave and me and the family we had created, and I was grateful beyond measure.

Since my dad had jokingly dubbed me the family historian years before, my siblings decided that I should take special family mementos and make a Hartrum family heritage museum of sorts along a wall in my basement. In addition, before my mom's passing, she had asked me to be gatekeeper of most of the family photos—meaning I would headquarter photos at my home and distribute any belonging solely to each of my siblings. I had my work cut out for me.

From Journal No. 10:

"Right now, I know the road is tough, and it's been long, but all I can see is what I've been given! Amen, and praise to almighty Father."

The night before my fourteenth wedding anniversary—the day that would open three days of struggle as I commemorated the start of our lodge trip two years before—I was pouring over old photos. I was looking through pictures of my dad as a boy, of my mom as a young woman, and of my siblings and me as children when I noticed a stack of fairly new-looking photos in a bag. As I reached for the bag, my eye caught the time on my phone. It was after midnight.

"Happy anniversary, babe," I said aloud as it officially began.

Bag in hand, I looked inside to see what treasure trove of photos awaited me there. As I pulled out the first photo, I couldn't believe what I saw. It was the first of a stack of pictures from our wedding. We got married in a small ceremony at the courthouse. My parents were our witnesses, and my dad was our photographer. And there in my hands were precious photos, my dad's copies of the shots he took that day. I had not seen them since the day Dave and I were married. I couldn't believe that out of all the old family photos before me—the black-and-white photos, the childhood pictures—I had run across photos from the day Dave and I got married. I was in awe, and as I poured over precious memories, in my spirit I quietly heard, *Happy anniversary, Sarah. I'm thinking of you today, too.*

That next day, on our wedding anniversary, I decided to attend to real life to keep my mind busy. I had a date with my siblings to continue going over items in our parents' house. Getting out of my house and spending time with my siblings was exactly what I needed that day. Every item we found, every picture we took off of a wall, every book we came across, every travel memento we removed from a shelf, carried a memory and represented our lives.

As I helped take things off of shelves, I looked at my hands. I had put Dave's ring back on my left hand. I had also been gifted with my mother's wedding ring and was wearing it on my right hand. I have since removed the rings from my fingers, but they were exactly what I needed to get through the three-day journey I was about to embark on once again.

Back home that evening, grateful that the time spent with my brothers and sisters had helped see me through my anniversary, I knew I had to prepare for what lay ahead the next couple of days. *Father, please guide me*, I prayed.

I awoke the next day, January 12, 2015, hoping and praying I would not dredge up every moment on the time line from my guys' journey two years earlier. But the memories threatened to overtake me, so I decided it was time to confront the grief head on, face to face, toe to toe.

"You've got two days!" I screamed to the darkness. "You have two days, and then it is done! Do you hear me?"

I was acknowledging the grief, the darkness, the memories, and the sorrow that wanted in. I fought every day to keep that darkness at bay. But I reasoned that if I ever felt the need to open the floodgates and allow myself to feel it, then those were the two days to do it. I resolved to allow myself to revisit any moment from that weekend two years earlier that I needed to.

The memories came crashing in—the sounds, the sights, the smells, the voices, the smiles, the anxiety, the worry. And I let it happen. *Father, help me*, my spirit cried, as I started to wonder if allowing myself to relive those moments was a good idea after all.

And He answered me. The idea hit me that if I was going to relive that time, then I might as well write down my memories as I was reliving them. I wrote on and off for two days.

I was nearing the end of the two-day journey, having allowed myself to examine every moment, every memory, and every word spoken two years before, and I found I had written pages and pages. My writing started as journal entries, and continued in my telling of our family's story.

I took a brief break from writing on the thirteenth, the boys' second heavenly birthday, to take the kids to our family's resting place to visit with Dave and the boys. We did not stay long, but as I stood alone, the children waiting in the car after having said their hellos to Daddy and their brothers, I looked at the stones before me. Those bleak, cold stones representing the lives of Dave, Dominic, and Grant. I thought, *They are more than this. They are more than these stones in front of me.*

I said aloud, "Guys, I don't know what to say to you this year. It has been quite a journey, and it has been quite a year this second year. But I will tell you this, I will tell your story. I will tell your story, boys, Dave. People will know, one way or another, however God chooses to do it, who you were and who you are. I will tell your story."

I walked away from those stones with hardly a tear. Instead, I was filled with a determination to get back to writing their story, to tell who they really were, and to say that their story continues, that their passing was not an ending but a glorious beginning!

From Journal No. 10:

"What makes the anniversary date of their heavenly birthday so hard? What makes it different from any other day that I don't have them, that their absence is with me, that their silence is deafening? At least with me, everything comes back. Not just memories, but smells, feelings, sounds, and the taste of sorrow returns. It's a literal taste. The time line plays in my head; major times on the time line scream out at me from the clock.

"And the first anniversary, I completely underestimated. I had no idea how hard it would be. I was woefully unprepared and came out mentally battle scarred due to my lack of preparation. I remember being at my parents' house a few days before the boys' first heavenly birthday and saying to my dad, 'If I can get through their birthdays, which are brutal, I can get through this.

It's no different than any other day; I miss them every day. I plan to honor them by doing a normal Monday.'

"I was so wrong."

For their second anniversary/heavenly birthday, I knew from my past mistake to prepare, to get my spirit ready, to respect the upcoming days, to honor the pain I knew was inevitable. And God is such a good God, He knew exactly what I needed to prepare.

I wrote a friend a letter a day after the second heavenly birthday of my family, describing God's protection from the despair that second anniversary:

> These last few days were as I thought they would be, a test of endurance and strength. It's so hard to explain to people who haven't gone through it. Your mind takes you to a place where all the smells, sounds, feelings, and heartbreak come back as if everything is happening all over again. In a way, I'm still at the stage of almost reliving it. But something was different this year—a sweetness, an honor to their story. And I just started to write. And I wrote on and off for two days.
>
> This year, in preparation to endure, I picked a focal point, just as when I was in labor with Kate and Dom. My focal point was family legacy, not just my family but generations past—photos, notes, and postcards from my great-grandpa to my grandma, from my dad as a child to my grandma, his mother. This helped me still to feel a part of something bigger and to see the contribution Dave and I made to that legacy despite our family's temporary separation. And I thought it was all my idea to keep my mind busy. God is a good God and knew what I would need for these days. I was prayed through these days by so many friends and family, and I am grateful.

Chapter 37

Leveling Out—and Meeting My Precipice

From Journal No. 11:

"Yesterday was a covered day of peace and calm, and I am exceedingly grateful. I woke after a pleasant dream I can't remember to a brilliant sunrise I felt was painted just for me. I looked to the sunrise and with a smile whispered, 'Good morning' to my Father in heaven. There was a sacredness in the peace, a peace I can't adequately describe with words. It was beyond what my human mind could understand (Philippians 4:7); it just was. I didn't know when it started or what brought it on, but I was grateful.

"On top of the peace, on the fringe, in the distance, on the horizon, was a hope I can't explain, either. Oh, I tried so hard to figure out the hope.

"'Lord, is it a hope of Your soon coming? Or Lord, is it because some blessing is coming around the bend?'

"Perhaps the hope was just for that day, for that moment. I remembered that mercies are made new each morning (Lamentations 3:23). Maybe it was a hope to carry me through just that day. Whatever the purpose, I felt it deep in my spirit on the horizon. And with that hope, coupled with the supernatural peace, I started my day.

"I felt a stirring in my spirit, a preparation. I realized the moments of stillness, of seeming inactivity, are a preparation. I could not quench my hope. There was (and is) a hope that lives in me, rises up in me, comes over me, and I am grateful.

"I readied for the day and enjoyed my Elise. We giggled, we joked, and I looked in her eyes and realized this is life, this moment. This is peace. This is hope. This is joy. And I realized how I take my sweet babe for granted—not realizing she and her brother and her sister are hope, peace, and joy. All that is good, right, noble, and pure is wrapped into those tiny bodies. And I was humbled as I saw the hope and the joy He gave me every single day through my babies. And I keep looking for more. 'What's around the bend, Father? I feel more is meant for me, Lord.' As love, light, and joy were staring me right in the face through those beautiful hazel eyes.

"I realized my job is to make her life as beautiful as I can. Too often, she, like her brother and sister, get caught up in my rolling sea, in my tempest waves; they are too familiar with the brutality of the grief process, of my grief process, on top of trying to shoulder their own confusions. They are too familiar with the deep, dark lows; yet the moments of calm. I decided in my spirit, in that moment, to try, by the power of the Holy Spirit, to provide for her more moments of calm and less exposure to my rolling seas."

The second anniversary of Dave, Dominic, and Grant going to heaven had come and gone, and I had survived it for another year. The weeks that followed were filled with ups and downs as I tried to get my footing and to engage again with real life.

One particularly hard night, while the kids were in church club, I was sitting alone in my car in the dark in front of my parents' empty house. My mom's car was still in the driveway, not driven. Usually, on church club nights I would pick up my mom and we would have dinner and conversation somewhere. But that night, there I sat in my car alone in front of a dark house, with no one to meet for dinner.

From Journal No. 11:

"I'm sitting here in front of this house, memories spinning. My family is swirling through my head—my parents as children, then as a young couple. Father, I feel lost. I feel like an orphan, a widow, and a mourning mother right now.

"I sit in the dark driveway, look at the dark house, the car not driven in the driveway. If I squint I can see shadows of lives past still roaming through the house, hear laughter, hear commotion, hear life.

"Lord, I'm tired of saying good-bye. Father, I'm tired of seeing others still live all around me—fathers, mothers, husbands, wives, children, even some grandparents, still intact, still thriving, still here.

"I know where they are, but I am here, and they are there. I feel very alone at this moment, my Father.

"I see darkness all around but refuse to believe this is all there is. Mom still laughs. Dad still rides. Dave still hikes. Dominic still builds. Grant still explores."

Another day, as I was out running errands, I heard a woman give testimony on the radio about how her husband had passed only two weeks before and about how she was steadfastly leaning on the Lord to see her through her trial. She sounded so sure of her peace, so calm, so composed at two weeks in. She sounded so confident in her healing. And all I could think was, *It has just begun, lady.* I was in a bad place in my spirit that day, and instead of being happy for that woman and praising God for the peace He had apparently covered her with, I got angry. I wanted to call her and tell her, "It's okay to cry, it's okay to yell, it's okay to be mad, and it's okay to question. As long as you come back up, get it out! Don't hold it in! Don't do what you think you are supposed to do, or your grief will fester and come back to bite you later. Get it out!"

I found myself wishing someone would tell this woman the reality of what she was about to face. I said so aloud to myself in the car and then went home to journal.

From Journal No. 11:

"I want to tell that lady I just heard on the radio who has such strength and resolve two weeks after her husband's passing that it gets worse. Hold on to that hope, comfort, and peace to get you through the initial pain, because it gets worse when real life hits and he's not there or when you open back up and the 'What now?' comes. Two years in, I can tell you it gets worse."

Entering year three of my journey after the second anniversary, I found that despite moments of resolve and progress on my grief journey, there were still moments that grabbed me out of nowhere. I realized that grief would rear its ugly head for the rest of my life and that it was up to me to remember how to control it and to recall how God had been faithful to save, guide, and protect me in the first two years of my journey. I had to remember what I had learned about how to harness each grief wave when it hit and sometimes how to simply fall into the arms waiting to carry me through each attack. And the attacks were sure to come. I had to allow God to guide me to the other side of each attack. God had laid a foundation of trust, of protection, and of guidance in the first two years of my journey; it was up to me to use the tools God had equipped me with and to recall the methods of handling my grief He had taught me. He had proven Himself as my protector. And like an impenetrable shield, always stood battle-ready to grab me by the hand and to run me through the flaming arrows the Enemy was waiting to throw at me.

Mercifully, as those January days progressed, my spirit got a little lighter, and I started to find my footing again.

I found a bright spot early in the new year when I gathered with my brothers and sisters and their significant others to celebrate my dad's sixty-sixth birthday—sixty-five on earth and one so far in heaven. We met at one of his favorite restaurants and toasted him, "To Dad! Happy birthday, Dad. We love you!"

We enjoyed a blessed evening of good food, laughs, memories, camaraderie, and family in honor of our dad.

Many relatives and friends continued to keep the children and me occupied. We went to a museum with my uncle and his girlfriend, visited with my aunts, and enjoyed many play dates. I had dinners out with my cousins and with my good friend Karen. My friend Heather encouraged and motivated me, and Becky listened to my latest revelations at our nearly weekly get-togethers. Kim and Chris, unbelievable friends to my children and me, continued to be like family to us. Chris helped to fill the male role missing in Finn's life and took him to see "manly movies." Kim and my sister-in-law Roxanne became staples at my home for play dates and for girlfriend talk. Those play dates with Roxanne and Kim became a welcome reprieve on my grief journey. Whether we were meeting at the park, at my home, or at one of their homes, I knew play-date afternoons with Roxanne and Kim were good for our kids and also meant fun, food, and many laughs for us ladies.

Though my days were becoming brighter, I still had questions. While my anger subsided again, the questions remained. Again, God whispered to my spirit that I would always question, that questions, like the grief waves, may be with me for the rest of my earthly life. The trick was learning how to continue to follow and to trust my God and His sovereignty even when I was asking questions that my Father was not ready to answer on this side of the veil.

From Journal No. 11:

"I look at my children, and I see how they've been called to walk this life without some of the basic loves that most children in a healthy home enjoy: their dad, two of their siblings, the love of my parents, their grandparents. I see my kids now asked to carry the burden of having one earthly parent, a single mom, because the dad who adored and cherished them has been called home to heaven.

"I see the void left by a man who was a father figure to most kids he met—a mentor, a friend—now absent from the lives of his own children. A man who dreamt of a brood of kids all around our dining room table, now absent from the family he helped create. There are empty seats at the table he wanted so much to fill to overflowing.

"I see my children, once rich in the camaraderie and friendship that come with a big family, with several siblings as their friends and their playmates, have to say good-bye for now to two brothers—Kate having to say good-bye to her best friend, Grant; Finn having to be the sole brother on earth, the sole male in our home. I hear Elise as she plays make-believe with her dolls explain from one doll to another that she actually has three brothers but that two live in heaven. I see the loneliness in Finn's eyes and the frustration in his spirit when he doesn't have anyone to play Legos with, anyone to run out in the woods with. Elise, his new buddy, tires after just so many rounds of wrestling, opting for gentler pursuits. (I am so grateful for school and for Finn's playmates there.)

"I see this family, once so testosterone-heavy, now wildly off balance as Finn is now far outnumbered. I see Kate, in her loneliness, be the only 'big kid' now on our Decareaux family day trips as I try to keep up that tradition of adventure Dave and I started for our family. I see her meander, bored to tears, through the preschool areas, the areas suited for younger kids, as we explore museums and parks when once upon a time, she would break off with her brothers. While Dave and I explored with the babies, Finn and Elise, the big kids—Kate, Dom, and Grant—would be free to explore the more age-appropriate areas for them.

"I hear Finn ask me why he's the only boy in our house. I hear him ask me why our family doesn't have a dad. I hear Finn cry out in frustration in his six-year-old innocence, 'Will you get a dad in this house, please?'—not realizing the enormity of what he's asking. As if it's as simple as that. Because in his mind, it is.

"My heart breaks for my kids. I think of my kids, having just lost their dad and two brothers, having to say good-bye to their grandpa and grandma not even two years later. Grandma cheered Finn on at every karate practice. Kate allowed Grandpa to call her Katie, the only person on earth given that privilege, for many years. Elise had known Grandma and Grandpa since she was two years old and we moved back to the States from Germany. Their presence in our lives had always been so constant and consistent, that she had never known, not knowing them. My parents proudly wore the titles of grandma and grandpa. And they joyfully lived out those roles. Kate got her artistic ability from her daddy, and also from my father, and my dad enjoying showing Kate how to draw upon their visit to us in Germany. My mom loved snuggling all of her fourteen grandbabies as much as she loved snuggling her children when we were small. The memories of her curled up on the couch in my home reading to itty bitty Kate, Dom and Grant in Italy, fill my mind. The images of her scooping up Finn and Elise in hugs and tickles in Illinois brings a sweet smile to my face.

"I wonder why, Father? Why the enormity of our losses? Why are You asking me to walk the road of mourning mother, widow, and earthly orphan? Why are You asking my children to be fatherless? Why did you bring home two of their best friends, their brothers? Why did You then take home so soon after, their grandparents, who had become constants in our lives in the absence of their daddy and brothers?

"God quietly reminded my spirit, Where I take away, I will always refill. Maybe not in the way it was before, but refilled all the same (Joel 2:25, Isaiah 61:7, Job 42:10).

"I feel such a surge of resolve to try to be the best parent I can be to my kids, to try to be mom and dad, but knowing I am only one woman. I know I will have to lean heavily on my Father in heaven to provide me with the strength, wisdom, provision, patience, and sheer will it is going to take to try to be two parents to my children."

Despite the ups and downs, the anger and the questions, as the year continued I began to feel a grand sense of purpose, of something coming around the bend.

I started to tell anyone within my circle of support who would listen, "I am believing God for good things in 2015. It's a bright new day. Now I must press on, knowing I am marching ever closer back to my boys as each day passes. I just feel like I am on the edge of a great precipice—like something is about to happen, and I don't know what it is yet."

And as I contemplated this precipice, I had to fight the urge to custom-tailor the restoration that lay ahead. God told me He would restore me, and it was up to Him how and when to do so. I simply had to trust Him. I had discovered this in the summer of 2014, and the lesson had been reinforced throughout the previous fall.

As I was driving and contemplating, God struck me with a simple but profound idea.

What if this is your redemption, daughter? What if your restoration is an acceptance of your new life? What if every day you tackle raising your kids alone, run your house, navigate grief and mourning, let go of anger, come to Me with your questions, reach out to others, and try to be a witness and an example, is your great redemption?

I fought the sentiment a bit, asking aloud, "God, but what about my precipice? What about a grand purpose? What about a grand design? What about being a foster mom or a wife again one day or adopting a baby? What if I should be a missionary or get a new job or …"

The list of dreams and possibilities went on.

I felt God answer my spirit, *Those are all grand dreams, My child, and yes, dream them, continue to dream, to hope in them, and perhaps some of those dreams may come to fruition as a restoration for you; some may be fulfilled this side of the veil. But if they are not, if none of those new dreams is fulfilled, is this enough for you? Is this enough as your redemption?*

Are depending on Me and being carried by Me through your journey enough? Is allowing Me to help you raise those children with the patience and the wisdom I will give you enough? Are the provision and the stability I will give you enough? Is the insight I will give you about whom to reach out to and how to minister to others enough? Are the precious moments spent with the children I have left for you enough? Are the friends I have blessed you with to overflowing, the family that I have made pillars of strength around you, enough? Is every day I wake you to a brilliant sunrise and lull you to sleep with the breeze through the trees outside your window enough? Is what I have already blessed you with enough, My daughter? What if your precipice is an acceptance of all I have blessed you with? Am I enough for you, child?

I was still a moment as I heard the questions spoken softly to my spirit.

And in my spirit, I answered, *Yes, my Father. Yes, You are enough.*

As I drove, I considered all that I had been blessed with, all the beauty that remained in my life, all the gifts that I had been given, and all the ways God had sustained me and continued to sustain me. And I decided, *Yes, He is enough.*

I decided to continue to dream, to continue to hope, but I also accepted what God had told me a year before—abundant life will come in many forms, and only He knew if my abundant life would come on this side of the veil or in eternity. My restoration would come in many forms—the seemingly small and familiar and, perhaps in time, the grand dreams I had pictured.

I realized I was at my precipice. The grand purpose had led me to accept what I still had and to say good-bye for now to all who had gone on before me. And I realized that if anything else were added to my life in the months or years to come, it would simply be an extra blessing. God was enough for me, and anything else He chose to bless me with would come because He is a good God.

As I realized God was my all and would always sustain me and would be faithful to carry me along the path He had called me down, I knew it was time to face good-byes I had been avoiding for two years. I knew it was time to release my family.

From Journal No. 11:

"Enduring grief has made me more aware of all of my blessings. When you are suffering, even what 'is bitter tastes sweet' (Proverbs 27:7). Everything means more. Even small, seemingly insignificant things are blessings, are joys."

Chapter 38

Letting Go into Capable Hands

While living in England from 2005 to 2007, we were stationed with a couple who lost their baby girl at four months old. Devastated for them, Dave and I kept the couple in our prayers and talked of them often.

One afternoon, Dave and I were on a drive with our little brood—our preschooler Kate, our toddler Dom, and our infant Grant—headed out for a Decareaux family day trip. As Dave drove us through the English countryside, I found myself thinking of my friend, a woman who had given birth to her daughter, only to have to give her back to God four short months later.

I just don't understand, God, I thought. *I don't understand how You could ask that of a parent. How could You ever ask a parent to say good-bye to a child?*

As I looked at my three babies in the rearview mirror, I was overcome with love and gratefulness as my beautiful, intact family continued down the road, headed to our latest adventure.

I had no idea that years later my Father would ask me to walk the same road of pain that had pierced my heart for my friend many years before. He would ask me to say good-bye for now to two of my children, two of the very children I had gazed at through the rearview mirror that beautiful afternoon.

As my mind came back to the present, the Father reminded my spirit that we were never promised an earthly life without nightmares or trials. We were never promised that this life would be smooth, that the waters would always stay calm, that the path would never be treacherous. In fact, we were told the very opposite. We were told we would suffer many trials (Acts 14:22, 1 Peter 1:6, 1 Peter 4:12-13, John 16:33).

A battle-scarred life is evidence of a well-lived life, of a faithful life, I believe.

As a mother, there was nothing more sacred then ushering my children into this life, then ushering two of them into their next life, into real life; into eternity. The very same children who were knit in my womb, who grew and were nurtured in me, whom I felt move and kick inside my body, whom I birthed. The same children whose first sounds I heard, whose tiny cheeks I kissed as their daddy carried them to me. The very same children I fell in love with from the moment I laid eyes on them, from the moment they said their first words, from the moment I watched them take their first unsteady steps. These were the children whose tiny hands I felt on my cheeks as they grabbed my face for goodnight kisses. These were the children whom I watched grow into a young boy, and into a young man. These children, these boys, I ushered into this life, and then I ushered out of it. And there is nothing more sacred.

We were never promised to be spared from nightmares. I am reminded.

But I was promised that the hand that reached out to save me from the waves of despair and brought me aboard His boat of reprieve during the storm, will continue to hold me. It's the same hand that held me when I said my earthly good-byes to my boys, as I lay with their bodies that would not respond to mine. The hand that guides me through every birthday, every special day, every holiday. God's hand holds me as I face every moment without my boys. He holds me up as I traverse the rocky path of learning to live again.

God assures me every day, that just as He holds and guides me; He holds my boys in the same mighty hands. They are the hands of my creator, their creator. He has a plan for my boys, He has a plan for me; one that extends beyond our limited life here on earth.

I released them to His hands. I released myself to His hands. I allowed God to take them and to hold me. I allowed Him to guide them along their new path of discovery and mission in heaven as He guides me along my new path of discovery and mission on earth.

I pictured Grant running to the Father for a quick hug and then taking off on another adventure. I saw him taming lions, playing with bear cubs, and swimming with sharks, all with no fear. I saw him watching animals perform their intricately designed routines, knowing now why they do all that they do. Grant knows why the birds sing. He knows why the wolves howl.

I saw Dominic, in all his curiosity, refusing to leave our Father's side. I saw him ask many questions. I saw him seeking to learn the secrets of life. I saw him direct his questions to as many historical figures as he could find. Dom knows the mysteries of the ages. There are no secrets for my boy now.

And that's only what my human mind can conceive. I have no idea of the heavenly wonders my boys are experiencing right now—all the while being guided by their daddy, my Dave, now joined by Grandma and Grandpa, and under the eternal loving care of our almighty Father.

The beauty of it all, the saving grace, is that one day those paths will cross again. And one day I will hold my Grant David, I will hold my Dominic. I will feel their tiny hands in mine, and will never have to release them again.

Chapter 39

A Releasing

Dear Dave,

It was you and me against the world with five little companions in tow. I miss you, my friend, but I know now that there is more. There is more for you. There is more for our boys. There is more for Kate, Finn, and Elise. There is more for me.

You lived on earth honorably and faithfully. I want to do the same, friend. It is more than my human mind can imagine, but that yours now can fully grasp, this mystery of our existence, of our purpose, of our mission. You can see how the threads of our lives form the tapestry of God's ultimate plans. The bright colors, as the blessed times in our lives, threaded alongside of the dark colors, as the obstacles in our lives, together make a stunning scene as you stand back and look at the full picture. You see that full picture now, friend.

I am ready for bright colors, Dave. I want to live again. I want to let God work through me in all His fullness. I have a fire to live. I'm back. I'm back, Dave. There are dark days, to be sure, but I'm at the point where the good days outweigh the bad. I owe all of that to our gracious heavenly Father, who revealed to me that this story is not over! So as my story continues, I will take courage! (Psalm 31:24). I am still finding out what to do with that fire. I was meant for more than to live on the sidelines in the darkness. But I will press on with patient endurance (Hebrews 10:36).

Thank you, my dear friend, for being the man you were to me on earth. The man you were to our children on earth. The man you were to the world on earth. The man you were for God on earth—a man among men, a man who set an example. A life well lived, indeed. And the best part is, the saving grace is, that you continue.

You continue to be that man in heaven—in perfection, in holiness, at completion. I am so happy for you, friend. You ran the race, and you ran it and finished it so well. You were born for, lived for, and went home for "such a time as this" (Esther 4:14). Your beautiful life here on earth was orchestrated by our Father, and He knew just how long you would be here, just how long our sons would be here, just how long I will be here, and you fulfilled His plan for you. How proud He must have been of you upon your entrance home. I am so happy for you.

Life here is so very short, and you lived it to its fullest. Now enter into your rest and continue your mission there. We still have a mission together. And while it looks a lot different than I thought it would, our mission continues because our family created a story. Our lives are a story. I am not the same person I would have been had I not walked alongside you for twelve years. The mark you made on my spirit has made me a better soul than I would have been had we never met that December night fourteen years ago. I am exceedingly grateful to our Father for knitting our hearts together, for knitting our lives into one those many years ago. The legacy you left here on earth will continue and will grow despite your residency in heaven. And I'm grateful I got to be a part of it. Now it would seem I walk this road alone. "Yet I am not alone, for my Father is with me" (John 16:32). I am in capable hands.

It's time, Dave. It's time for me to throw the gates wide open and allow the Father to use me as He needs to until it is time to finish my race. I am frightened. But I have you to use as my example. You lived here with boldness, with fullness, with passion, with dignity, with strength. You unabashedly allowed Jesus to be the anchor of your soul, and you were not afraid to let the world know.

So here I go. I will step out into this great unknown. Here I stand, willing to hand God all the broken pieces of my heart, of my spirit, and to see how He rebuilds me. There is a part of you in the healing balm He uses to restore me, a part of Dominic, a part of Grant. Thank you.

You started out on every trail in life with confidence, and so will I. Until those trails meet in eternity and I get to see your face again, I will press on.

Thank you for paving the way down this rocky, uncertain path. Led by the strong hands of our Father, I will follow the trail blazed by you. As I set out, I am grateful knowing that no matter where our paths may lead, they meet at the same place in the end. And that place is not an end at all but our true glorious beginning.

Until then, friend.

Chapter 40

A New Beginning— Continuing the Climb

From Journal No. 11:

"I can't wait to one day meet my Savior, meet Jesus, meet my heavenly Father. To one day put a face to the unseen hands that have held me my entire life but that I had never felt before as I have the last couple of years. To stand before the very One who made me, who knew this would be my path in life and allowed it, assuring me He would walk it with me. The One who speaks softly to my spirit through revelations and dreams, through His words as I seek His instructions in the Bible. That still small voice that beckons at the depth of my spirit. I can't wait to meet Him, to get to walk side by side with Him and see who I am talking to and who is talking to me. I know one day He will walk with me and will explain the purposes behind every intricate detail of my life, behind the things He allowed in my life. I will see the grand design, the plan, and the purpose."

As 2015 continued, I recalled a conversation I had at a ladies' group during our time stationed in Germany. I was attending a Bible study and was in a small breakout group of about four ladies. We were each asked to talk about our life dreams and how we could achieve them. We were also asked to try to decipher what calling God may have given us—what we felt we were meant to do. When it was my turn to speak, I looked at my list and said, "My dreams were to become a teacher, a wife, a mother and to travel. I have achieved my life dreams. God has granted me the 'desires of my heart'" (Psalm 37:4). I said this not with pride but with gratefulness and as a testament to God's goodness.

As we continued around the group, most women found they still had many unfulfilled desires left on their lists of life goals and dreams. As I listened to the other women read, I was overcome with gratitude; I felt like I had arrived. I felt that I had achieved my life goals and that my dreams had come true.

I was grateful to God for answered prayers, but one thing nagged me. *God, I'm only in my early thirties. If I've arrived and my goals are achieved, what is next for me?*

As I left the ladies' group that day, I thought that I had summited, that I had arrived at the top and had achieved all that I ever thought I wanted out of life. Yet God had more planned for me for His purposes.

As I returned to the present, God softly reminded my spirit that I had not summited that long-ago day. Sure, I felt like I was at the top. The view was beautiful, the skies were clear, and I was fulfilled and accomplished. But God revealed to me that I had merely plateaued. There were greater heights to achieve, more to work toward and to overcome. There were dreams, plans, goals, and desires I did not even know I had. He quietly reminded my spirit that my life goals before were merely self-seeking; while they were not wrong, they were simply geared toward my happiness. He reminded me that He had goals and dreams for me that would also serve a purpose for His kingdom. I felt God asking me, if all were taken away, if I were brought to my knees, would I continue the climb with Him? And in my spirit, I answered yes.

I felt my Father say to my spirit, *Daughter, there is more to go, more to climb. I gave you a brief reprieve with the blissful years on your plateau, but it is time to move on. Move up; keep climbing. Continue on with Me. Continue the climb, and daughter, believe Me, when you do summit, you will know. The view will be breathtaking and will last forever, My child.*

One afternoon early in 2015 when I was substitute teaching at Finn's school, I found myself with playground duty during recess. As fifty or more kindergarteners played around me on all sides, another teacher and I kept close watch, making sure the children played nicely and safely.

"Hi, Mom!" Finn yelled as he ran past me while in hot pursuit of a classmate he was trying to catch during a game of tag.

That's one of the blessings of occasionally subbing at Finn's school—getting to see my boy throughout the day. Since I was a sub, I was somewhat of a novelty, an unfamiliar face, to those precious five- and six-year-olds. Several children were crowded around me, asking me questions. "You know Finn?" asked one.

"Hey, why did Finn call you Mom?" asked another.

"How do you know Finn?" asked yet another.

I was bombarded with questions along with the occasional requests: "Will you tie my shoe?" "Can you zip my coat?"

I was trying to answer every question and to tie every shoelace presented to me when off to the side I noticed a little girl. She had her head hung low, and as I neared her, I could see she was crying.

"What's wrong, dear?" I asked.

"My … my card had to be m-o-o-v … moved today," she said through sniffles and sobs.

She was referring to her behavior card having to be moved from the "good behavior" column to the "not-so-good behavior" column in her classroom earlier that day.

"Oh," I responded sympathetically as I knelt down beside her.

"Guess what?" I said, trying to comfort her best I could. "Tomorrow is another day. It is a bright new day, a new day to make better choices and a fresh start."

As I stood to gather the children into line and to help lead them back to their classrooms, I smiled and shook my head at myself. I wondered why I didn't take to heart the advice I had just given a six-year-old girl. As I led the kids back to their classrooms and settled behind the desk of the room I was in that day, I resolved to take the advice God had inspired me to give that child.

Tomorrow is another day; tomorrow is a fresh start.

In the early evening, I drove home from teaching and running errands, the school bus carrying my kids having beaten me home hours before. As I pulled into my driveway, turned off the car engine, and got ready to hop out of the car, I saw something in the corner of my eye—a bright neon index card shoved in the console of my car. Not knowing what on earth it was or remembering that I had put anything there, I was curious to see what it might be. I grabbed it and found one of my mom's many prayer cards, as she called them.

For years, my mom had been in the habit of writing her favorite Scripture passages on index cards and of writing on the back what a particular passage meant to her.

I read the card.

"Give us aid against the enemy, for the help of man is worthless. With God we will gain the victory, and He will trample down our enemies" (Psalm 60:11–12).

On the back, my mom had written, "David found satisfaction only in his relationship with God. God refreshes and fulfills him."

As I sat on the edge of the driver's seat, I thought, *Thank you, Mom. I hear you.*

As I walked to the front porch, I thought about all the ways God had trampled my enemies and would continue to trample them—the enemies of despair, confusion, darkness, death, sorrow, and anger—and I realized that God was refreshing and fulfilling me every day.

As I climbed the porch stairs toward my front door, I could see light in the house; it seemed every light was on. I heard laughter, voices, commotion, and footsteps as the children hurried from one task to the next. I knew warmth and hugs lay just beyond the door. I knew life was thriving just over that threshold.

As I turned the doorknob, I knew that God was enough and that everything He had already blessed me with was enough. And I was exceedingly grateful in my spirit.

Epilogue

One fine day, my mission will be complete, my earthly road will come to an end, and I will rejoice in a glorious new beginning. I will see Dave, Dominic, and Grant David again.

Until then, I will press on. I will move. I will continue forward. I will be patient with myself, as I still have much to learn, many ways to grow, and more healing to do. There are days when I take grand strides and days when I feel I've taken two steps backward. There are many days when I want to wallow, to stay stagnant and still. I don't want to grow. But God demands of my spirit that I stop playing in the muck and the mire and rise to the life to which He has called me.

I have come to realize that the grief road is a never-ending one. There will never be complete healing or a finish line, at least not on this side of the veil. There are still lonely days, and there are still tears. While my life does not have to be defined by grief, I have come to accept that grief will be a constant companion. I must learn to rely fully on God to get me through the tougher days, the choppy seas, and the treacherous paths.

But I have also learned that there are days when He will fill me with joy to overflowing. On some days, grief takes a back seat, and my life feels full. God reminds me of all I still have and of all He will restore to me in one way or another. I will take one step at a time, one breath at a time, enjoying the level parts of the path and asking God to lead me through the steep areas. I resolve to enjoy the view as I continue on my way. I feel I owe it to Dave and our sons not only to endure this journey in front of me but to revel in it, to find joy, purpose, and beauty in it. All the while, cherishing all the times they brought joy, purpose, and beauty to my life.

Dave, Dom, and Grant left a legacy of love, endurance, loyalty, and peace. How can I do any less than to strive to leave just such a legacy with my time here on earth? Until I reach that place where grief is no more, tears do not exist, good-bye is no longer a word, all paths are level, all views are bright, all skies are clear: the best yet to come.

"Be strong and courageous. Do not be afraid; do not be discouraged, for the Lord your God will be with you wherever you go" (Joshua 1:9).

From Journal No. 12:

"'The skies proclaim the work of his hands' (Psalm 19:1).

"I was walking back from the kids' bus stop this morning and caught the sun rising to my right, coming out of the east. It had a brilliant orange glow, casting yellows, blues, and purples on the surrounding clouds, the colors coming together to make a stunning morning sky.

"As I passed the tree in my front yard, the bare branches started to obstruct my view of the sunrise and the brilliant sky, so I started to back up to return to where I could see the beauty unobstructed once again.

"But I felt the Holy Spirit whisper to my spirit a revelation spoken softly to my soul: 'Don't back up to see the beauty again, but step forward beyond the tree, the obstruction, and you will see the beauty once more. Don't go back. Step forward.'

"And sure enough, there it was, there it remained—the beautiful sky. I got a different view seeing it from in front of the tree than before the tree's obstruction, but it was stunningly beautiful all the same. The beauty remained. The view was slightly different, but there was still stunning beauty. And all I had to do was allow the obstruction, that brief interruption in my view, for a moment to see that the beauty was always there.

"I had to walk past the tree and step forward to see the magnificent skies open up before me."

The kids and I—the Decareaux family; Thanksgiving 2014, Illinois.

Kate, Finn, and Elise, fall 2014, Illinois.

Left: Kate, almost thirteen, fall 2014, Illinois.
Right: Finn, six years old, fall 2014, Illinois.

Left: Elise Marianna, four years old, 2014, Illinois.

Right: Bear, two and a half years old, fall 2014, at our creek in Illinois.

Kate, Finn, and Elise, winter 2014, Illinois.

AFTERWORD

April 15, 2015

As the second anniversary of my husband and two sons entering heaven approached in 2015, I prayed and asked my Father in heaven how to prepare for the days ahead of me. I felt Him tell my spirit to start writing. Six weeks later, I had completed the story of my family, of our life, of our journey. How this book came about is explained in detail in the chapter "Two Years."

Writing this book was a balm for me. I started writing that morning of January 12, 2015, as part of a healing process. Interestingly enough, I could only write about the events of January 13 from two years prior, on January 12; and could only write about the events of January 12 from two years prior, on January 13. I could not write about the day, on the actual date. That hit too close to home; it was too hard. I wrote for two days, and when I was finished, I had the hardest parts of the story done. I continued to write every few days, and by the end of February, I had completed the book. I wrote as God laid certain subjects on my heart. I wrote whatever He placed on my heart at any given time. When the writing was completed, I put the chapters together like puzzle pieces. I did not write in chronological order. As an example, I put off writing about the funeral of my husband and sons until the last week of the project. I wasn't ready to put myself in that place. As I buckled down to write that chapter, I was so emotionally involved that I was becoming physically ill. I had to periodically step away from writing and to reengage after I had regrouped.

My goal with this book was multilayered.

I wanted to share my testimony: "We overcome by the blood of the Lamb and the word of our testimony" (Revelations 12:11). I believe firmly that it is a slap in the face of the Enemy when we share our testimony. He will not win this story; he will not win this life. We have already won the war and are fighting mere battles until our ultimate rescue by our Savior. I wanted to use the story of my family to recount a victory for our side, a victory for Christ, and as a testament to how only He can bring "beauty from ashes, strength for despair, and joy for mourning" (Isaiah 61:3). He can rebuild a life from broken pieces, creating a beautiful, albeit different, existence. If He can do it for me, He can do it for anyone.

I also wanted the book to be a message of hope for the hurting. I know too well the arduous, brutal journey that grief is. I wanted to share my family's story to give hope to those also suffering. I wanted to show that God is faithful to guide, that there is hope, and that death is not the end for believers in Christ. One may ask why I was so willing to open my heart to strangers, to share the details of my loss through my prayers and my journal entries, to spell out my grief journey, my thoughts, my emotions, and my struggles. I wanted to lay out the grief process—the good, the bad, the ugly, and the strangely beautiful—as a guide for those suffering any form of pain. I wanted those going through what I am enduring to read my words and to know that they are not alone. I didn't write my book on the other side of pain; I wrote it while in the midst of the pain—at the height of the storm, in the rolling seas, some days still wallowing in the muck. I was not (and am not) at a place of completion, trying to tell readers how to get to the destination I have reached. I wrote from the battlefield in a waged and raging war. I wrote as a fellow soldier, still fighting toward victory, still trying to find my way. I wrote from messy places; I wrote some days with a heavy heart.

There is no clean, crisp healing. There is no ultimate victory this side of the veil. Life on earth is a battle, and these tragedies have been nearly mortal wounds. But without fail, God has lifted me back to my feet, has righted my path, and has battled before me and beside me. I wanted to write as I continued the fight so that others on any journey of pain and healing could know they are not alone. We battle alongside each other, each in our own way, each in our own struggle, but as brothers and sisters, and as sons and daughters of the King. We are together in the fight.

I also wanted my book to serve as a thank-you to everyone who has accompanied me and my children in our grief journey and on this new path we been called to take. I would not be functioning if Christ's followers had not acted as His hands and feet. God's love, shown through family, friends, and sometimes even strangers, built a bridge that helped carry me and my kids over the most treacherous stretches of grief. God's people are heaven on earth, a preview of the great kingdom to come, and I am eternally grateful for them. I have seen angels. Of that I am certain.

Finally, I wanted to write the story of Dave, Dominic, and Grant. This book is one of the many parts of the legacy they have left us. It is their story, a testament to their strength, endurance, and perseverance. I pray we all learn from the lives they lived, the strength they showed on their final earthly journey, and the tenacity they displayed as they exited this world and entered the next. Their lives each go on. While they exist out of our earthly view, they are no less alive; in fact, they are more alive than we are, living to the fullest extent meant for them and for each of us. I pray that as you read our family's story, you were able to discern that there is a loving God. He is sovereign, His ways are good, and while it may not always seem so, He has a grand plan far beyond anything our human minds can comprehend or imagine. I pray you will trust Him with your hurts. I pray you will trust Him with your life. If you do, your life will continue far beyond this world, reaching the fullest extent intended for it.

This is a story of mission, of purpose, of the true meaning of abundant life, of enduring, of battling, of learning, and of thriving.

Those themes are woven into this account. This is also a story of spiritual warfare, of leaning on the Father to fight for you and with you. Allow Him to walk with you, to carry you, to push and pull you along your path of grief or pain. This is a story of calm waters and rolling seas, of smooth paths and rocky trails. This is a story of life. This is the story of the Decareaux family, from a golden time, to our separation, to the journey Kate, Finn, Elise, and I have taken as we learn to live again. But more than anything, this is God's story—a story of hope, of true life, of the best yet to come. He never promised to save us from nightmares, but He promised that He would see us through them.

As you have read my story, our story, God's story, I pray you were able to recognize all the ways in which God sustains, shields, teaches, guides, and loves His children. I pray you can apply the truths of His promises to your life as well. There will be calm at the end of the storm, peace at the end of the fight. I pray this story served its purpose, providing hope and guidance—and most of all a reminder that the best is yet to come.

—Sarah J. Hartrum-Decareaux

A Note on Grief—and Hope

Early in 2015, I was asked to write a friend of a friend—a woman who had lost her husband just weeks before, a new young widow—to provide encouragement. I offer the message I sent her to those facing any kind of loss.

"I am praying for your heart. I am praying that the peace you cannot understand will enfold you right now as you step out on this grief journey. I too am a young widow. My husband Dave (only thirty-six) and two of our five kids—sons Dom (ten) and Grant (eight)—all went home to heaven in a hiking accident in January of 2013. God is absolutely sustaining, redemptive, faithful, and mighty. There is healing. Oh no, life will never be the same! But more than two years in, I can tell you, have faith, claim hope, and there will be light for you and for your children. Please, for now, just take one breath at a time. Expect nothing more from yourself than to breathe. Survive. Please cling to the Father for every need. Be patient with yourself, since this tragedy is still so very fresh for you. In time you will look back and see how you were held, even if it doesn't feel like that now.

"There is so much to say. I know I am asking a lot when I say, for now, just trust Him and lean on Him. Again, just breathe. And let Him tell you where to step and when. You are just starting, but I can assure you that if you allow it, He will walk right beside you! This will be a spiritual battle. I will be honest with you. You will have to lean on the Almighty to fight for you. Just know that your husband goes on! He made a transition, but he is more alive in heaven than we are here! That idea takes time to sink in and to accept. I understand that. But I am throwing it out there for you to consider. You can let it seep into your spirit when you're ready.

"God bless you and hold you in His mighty arms as you lie down to sleep tonight. May He send angels to form a hedge of protection from the enemies—the demons of hopelessness, despair, and sorrow—around you, your children, and your home! Amen. God bless you."

From Journal No. 12:

"Sometimes grief is dull, sometimes it is very heavy, sometimes it is sharp, and sometimes it seems unbearable. Sometimes I defy it. I laugh despite it. I hope despite it. I dream and plan and pray despite it.

"Sometimes I give in to it. Sometimes I want to dwell in it, to feel it, to put it on, to absorb it, and to live in it. But God quickly knocks those notions out of me. To stay there is to die—maybe even literally, but absolutely spiritually, emotionally, and mentally.

"And sometimes I don't want to give in to it, but it overtakes me. I try to fight, but I get tired and weak, and my immunity wears down. I am right where the Enemy wants me, and I cave in under the weight. I can almost feel the attacks—the jeering, the laughing, the poking of fingers at me and at all of my trials by the Enemy and his minions. But a godly defiance rises

up in me, and I rebuke that darkness away from me in the name of Jesus! Did the Enemy think I didn't know I had that power in Jesus' name? Think again.

"I will be bent but not broken. I will not be snuffed out. I belong to the side that has already won the war! We are fighting mere battles.

"Grief is spiritual warfare. I find when I get on a high, hear a revelation from God, or feel hope, peace, and contentment, the Enemy doesn't like that much. I get attacked, dragged down, confronted with reminders of all I've lost: the should-haves, the used-to-haves, the would-haves. This is when I am avoiding grief but it finds me. My only choice is to fight, to move forward, to press on, and with every step through that gauntlet, the Enemy loses his grip. I fight by keeping my thoughts pure on purpose. There must be purpose.

"'Think on what is pure and lovely' (Philippians 4:8).

"I fight by quoting Scripture in my head; I fight by refusing to give in to the norm, or public opinion, and by refusing to keep up with the Joneses or to compare myself to others. Those are easy fixes, things of the world, making it appear as if grief is healed. That's where the Enemy would like me to be, because then I am not fighting but merely content to be stagnant.

"Further, I fight by listening to praise music; I fight with the Word—the sword of the Spirit, the Bible; I fight by being still and listening for my valiant Savior and by calling on His name.

"Would it be easier to try to cure grief, to put a Band-Aid on it, to try to get through it? Sure. But that is a temporary answer and of the world. No real healing in that. Healing will hurt. It may even leave you ostracized, making you feel alone at first. That's because healing is hard work. It's God's work, and God's work is not done by the world's standards. Grief healing means reaching out beyond yourself, helping another, praying for another, climbing

out of the mire and stepping forward in faith. By fighting in all the ways mentioned above, you will not find instant healing for grief; you have to work through it, hurt through it, fight through it, never forgetting that the Enemy is responsible for it and is trying to bring you down.

"To truly work through grief is to hurt, to fight, to be aware, to reach beyond yourself, to call out to our Father, to defy the Enemy, to be still and listen. It is to press on, to endure, and never to stop hoping! Allow hope. Let it rise up in you. Dare to hope. Dare to believe in restoration! Don't write it off as false hope. Grab hope with both hands and don't ever let go! Believe God is restoring the desires of your heart. Hope is a slap in the face of the Enemy. Hope is good, pure, and right. If you feel it, let it run through you. Don't try to figure it out; just be grateful for the glimpse of the Father and for a reprieve from your battle."

ACKNOWLEDGMENTS

To my children, my treasures, my "quiver full" still with me here on earth, Kate, Finn, and Elise Decareaux: Thank you for keeping me laughing, busy, crazy, smiling, hugging, snuggling, scolding, playing, and all other ways you keep me mommying. You are my purpose on this earth. Love, hope, peace, comfort, and joy are thick when I hear you laugh, see you smile, and watch you grow, learn, and discover. I see your daddy in your eyes, your mannerisms, and your smiles. I see your brothers Dom and Grant in your innocent, pure, adventurous spirits. Daddy and your brothers will be at every graduation, every birthday, every special day; they are present and aware. While we can't see them with our eyes, we can feel them with our spirits. I love you, my beautiful Kate, my adventurous Finn, and my precious Elise. Let's keep making our guys proud together.

We are still the Decareaux family. I will cherish the past, and hope for the future. But you three are my full and grateful present. I love you!

"Children are a heritage from the Lord … Blessed is the man whose quiver is full of them" (Psalm 127:3, 5).

To Dominic and Grant Decareaux, my joys, my boys who preceded me to heaven with their daddy: Thank you for teaching me what life is all about. Your resolve to press on in the face of trials proved you are mighty warriors housed in little-boy bodies. You are no longer bound to your bodies, and I can't imagine the work you are doing for Christ's kingdom now. I am so proud of you both, and I can't wait to see your sweet faces and to hold each of you in my arms again. Your sheepish grin, Dominic, and your sunny smile, Grant, are often the last things I see before I drift off to sleep.

Some may say I gave you the gift of life in birthing you, but you taught me what true life is in the joy you brought me on earth—the laughs, the giggles, the jokes, and the stories, the afternoons snuggling on the couch watching our shows, the adventures we shared, the hugs you so willingly gave. You continue to teach me what true life is, giving me the gift of life every day in the way you modeled for me what perseverance, endurance, and strength look like. Thank you, my sons. I will do my best to make you proud every day. I can't wait to continue our snuggling, our laughing, and our adventures together again one day in heaven. I love you, my sons. I am humbled at the gift of you both.

"I thank my God every time I remember you" (Philippians 1:3).

To Dave, my partner and my friend: Our bond is infinite, no matter our title. Thank you for guiding, protecting, and loving our boys. Thank you for sacrificing yourself to try to give them a chance. Thank you for the person you were and are, for the father you were here on earth, and for the husband of integrity you always were to me. I said that night in the restaurant while we were dating that I felt we had a mission together. I think this is it: our five beautiful kids, our family. I pray our family continues to be a story of love, of legacy, and of an unbreakable bond that overcomes death upon our reunion one fine day. I love you, Dave.

I will do my best to care for our babies left with me—Kate, Finn, and Elise—with the same love, adventure, fun, and life that we gave them together. With the Holy Spirit's guidance and power, I will do my best to make you proud. Just as I felt you at Finn's kindergarten graduation and at so many other points along this journey, I know that you are here and that you are aware of how our babies are thriving. They are beautiful little people, and we made them. I know, too, that not only are our boys Dominic and Grant under our Father's loving care but that they have their daddy right beside them, still guiding, loving, and teaching. I am forever grateful that God used the best of you and the best of me to make the five little souls we call our kids. Until we meet again, you've got those two and I've got these three. We will see you on the other side, my dear friend.

It's you and me. Love, your Sarah

To Dad and Mom, Keith and Mary Hartrum, who entered heaven months apart, less than two years after Dave, Dom, and Grant: Thank you for teaching me what family is. Thank you for teaching me the importance of tradition, heritage, legacy, and love. Thank you for the proud stories and the lessons learned, for the faith you instilled in all your children, Mom, and for teaching me there is no hill too steep, Dad. Thank you for the memories of how we traversed Europe together during your many visits to my family overseas. These memories still comfort me. We will recall all our precious moments together one fine day in bliss and glory. You both are safely home with my boys, all three. Thank you for teaching me to fight and to always stand. Thank you for showing me the meaning of endurance as you both fought the good fight. May you both rest in eternal peace. We'll see you again. I love you, Mom and Dad. Enjoy the grand reunion and save a place for me. And Dad, may it be as Elizabeth dreamed that autumn day last year. Pure white light…immeasurable peace. And then Grant running to you, grabbing your hand, and saying, "Come on, Grandpa. You've got to see this."

To Dave's parents, David Sr. and Carmen: Thank you for raising such a fine man. Thank you for instilling all you did in Dave to help make him the outstanding soul he was and is. Thank for teaching him what hard work looks like. Thank you for being the Nana and Popsie you are to the children. Thank you for the visits, the goody boxes, the smiles, and the laughs. Thank you for our visits in New Orleans spent fishing, swimming, and boating; thank you for your visits spent exploring all kid- friendly places in St. Louis. Thank you for the memories as we traveled across Europe together on your visits to our family overseas. And finally, thank you for that last magical Christmas celebration we had at your house in January of 2013. With Grant's scavenger hunt and Dom's midnight fishing trip, you helped bring joy to some of my boys' last days on earth. The treasured memories of that day out on the lake and at the lighthouse are forever etched in my spirit. I will forever ponder them in my heart. Thank you. We love you!

To Deanna, Elizabeth, Becky, Heather, Kim F., Roxanne, and Faye: Thank you for being my constants. You ladies, as a group, have walked by me through the brutal, suffocating days of grief. Whether through a call, a note, or a visit, by holding my hand or by babysitting, you have been my constant companions. I have built my healing around your unabashed love and support, and I could not have come this far down the grief road without the love of Christ manifested in each of you. God used you all individually and brought your love together as one shield around my children and me. I am grateful.

To Deanna, my sister: There are not enough words to thank you. From the first day, your love, concern, devotion, and support have accompanied me everywhere. Through the dark, horrific early days of grief to my tentative efforts to find my way again, you have been there. I know you prayed to take some of my burden, and in a way, God allowed you to do that. If I were to mention all the practical ways you've helped my family—babysitting, visits, phone calls, keeping Finny occupied—it would be a book in itself. You have listened to my latest spiritual revelation and texted me to look outside at the sunset. Your love and care have carried me further along this road than I would have come without you. You have been a pillar to me, a cornerstone in rebuilding my life. Mom and Dad are overflowing with pride, I am sure, at their eldest child, a woman of character, resolve, and faith who manifests her love for others. I thank you for walking closely with the Father and for being my spiritual partner on so many days. There are not enough words, but I offer this: I love you.

To Elizabeth, my sister: My gratitude to you goes beyond any words I can find. You are a realistic, practical voice of truth amid a complicated mess of sugar-coated flatteries and platitudes. I'm grateful for your help in the early days of my journey—babysitting my kids and visiting with me. But I thank you even more for the example you gave in the practicality and the realism of your everyday life. You reminded me that when the layers of grief and mourning are pulled back, there's still a life that must be lived. And each time I am with you, a piece of that practicality is restored to the fabric of the life I am trying to rebuild. Mom and Dad must be beaming with pride at their middle child. You never shrink from a task. You do what needs to be done, and they must be smiling ear to ear, knowing you will do it well. You are a witness to me in my rebuilding, showing me how to get things done in this life. I am grateful. I have mere words to offer, but my spirit is overflowing with: I love you.

To Richard, my brother: Your constant support from the earliest moments on my grief journey has kept my head above water these last two years. For your help in gathering the information to piece together Dave and the boys' last hours on earth, I thank you from the bottom of my heart. The information you and David recovered helped me to rest, knowing that my boys went to heaven in their daddy's arms. This knowledge was absolutely priceless and lifesaving for me. I could have asked for no greater gift in those early days of grieving. For accompanying me on the trail that took my guys home that early winter morning, I thank you. Thank you for reminding my kids that their father is a man among men, an example, and that he carries with him the spirit of the bear. Thank you for being a friend to Dave, a hiking buddy, a brother. Thank you for allowing me to talk your ear off in those spring days of 2014 as you painted in my basement. You embody the best of both of our parents—the kind heart of Mom and the intelligence of Dad, and I am grateful to have you by my side as my brother. I love you.

To David, my brother: There are not enough words to thank you for the help you have offered me from the earliest moments on my grief journey. As you hiked with Richard that day to recover information about Dave and the boys' last moments on earth, you couldn't have known the lifesaving gift that knowledge would be for me; thank you. For the afternoon we hiked along the trail that took my boys home, piecing together their time line, thank you. For the signs you made to prevent other hikers from losing their way, I thank you. The day you and I hiked that trail again to hang the lodge signs was one of the first bright spots for me as I started out on my grief road. That day out on the trail brought a purpose back to my life and gave me a hint of the purpose I could find in Dave and the boys' journey—to help others. You rose to the challenge and walked Mom and Dad through their last days of this life with a tenderness, care, and compassion not usually seen in a young man. I count myself blessed to call you my brother. I love you.

To Roxanne, my sister-in-law and a sister: Thank you for your caring, compassionate heart. Thank you not only for all the practical help from early on in my grief journey—visiting, bringing meals, keeping the kids occupied—but for your friendship as this journey has progressed. Thank you for always listening as I talk too much on our play dates for the girls. Our afternoons together have become a welcome reprieve from my journey, and I am grateful. You set the bar on motherhood—and on baking. I am grateful you will forever be a part of my life. I love you.

To Aunt Chris and Uncle Bob: A special thank-you, not only for all the practical help when disaster first struck but for being friends to my children and me. Your love, support, and friendship has been invaluable to us. I will always remember the stories of Bigfoot that you told to my five babies in January 2013; our day at the St. Louis Zoo in the summer of 2014 with Kate, Finn, and Elise, and our adventure at the New Orleans Aquarium in the spring of 2015. You continue to fill our lives with joy. Our last visit as a family of seven with you and Maw Maw meant so much to all of us. Our family treasured that night at your home. I especially thank you for supporting me through the passing of my parents; your care, compassion, and love meant more than I can say. We love you dearly!

To Becky, my best childhood friend, my other sister, and Kate's godmother: Thank you for a friendship that has lasted decades. I will always be indebted to you for writing my number down for Dave that night he and I met. No wonder he called you our angel. Thank you for walking right beside me on every step of this arduous journey. Thank you for your loyalty, your love, your words of wisdom, your insight, and most of all your ears, which never tire of hearing my latest revelation, complaint, worry, sorrow, or joy. I still recall lazy summer days hanging out at your house as thirteen-year-olds and plotting out what our futures would look like (living next door to each other with husbands who were best friends). Our lives don't look exactly as we had planned those many years ago. Life took me across an ocean, finally brought me back home, and shortly after brought me to my knees. But God has a plan that far exceeds anything we could have hatched as little girls. Thank you for always reminding me of what He has overcome for me and of what He will continue to do. Your dad is in awe, I am sure, as he watches you from heaven and sees the woman of integrity, wisdom, and character you are. Dear friend, you are a gifted listener, and I am all the better for having you in my life. I love you, sister!

To Heather, my treasured friend: Thank you for all the memories, from kindergarten, to walking down the high school graduation aisle together, to being my nurse when Dom was born, to our long-ago play dates with babies Kate and Nola, to our play dates now with a bigger gang. Thank you for being my friend, my confidante, my sister in Christ. Thank you for being the consummate cheerleader; your motivation is a gift from God! Your constant encouragement and positive attitude are bright spots on otherwise dark days. God uses you, your smile, and your words of encouragement mightily. Thank you! And I know of no one else who would force me—or help me—to clean my room until 4:00 a.m.! I love you, dear sister!

To Dave's sister, Brittany, and her husband, Joel: Thank you for taking care of Bear during our early grief journey. Thank you for all the ways in which you helped and supported the children and me that first week after our boys went home. Thank you for your words, Brittany, at the services for Dave, Dom, and Grant. Thank you for reminding me that besides being a stellar husband and father, Dave was (and is) a brother, a son, a friend, and a cousin. He wore so many hats, and I am grateful I got to be a part of his existence. I count it an honor to help keep Uncle Dave and cousins Dom and Grant alive for your precious little girl in any way the kids and I can. "Uncle Dave's family" will always be here for your family. And I pray that your little girl grows to be just like her Uncle Davey and as adventurous, curious, and joy-filled as her cousins Dominic and Grant. By the grace of God, we have her cousins—Kate, Finn, and Elise—to show her just how it's done. We love you and God bless you!

To my cousins, Colleen and Hilary: How do I thank you for a lifetime of friendship, camaraderie, laughs, memories, and fun? Thank you for walking with me through my grief journey. Thank you for that first Valentine's Day after Dave and the boys went to heaven, for your company, your willing ears, your common tears. Thank you for every moment along the way—for our visits, our laughs, our travels, our talks. There are no other people I would rather travel with than you two. From the balled-up map pulled from your pocket in Paris to the attack birds in Stratford, England, you two have made my life an adventure. Your love for Dave, Dom, and Grant remains forever in my spirit and is one of the many reasons I am grateful to have you as friends and cousins. I know my loss was also your loss. But we will all enjoy the ultimate victory as one day we sit around heaven recalling our many adventures together—from Dave freaking out at almost running out of gas in the middle of the night in Germany, to Dom talking your ears off about piranhas and World War II on the way to Rothenburg, to Grant's sweet smile covered in chocolate ice cream as an itty-bitty toddler during that Valentine's Day dinner in England. We will laugh and smile and make even more memories together. I love you, my cousins, my friends, and I am so glad I have you both by my side. What's our next adventure? I'm always down if you are!

To Kim and Chris: I am so blessed God chose to bring you near us upon your move to Scott Air Force Base. He knew we would need each other. You were family away from family to us. You continue to be "Auntie" and "Uncle" to my kids, and I am grateful. How do I thank you for the love and the bond you formed with our family in Germany from our first meeting on July 4, 2009, to our annual Halloween get-togethers? I treasure the memories we made at each birthday, each special day, and each play date. Dom and Grant loved hugs from "Ms. Kim" and wrestling with "Mr. Chris," and you helped make my boys' days bright every time we got together. Dave and I treasured our time with you as our families grew together with the births of Sydney and Elise so close together. I continue to count myself blessed to have you in my life. Thank you for your continued support as you wrap your arms around the kids and me—from play dates with Elise, to mentoring Kate, to "man movies" with Finn. I love you both and your sweet baby girls!

To Faye, my dear friend and babysitter extraordinaire, and your remarkable young men, Corey and Jesse: Thank you for being there when I need you. I never fear a moment when my children are under your care, knowing they are in the best hands. Thank you, guys, for being young men of character whom Finn can look up to. Faye, you are doing an amazing job with your young men, and I look to you as an example of how to raise my boy when he gets to be a teen. Your boys are outstanding gentleman, and that is a testament to your parenting, my dear friend. Thank you for being the friend you are to me, for the family you three are to my kids and me. I treasure our get-togethers whether it be a Christmas dinner or a Mother's Day lunch. I am grateful my kids and I can count you as family. We love you!

To my siblings' friends and significant others, Aaron, Dale, and Rebecca: Thank you for making my siblings happy and for walking with our family on this journey as Dave, Dom, and Grant and our parents entered heaven. Aaron, thank you for your encouragement, your spiritual inspiration, and your insight. Thank you for keeping Finny blissfully occupied anytime he sees you. Thank you for all you bring to our family. Dale, thank you for your big bear hug that summer day in 2013 when my world was falling apart. God used you mightily that day, and I am forever grateful for the change in my spirit you brought about. Rebecca, thank you for your kind heart and for your sincerity as we visit. Talking with you and enjoying your wealth of knowledge about all things German, I return to beautiful, blissful memories. Thank you. I look forward to getting to know you even more. God bless you!

To my nieces and nephews, Jacob, Hailey, Damian, Riddick, Michael, Megan, Nicholas, Maggie, and Ellie: Thank you for keeping me laughing and smiling. Thank you for keeping Kate, Finn, and Elise happily occupied as we get together for play dates, holidays, and barbecues. Thank you for your jokes, your hugs, your stories, and thank you for being such good cousins to Dom and Grant. Jacob, thank you for your dry, grandpa-style humor. It keeps me smiling every time I see you. You are so smart, and I cannot wait to see what you do in this life. Hailey, thank you for your sweet and gentle nature. You are smart and determined and are destined for great things. Jake and Hailey, I bet your dad is beaming with pride up there with my guys, watching you two grow. Damian, thank you for your hugs and your patience with Finn and Elise. Your sweet smile makes me smile, and I believe good things for you! Riddick, thank you for being such a good friend to Grant. Thank you for your crazy sense of humor. I cannot wait to see what you do as you grow up. Michael, thank you for keeping Finny occupied when we are together. You have a strong spirit, and I look forward to seeing you grow. Megan, thank you for being a friend to Kate. You are smart, strong, and beautiful and will make a difference in this world. Nick, your gentle spirit is a gift. You are blessed with a huge heart and unbelievable artistic ability. I cannot wait to see how God uses you. Maggie, thank you for being Elise's best buddy. I don't know how I would ever keep her occupied if it were not for your sweet face. Ellie, thank you for your smile. It lights up any room. Your precious face makes me giggle every time I see you smile. It makes me smile every time I see you. I love you all. You make my heart fuller every time I see your faces.

To Aunt Mary and Uncle Tim: Thank you for loving my children and me. I cannot attempt to list the many ways you have been there for me. Thank you for the visits, the laughs, and the consistent company. Uncle Tim, thank you for keeping Finn blissfully occupied during our visits. Aunt Mary Colleen, thank you for being my friend. You are always there to support me, love me, and guide me. You are a grandmother figure for my children, and I am grateful for all you do. The day you went with Finn to Grandparents Day at his school, he could not stop smiling. He was so proud to have Aunt Mary there. I love you. Remember: one breath at a time, and one day you will see your Eric again. He is more alive than we are here, and he is looking down on you, urging you on as you continue this race. I will never forget the Christmas celebration my family of seven spent at your home in 2012.

The memories we created together are forever cemented in my spirit. Love, Sarah Jean

To Aunt Lee, my godmother: You have been a rock for our family through all of our ups and downs. Thank you for being the glue that held everything together as life started to go crazy that summer of 2014. You are intelligent, giving, loving, unbelievably considerate, and the most creative woman I know. You are amazing and never cease to give your all to so many. I will always remember your loving care as I underwent surgery, how you came to Finn's Christmas concert just days after his grandma passed to heaven, and how you attended his kindergarten graduation. These are just a few examples of the selfless love you show everyone around you. Uncle Darrin called you Mom's guardian angel, and I couldn't agree more. Your big sister is looking out for you now as you so often looked out for her on earth. I picture the pride, Mom, Uncle Tony, Grandma, and so many more have as they watch you fulfill your many missions in this world. I love you, Aunt Lee, and am grateful to have you in my life.

To Aunt Cindy: Thank you for showing me what a young, vibrant, beautiful widow of dignity looks like. May I hold my head as high as you continue to hold yours. I love you!

To Uncle Darrin and Stephanie: Thank you for your love and support—and for your help with yard work. Thank you for reaching out and spending time with my children and me. Thank you for loving my mom and dad so much. You were both there as they took their last earthly breaths and entered into glory, and I am honored that you shared in these sacred moments. And that day you spent with the kids and me at the City Museum in early 2015 reminded me of how my dad and his generation are kept alive by the love shown by my aunts and uncles. Thank you. We love you and look forward to our next outing! And Uncle Darrin, I will remember that gardening is most certainly an exercise—"It's a sorta stretch" (cue British accent)—and to "Viva la Dungeon Slide."

To Aunt Nancy: Thank you for always being there. Thank you for the joy you brought to Finn and Elise as they participated in Vacation

Bible School with your church. Your thoughtfulness is a gift from God. I love you!

To the extended Decareaux family and family friends - Maw Maw, Uncle Kenny, Aunt Mae, Aunt Chris, Uncle Bob, Aunt Kathy, Uncle Larry, Uncle Ted, Aunt Edith, Uncle John, Uncle George, Aunt Toni, and all aunts, uncles, cousins, and family friends: Thank you for coming up to Illinois in droves to be there for the kids and me that first week and/or showing your support and love at the Louisiana memorial. Whether you changed a diaper, held a hand, made a meal, or cleaned the house, I am grateful. Thank you for sharing in stories and photos Davey, the little boy you remember, with the kids and me, keeping Daddy alive for our children in a whole new way. Maw Maw, Dave often told the kids and me how he loved you so much. He still loves you. He shared his sweet memories of burying action figures in your backyard and of many other boyhood adventures during his visits with you while you were neighbors. He treasured his time with you and his Papa. Dave was always proud to have gotten your eye color, which he passed to Grant and Elise. He lives on in all of us. I thank you for the love you show the children and me. We love you, Maw Maw! Uncle George, I am honored to think of Dave and Aunt Glenda in heaven, cheering us all on as we finish our races here on earth, and Uncle Larry and Aunt Kathy, I can just see Dave and Anthony together on many adventures up there. I am sure they will have many stories to tell us upon our entrance home one day. We love you all!

To my aunts, uncles and cousins on both sides of my huge family - Uncle Greg, Aunt Leslie, Tom, Aunt Mary Colleen, Uncle Tim, Aunt Marsha, Aunt Cindy, Aunt Judy, Aunt Janet, Uncle Darrin, Stephanie; Aunt Mary Ann, Uncle Beas, Aunt Bonnie, Aunt Nancy, Uncle John, Aunt Lee, Uncle Charles, and my many cousins: Thank you for your support at the services for my family. Thank you for your words of encouragement, your hands of support, and your hugs of comfort. I am so proud to be a part of such a large family. The stories, the good times, the tough times, the lessons learned, the humor shared—I have carried that foundation, and the lessons learned through it all, with me from my days as a little girl at family gatherings to our visits in adulthood.

I am proud to be a part of something more, something bigger—our family, our story, our legacy. Thank you to all of you. And while Dad, Mom, Grandma Mary (Hartrum-Thebeau), Grandma Dorothy, Grandpa Dick, Grandpa Bob, Aunt Kathy, Uncle Rich, Eric, Dave, Dom, Grant, baby Julie, Uncle Tony, and many more have gone before us, let us never forget that they are alive. They are well, and they have found fulfillment. May we continue their legacies of love as we live out our missions here on earth. I love you all!

To Heath, Dave's cousin, a brother and a friend: Thank you for loving Dave so much. Thank you for being good to him and for being his friend. He loves you very much! I am forever grateful for the continuous support and love you have shown the kids and me as we have walked this grief journey. Thank you for your messages, your concern, and your love. We love you!

To Dave's cousin Jamie: Your messages of love and support calm my soul and bring encouragement to my spirit. I am grateful to see our friendship grow. I look forward to hearing more about "Davey" from your memories. Never forget how much Dave loves you, and if you ever need a giggle, just remember his pizza-man prank phone call in January 2013. I love you!

To my cousin Randy and your beautiful wife, Valerie: Thank you for taking me under your wings from early on in my grief journey. Thank you for the visits, the notes, the prayers, and the meals. The light boxes you gave us to illuminate the many names my guys went by—father, husband, son, friend, cousin, leader, brother—stay lit in my living room twenty-four hours a day. They offer constant comfort and remind me of the legacy left by my guys and of the gifts they continue to hone in heaven. I love you both and am grateful for your love. May you receive back tenfold the love and encouragement you so willingly gave to me.

To Doug and Julie, my parents' dear friends: Thank you so much for the outstanding friends you always were to my parents and the friends you continue to be to us, their children. Doug, I am forever grateful to you for singing my dad into his next life with your soothing voice and soft guitar chords. What a testament to your decades-long friendship with my dad to see you do all you could to make his transition to heaven smoother! Thank you for playing your guitar at Mom and Dad's services. How fitting to have you play after you so willingly came to play as they were preparing to enter into eternity in their last earthly days. Thank you, Doug and Julie, for the help you gave me in building the shelves and tending to my garden in those early days on my grief journey. Thank you, Doug, for your brother, Dave, and thank you, Julie, for your sister Stacy, who helped as well. Thank you for the support you continue to show my family in the messages sent, the cards made, and so much more. You embody the love of Christ in acts of love and selflessness. You are gifted with love to overflowing for your family and friends. Thank you. We love you!

To Dustin and Tonya: Thank you for your love, encouragement, generosity, support, and friendship, especially in those early days of our grief journey. Dustin, thank you for being the dear friend you were to Dave. He loved you like a brother and, as you know, considered you the brother he never had. I am so grateful he had you in his life. You remind us of what a loyal man Dave was, and I am forever grateful for the dear (and sometimes hilarious) stories you share with my kids about their daddy and his boot camp and tech school days. We love you!

To Mike E.: Thank you for being a friend to Dave. His stories of your humorous adventures through high school were among the first things I loved about him. They showed his sense of humor and of adventure. He treasured your friendship and loved you like a brother; he still does. Thank you for the friend you have been to the children and me since Dave entered heaven. Thank you for the support drive you organized at your twentieth high school class reunion. The support shown to the children and me was overwhelming and was a testament to what Dave meant to so many of his classmates. Thank you.

To my dear friend Amy S.: Thank you for always keeping it real. Thank you for the giggles, the texts of love, the jokes, and the encouragement. Thank you for the memories from our days together in the Azores onward; thank you for loving Dave, Dom, and Grant. Thank you for encouraging me to keep journaling. Thank you for giving Kate her nickname, Baby Kate. Amy and Steve, our visit at the park in Germany remains forever in my heart and my spirit. As we often told you, Dave and I wanted to be just like you two when we grew up. Dave surpassed us all, but I am still striving every day to be like you, to make friends as close as family, as you so beautifully demonstrate. Thank you. And Amy, thank you for reminding me that Dave is up there looking down on me and saying – "Tag, babe; you're it." We love you guys!

To Kim B., my dear college friend: You are a mighty prayer warrior, and I am grateful you continuously bring my family and me before the throne. Your unabashed faith in the power of prayer is an inspiration to me. I am so grateful you were able to come see my family twice in England. The precious memories we made with itty-bitty Kate, Dominic, and Grant are forever in my heart. I will always remember the broken bus seat in Dublin and the city map turned sun visor in London. I will always remember you saving Kate from the geese in Stratford, your delight at the huge smile on Grant's toddler face, and your sweet and patient nature as Dom talked your ear off during that trip. You are a dear sister to me, and your parents are kind and remarkable people who raised an awesome woman of God. I love you!

To my male friend: Thank you for the part our friendship and conversations played in my awakening. Thank you for the late-night talks and laughs. God bless you as you allow our Father to lead you on your journey. May your skies be bright, your paths be smooth, and your direction be clear. Romans 8:28.

To Allison E.: Thank you for your encouragement, especially early on my grief journey when there was darkness all around. Your e-mails helped to dispel the darkness and to allow a little bit of light in with each message of hope you sent. Thank you!

To my spiritual rocks, dear friends, and sisters in Christ, Jen D., Christy S., and Ami E.: You took me under your wings, encouraged me, and pulled me along when I could go no further on my own. Though you didn't know one another, God used you three together to form a hedge of divine wisdom, love, hope, truth, and strength through your words, messages, and prayers.

To Jen: Thank you for reminding me that I am nothing less than a daughter of the King. Thank you for your messages, which arrived exactly when I needed them. I am humbled by your continuous support, encouragement and love. You are gifted in many spiritual gifts and I am honored to fight alongside you, dear sister.

To Christy: Thank you for showering me with love. I always take one thing away from your messages—that above all else, I am immensely loved by our Father. You so beautifully convey this truth to me. Each message you send pours forth care, concern, and sincerity. I am overcome with hope when I read your words. Thank you!

To Ami: How do I even begin to thank you? You pulled me to your side so early on my journey, coaching me, plunging into the depths with me, and going before the Father for me. You love me with a love that only a mother who has experienced my pain can offer. You are a beautiful gift, my sister, and I love you. You help me walk a road no mother should ever have to walk. In your own pain, you reached out to me, and I'm humbled. You remind me that my boys are in heaven and that I will see them again. We will walk this arduous journey on earth together until that glorious day when we hold our boys and never have to say good-bye again. Death is a lie! I can't wait for that day when we are reunited with our sons. We will look at each other, knowing we can lay our burdens down forever. I hope I can give you a fraction of the support that you have given to me. There are not enough words to thank you. I love you!

To Rachelle, Elissa J., Renee P., Trinity M., Karen M., and Carolyn M.: Thank you, ladies, for being the prayer partners, encouragers, friends, confidantes, and mighty women of God you have been to me. Rachelle, our play dates for the girls are a breath of fresh air. Elissa, your wise words and encouragement are a gift from God. Renee and Trinity, your friendships across the miles brought comfort to my aching heart early on my grief road. Karen, God works in crazy ways, and I am so grateful our paths crossed and we formed a friendship. You are a sister in Christ, and I am so grateful for your messages of love and support. Carolyn, thank you for your wise words, your mentoring, the love you show my children and me, and your many forms of encouragement.

You are a woman of dignity and have been a beautiful example to me of how to walk this widow road.

To Dori, Kelty, and Heather: You are beautiful inside and out. I am so grateful our God saw fit to make our moms best friends and then to make us like family. I love each of you deeply and count you as my sisters. My mom loved you as daughters, as you know. Dori, your continuous words of encouragement are a gift from God. You are immersed in the light and the love of the Holy Spirit and are blessed with many spiritual gifts. You embody what a woman of God should strive to look like, and I am grateful to have you in my life as a Christian sister. Kelty and Heather, your children are blessed to have moms with such huge hearts and determined souls guiding them through this life. Ladies, your mother has got to bursting with pride at the way her three little girls have grown into women of character, resolve, determination, and strength. You are examples that any young lady should count herself blessed to look up to. I can't help but wonder what mischief our moms are getting into together in heaven. I love you ladies!

To Glenda, breeder turned friend: Thank you so much for your kindness, your friendship, and the love shown my children and me during our visits. Your kindness in naming a memorial litter in honor of Dave and my boys touched my heart and comforted my soul. Your generosity was a gift. Thank you so much for all you have done and for the friendship you give.

Thank you to all who helped organize the memorial in Germany in honor of my family: Kim, Chris, Cub Scout Pack 113, all packs in the Stuttgart community, Awana friends, American Heritage Girl friends, Girl Scout friends, and Dave's work friends. Thank you for the beautiful ceremony honoring my boys. Dave loved leading the Cub Scouts there and gave everything he had in him. What an honor to see the love he had for your families returned to him. I am grateful.

Thank you to all who organized the Louisiana memorial Mass for Dave and our boys held at St. Paul's High School. It was an honor to have been there to see the outpouring of love from Dave's family, his alma mater, and his hometown. Thank you so much!

Thank you to all on Scott Air Force Base who organized the memorial held in honor of Dave and our sons. I am blessed beyond measure to have been able to witness the missing man ceremony, a moving tribute in honor of Dave. To all those who spoke in honor of my husband, thank you. To the Scott homeschool group that provided a wonderful spread of refreshments afterward, thank you.

To Pastor Steve Neill and all at the First Baptist Church of Waterloo, Illinois, my home church: Thank you for your outpouring of love and support. Thank you for the beautiful meal the church prepared after the service for Dave and our boys. Thank you for your continued support as you helped guide my family through the passing of my mom and dad to heaven. Your love is overwhelming, and I am grateful. Thank you, Pastor, for reminding me in those early days after Dave, Dom, and Grant entered heaven that this is not the end. Thank you for reminding me of the new heaven and the new earth and of all we have to look forward to. I am eternally grateful.

To Father Osang of St. Peter and Paul Parish in Waterloo, Illinois: Thank you for your words of encouragement at the service for Dave and our boys, for your prayers, and for reminding us that God is in control. The sincerity of your faith is refreshing.

To all at Concordia Church in Belleville, Illinois: Thank you for your care, concern, messages of support, prayers, and practical help in the form of groceries early on our grief journey. Your thoughtfulness is greatly appreciated. The week the kids spent at your Vacation Bible School was one of our first bright spots as we stepped back out into the world.

To the United Methodist Church in Freeburg, Illinois, Journey Church: Thank you for the many Sunday mornings and early afternoons spent helping me with yard work. Thank you for so beautifully displaying Christ's love by offering your time and energy. God bless you all!

To Doug and Sherry: I thank you not only for being the best neighbors anyone could ask for, not only for being so patient when Finn and Elise show up at your front door unexpectedly, but for organizing the church's work days in my yard. Thank you!

To my counselor, a wise woman of God whom Kate and I have seen since our grief journey began: Thank you for always making me strive toward that next step and for helping me remember that no matter what God allows into my life, He also supplies what I need to get through it.

To all lodge personnel, to all who searched for my husband and my boys, to all first responders and hospital personnel who worked valiantly on my boys, and to the first responders I had the privilege to talk to (you three know who you are): From the bottom of my heart, I thank you all. I thank Mavis and Jordan for their continued support and love. I thank Annette and Nikki for being my angels and guiding me through the most horrific day I have experienced. I thank my angel of a nurse, Karen, who was by my side throughout the battle for my boys in the hospital. Thank you for all you did to try to bring my loved ones back to me. Thank you for showing me Christ's love, which I continue to feel even now. Your acts of bravery, love, commitment, and determination have stuck to my soul, and I will never forget what all of you did for my family. May God bless every one of you for the difference you have made in my life and for the impression you have made on my spirit. I cannot wait until you meet my three guys, whom you worked so hard to rescue, on the other side in bliss and glory and get to see them whole, in perfection—full of love, light, joy, smiles, and laughs. Thank you from the deepest part of my spirit.

To all in Waterloo Cub Scout Pack 323, American Heritage Girls Troop MO2005, the Scott Air Force Base homeschool group, Colleen G., and so many more: Thank you for supporting my family and me in so many ways. Colleen G., you have a huge heart, and the love, compassion, care, and kindness you showed the kids and me from the earliest part of our grief journey will never leave my soul. Thank you for organizing the memorial fund that sustained my children and me. I am forever indebted to you and to all in the pack and the community. My heart overflows with gratitude. I thank all those in the American Heritage troop who supported Kate and me with messages of love and compassion and with your prayers. And the honor you paid Dave in canceling the father-daughter dance in January of 2013 touched my heart more deeply than I can tell you. I am grateful and humbled.

May God repay you for the kindness and the honor you showed my family. And how can I thank everyone in the homeschool group? You were constant supporters of my kids and me in every way possible, babysitting, doing yard work and laundry, providing a dishwasher, offering food, Christmas and Valentine's gifts, visits, laughs, and tears. There is not enough space to list every way you showed us love. I could not have made it through a day in those early weeks without your companionship, conversation, prayers, meals, and help. Thank you, Amy, Deb, Jen, Michelle, Faye, Beth, Shannon, and many more. You so beautifully demonstrate the love of Christ in action. You practice what you preach, and I am forever grateful!

I offer a special thank-you to every person who said a prayer; sent a card, a gift, or a text; or came to visit, brought a meal, wrote a letter, made a call, ran an errand, folded laundry, did my dishes, walked my dog, mowed the lawn, helped with yard work, held my hand, played with my kids, planted flowers, took out the trash, changed a diaper, sent money, babysat, or honored my family in any way. I thank you for your words of comfort, words of wisdom, and acts of love. I am overwhelmed by your love.

I offer my eternal gratitude to those of you I did not have the opportunity to thank personally. We received hundreds of notes of comfort and love in the first several months after Dave, Dom, and Grant entered heaven, and I wasn't in a place to pull my thoughts together to properly thank anyone, much less everyone. After I started writing thank-yous, I got a couple hundred finished and was emotionally exhausted. If you did not receive a thank-you from me, please know that your note, card, prayer, Scripture encouragement, or act of kindness did not go unnoticed and was no less important on my healing journey than any other gesture. I read every note, e-mail, text, and card, and every one played a part in relighting my spirit one kind word, one prayer at a time. Thank you. I also thank those of you who sent anonymous gifts, cards, books, Scripture encouragement, and gift cards. You know who you are. The acts of love, support, and kindness shown my family have been so numerous that I couldn't attempt to list them all here. Thankfully, we have a God that knows exactly who you are and exactly what you've done in His name! I am humbled by your love. Every act of kindness moved me and my family that much further along on our healing journey.

Finally, I thank God for allowing me to play a part in the lives of Dave, Dom, and Grant. Thank You, Father, for leaving me Kate, Finn, and Elise to nurture, to raise, to love, and to enjoy. I love You, my Father, and I thank You, Jesus, my redeemer, my protector, my friend, my companion, my confidant, my all, for walking with me from the time You whispered to my spirit on the cold barn floor, to all the moments along this journey when my reserve has run dry and You have filled me up, to now as we continue to walk this road of discovery, mission, revelation, redemption, and hope together. Will I still praise Him? I will (Psalm 43:5).

—Sarah Hartrum-Decareaux, Spring 2015

About the Author

Sarah Hartrum-Decareaux is the mother of five children, and the best friend of Dave Decareaux. In January of 2013, her husband, Dave, and two of their sons—Dominic, ten; and Grant, eight—entered glory. Sarah and her three remaining children are forging forward, picking up the pieces, and finding pockets of joy in the ashes. A seven-year homeschooling veteran and a teacher by trade, Sarah put her kids in the public school system in the fall of 2014. Sarah substitute teaches at her children's schools. Sarah, Kate, Finn, and Elise stay busy with extracurricular activities, doing homework, and performing other blissfully routine daily goings-on. When Sarah and her children are not on day trips in the surrounding area, out to eat, cooking, watching movies, gardening, or spending time with family and friends, they can be found at home relaxing, surrounded by their faithful canine companion, Bear, their many farm cats, their chickens, their gecko, their bunny, their hermit crabs, and their fish. Sarah, Kate, Finn, Elise, and their menagerie reside in Millstadt, Illinois on their few acre sanctuary.

Printed in the United States
By Bookmasters